LEGENDARY LOCALS

OF

ORLEANS COUNTY

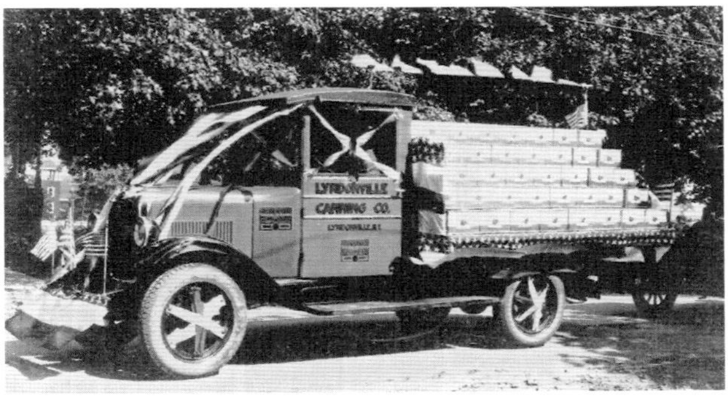

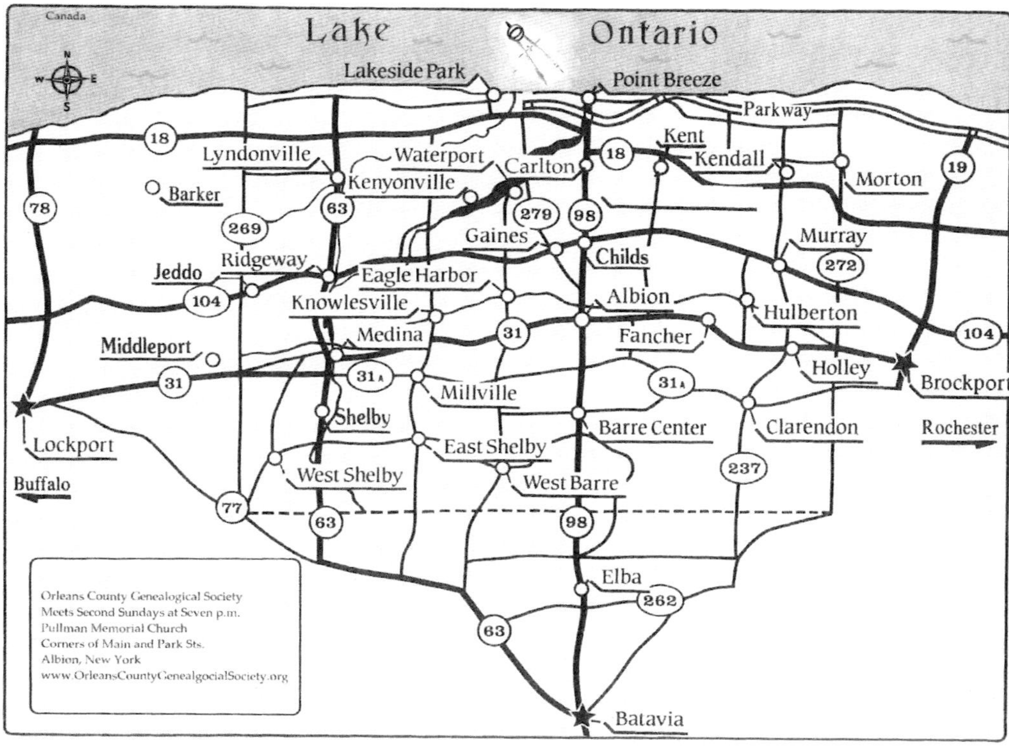

Page 1:
Agriculture has always played an important role in Orleans County. Since Rachel Lovewell planted the first apple tree around 1803, apple orchards have dotted the landscape. Today, farmers continue to harvest apples using advanced knowledge and technology—one can now easily find over a 1,000 apple trees in just one acre! Throughout this book are several stories related to apples and apple growers. The Lyndonville Canning Company is just one of these stories. The truck on the previous page represents a time gone by, and is perhaps symbolic of the economic importance apples were—and are—to Orleans County. (Courtesy of Scott Goetze.)

Page 2:
This map provides a visual glimpse of Orleans County's hamlets, towns, and villages; Albion is the county seat. It has approximately 42,883 residents (2010 census) and measures 24 by 17 miles. (Courtesy of Orleans County Genealogical Society.)

LEGENDARY LOCALS OF ORLEANS COUNTY

HOLLIS RICCI-CANHAM
AND ANDREW CANHAM

LEGENDARY LOCALS

ISBN 978-1-4671-0010-6

Published by Legendary Locals, an imprint of Arcadia Publishing
Charleston, South Carolina

Printed in the United States of America

Library of Congress Control Number: 2011941153

For all general information, please contact Arcadia Publishing:
Telephone 843-853-2070
Fax 843-853-0044
E-mail sales@arcadiapublishing.com
For customer service and orders:
Toll-Free 1-888-313-2665

Visit us on the Internet at www.arcadiapublishing.com

Dedication

From the nascent development of the Orleans County Genealogical Society, Virginia Kropf has consistently recorded and preserved our educational events and community stories. Her generous contributions to this book are greatly appreciated—Ginny, thank you!

On the Cover: From left to right:
(TOP ROW) Claude Bennett, World War II pilot and POW (Courtesy of Douglas Bennett; see page 13), Charlie Owen, World War II armament specialist and POW (Courtesy of Charlie Owen; see page 16), Dan "Spaghett" Paul, veteran and community servant (Courtesy of Debbie Russo; see page 96), Tim Archer, teacher (Courtesy of C.W. Lattin; see page 68), Carl Fischer, MLB player (Courtesy of C.W. Lattin; see page 85).
(MIDDLE ROW) Grace Denniston, outstanding volunteer (Courtesy of Monica London; see page 91), Mike Monacelli, coach (Courtesy of Michael Johnson/*Livingston County News*; see page 83), Gretchen Sepik, storyteller (Courtesy of Pat Mead; see page 72), Stan Vanderlaan, archaeologist (Courtesy of Stanley Vanderlaan; see page 67), Hank Porter, Disney artist (Courtesy of C.W. Lattin; see page 61).
(BOTTOM ROW) Sgt. Trevor Cook, US Marine Corps (Courtesy of David Cook; see page 19), Richard Gordineer, former slave, businessman (Courtesy of Orleans County Department of History; see page 99), Frank Cushing, anthropologist and ethnologist (Courtesy of Neil Johnson; see page 66), Joy Huff, NASA (Courtesy of Joy Huff; see page 97), and Kathy and Neil Samborski, clowns and puppeteers (Courtesy of the Samborskis; see page 64).

"Unselfish and noble actions are the most radiant pages in the biography of souls," noted early American writer David Thomas. To each of you, thank you for kindly supporting our work by way of suggestion, photograph, or "juicy tidbit." The book is better because of you.

Contributors, listed alphabetically, are Dick Anderson, Tim Archer, Sue Webreck Alman, Helen Bachellor, Matthew Ballard, Robert Batt, Joann Baxter, Timothy Bellavia, John Belson, Douglas Bennett, Janice Bennett, Julie Bennett, Richard Bennett, Frank Berger, David Bertsch, Heather Bertsch, Sharon Bertsch, Tracy Bettilyon, Diane Biemans, Dwight Bliss, Roosevelt Bouie, Margo Bowerman, Deborah Brundage, Evan Cady, Bud Canham, Elaine Canham, Mikken Canham, Carl Catraccia, June Chamberlain, Fay Ciarico, Joseph Ciarico, Susan Colby, David Cook, Catherine Cooper, Virginia Cooper, Grace Denniston, Lorraine Dibley, Susan Dowe, Alyssa Downs, Trina Dreschel, Kathy Dreyfus, Tiffany Frary, Sandra Freeman, Glen Gaston, Scott Goetze, Larry Grimes, Jim Gommenginger, Eugene Haines, Nadine Hanlon, Mary Keppler Hebert, Joy Huff, Melissa Ierlan, Hugh James, Michael Johnson, Neil Johnson, David Kast, Kathy Kast, Jim Kennard, Sharon Kerridge, Terri Kinser, Barbara Kludt, Virginia Kropf, George Lama, George Lamont, Roger Lamont, Pauline Lanning, C.W. Lattin, Julie A. Lewis, Kim Martilotta, Aaron Massey, Gene Massey, Helen Mathes, Joe McCracken, Pat Mead, Andrew Meier, Garland Miller, Jonas Miller, Audrey Monacelli, Tony Monacelli, Wilbur Mull, Sean Narburgh, Ted Narburgh, Edward Neal, Jody Neal, Darrel Oakes, Wendi Pencielle, Kim Eddy Remley, C. Dan Ricci, Merle Ricci, Homer Rietz, Tom Rivers, Linda Rosenthal, Debbie Russo, Kelly Russo, Nick Russo, Carolyn Rustay, Mark Rustay, Idris Silah, Kathy Samborski, Neil Samborski, John Sawyer, Claire Saxon, David Schlabach, Gracia Schlabach, Paul Schwenck, Gretchen Sepik, Leeann Serrato, Julia Sheppard, Kathy Sillick, Gary Simboli, Ellen Smith, Mary Stack, Sue Starkweather, Roland "Chip" Stevens, the Stielow Family, Joan Sullivan, Ted Swierzinski, Michael Thaine, LuAnn Tierney, Holly Toal, Marcia Touhey, Stanley Vanderlaan, Jack Wasnock, Karen Watt, Kris Watt, Larry Weed, Tammi Weed, Lynn Williams, Gary Withey, Eleanor Yungfleisch, Alice Zacher, Frank Zicari, and Christine Zinni.

In addition, we would like to thank the following entities: the Buffalo Bill Museum and Grave, Golden, Colorado; the Batavia *Daily News*; Cobblestone Museum; the Joseph F. Glidden Homestead and Historical Center, DeKalb, Illinois; the Kansas State Historical Society; National Archives; the *Livingston County News*; National Anthropological Archives, Smithsonian Institution; *Revolution Magazine*; University of Rochester, Rush Rees Library; the University of the Sciences in Philadelphia; and finally, the Towns of Albion, Barre, Carlton, Clarendon, Gaines, Kendall, Murray, Ridgeway, Shelby, and Yates.

We are specifically thankful to Ginny Kropf, who has been a wonderful community advocate by helping generate ideas, tracking down details, and, most importantly, accepting responsibility for errors found in this book. We wish to extend a special thank you to our immediate family members for their encouragement—and tolerance!—of this project; you, too, are legendary.

Nestled on the southern shore of Lake Ontario, between the cities of Rochester and Buffalo, Orleans County is considered part of western New York State. It was separated from Genesee County in 1824, and the county seat is centrally located in Albion. Forests, not grass, were indigenous to this area. The canopy formed by the dense foliage of trees allowed little sunlight to penetrate and thus the northern area came to be called "the black north." The first white settlers to reside in the county arrived by boat from Canada. Brothers William and James Wadsworth built cabins at the mouths of Oak Orchard River and Johnson's Creek, respectively. William arrived first with his family, having crossed the lake in an open boat in May 1803. James followed soon after. Attracted by land offered by the Holland Land Company, the area saw steady growth; the use of the Erie Canal in 1825 ensured that most parcels were sold. The soil was rich, and cleared for farming. The discovery of sandstone provided quarry jobs for stonecutters. Together, farming and quarrying provided opportunity. Though little quarrying continues today, farming and agritourism businesses continue to thrive. In 2011, Orleans County offers two banking operations centers, two state correctional facilities, and one hospital; these are among the county's major employers.

Orleans County is certainly a quiet rural community. However, much goes on that those passing through might miss. Albion now offers a European-style art gallery, owned and operated by Kim Martilotta and her husband. The Medina Railroad Museum is a big tourist attraction, and several wineries have opened over the past few years. The Oakes family went beyond general agritourism—they planted an orchard that is a living museum of antique apple trees. The orchard produces varieties from yesteryear with "stories" of their own.

Time passes and we must move with it, accepting changes to our traditional way of life. Change is not always easy, even for the most progressive thinkers among us. Some changes are welcomed, some seem to go practically unnoticed, and some, well, are full of controversy. The county has its first wind tower, which proves the old adage, "it isn't easy to be first." Another sign of the times is Intergrow. Acres of tomatoes are grown indoors, under glass, with a computer-controlled, sustainable, closed environment producing tomatoes on the vine in a class all their own. Here! Well, there's the beauty of life in Orleans County. We smile approvingly as we witness the Amish preserving time-honored agricultural processes, and a few miles away we stare in awe at the advances of technology that are now part of our little farming community.

Citizens here are essentially good neighbors. More than a few farmers have been known to haul their tractors out and go up and down their road unblocking driveways inevitably plugged up with snow from the highway plows. The occasional blizzard does happen and most are prepared for it. It's a nice feeling, though, when the roads are impassable, to hear the engine of that friend's snowmobile coming to take you home. Ted Narburgh, president of the Orleans County Snowdrifters snowmobiling club, makes sure the trails and bridges are well maintained, and properly marked. The group participates in rescue drills and stands ready to be of service when called upon.

Rural people and farming people often hunt well. It is a practical matter. We are raised to be self-sustaining, to stock our freezers and put up food to take us through our long winters. Tending livestock is hard work, but overall a pleasurable activity. There are some sad aspects, though, such as predatory animals. Sometimes we need to be good with a gun to eliminate threats to our livestock. Sometimes we are only good stewards if we hunt for population control. The area boasts many experienced and fine hunters. One such fellow is Doug Bennett. He has many hunting stories (and as a charter captain a few fish tales, too) and you'll see an image of the record coyote he killed a few years ago. The local conservation office believes the county's high coyote population now is due to the decline of smaller "Mom and Pop" farms. Where barnyards and pastures were, we now have trees. In fact, we have more woods now than we did 100 years ago—creating the perfect habitat for coyotes.

Our community actively participates in social clubs and has its fair share of member-organizations such as the American Legion, Catholic Daughters, Eastern Star, Elks Club, Knights of Columbus, Lions, Masons, Orleans County Historical Society, Rotary Club, and scouting troops. Groups featured in this book are the Orleans Community Choir, the Future Farmers of America, a sampling of 4-H–related offerings, the Salt Port Vigilance Committee, and a glimpse into academically affiliated activities such as the Medina Marching Band and the Mt. Albion Ghost Walk.

We have an amazing number of outstanding and notable people from Orleans County. We can, and do, brag that Charles Howard, founder of the world's first Santa Claus training school, hailed from Albion. You'll read about Howard on a few pages as he was multitalented and made wonderful contributions to the community. George Pullman, of railroad sleeping car fame, hailed from Albion and built our Universalist Church as a memorial to his parents. You'll read about the inventor of barbed wire too. Hank Porter, famous Disney artist, George Stebbins, musician and composer, and Peace Prize winner Donna Rodden all called Orleans County home once upon a time. Many Legendary Locals are living people, currently contributing to our community; this book highlights a selection of them too.

Government, Politics, Military, and Law

Citizens who work in these disciplines all have tough jobs. They perform important duties every day, and they make difficult decisions that often directly affect people's lives and lifestyles.

Generally, these positions are held by honest, hardworking people trying to make the world a better place; but, when something goes wrong, it can go devastatingly wrong. Such was the case for wrongfully convicted Orleans County resident Charlie Stielow. During his trial, ballistic evidence was used in a courtroom for the first time anywhere; read further to learn why his wrongful conviction case is still taught in law schools across America. Also included in this chapter is Sheriff Herbert Clark, who, 10 years later, introduced Orleans County to the use of fingerprinting for evidence collection.

And, while it is true that every society has its share of growing pains, this is a community historically rich with great people who genuinely wanted to protect and improve our way of life. Read about brave military veterans and their accounts of prisoner of war experiences, and their resolve to survive and return here—to return *home*. Orleans County has welcomed many servicemen home and mourned the loss of our fallen. This chapter is rich with contributors—both past and present. Together, they represent Orleans County's storied past, and the promise of a new day.

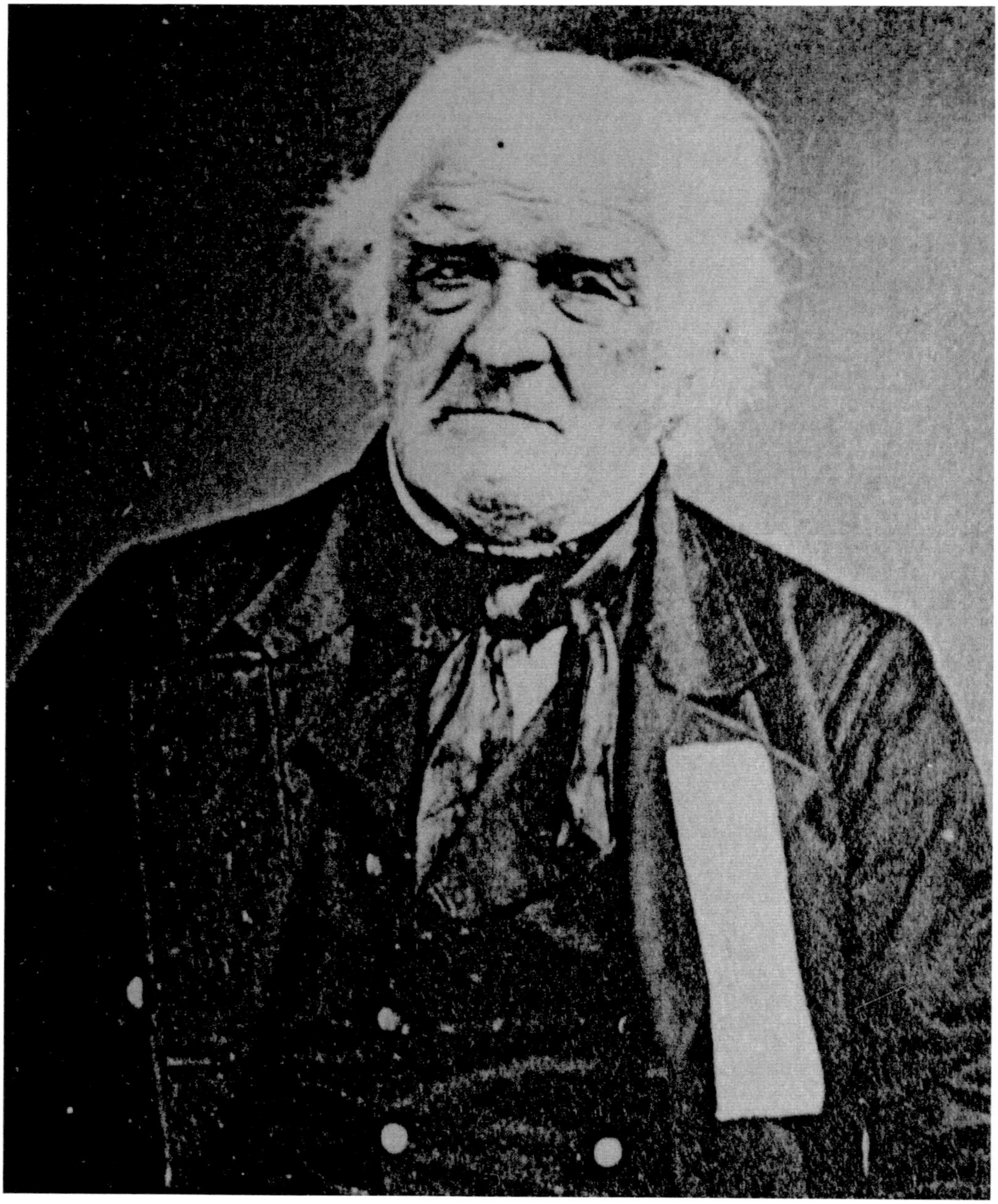

Cook (1759–1866) joined the Continental Army at age 16. He served in the Virginia campaign, fought at Brandywine on September 11, 1777, as part of the Philadelphia campaign, and was present at General Cornwallis's surrender at the Battle of Yorktown in 1781. Later, Gen. George Washington signed Cook's honorable discharge in 1784. After the war, Cook married Hannah Curtis and eventually moved to Clarendon, New York, where he lived his remaining years. Upon his death at age 106, Cook was given full military and Masonic honors. He was also considered by many to be the last surviving Revolutionary War veteran and longest to be on government pension rolls. (Courtesy of Holly Canham.)

Clark (1755–1834) served as courier to Gen. George Washington during the American Revolutionary War. He was responsible for delivering the news to General Washington that the British had landed at Throg's Neck as part of their attempt to trap Washington and his Continental Army on Manhattan Island. This event was part of the Battle of Pell's Point (about October 18, 1776). (Courtesy of Holly Canham.)

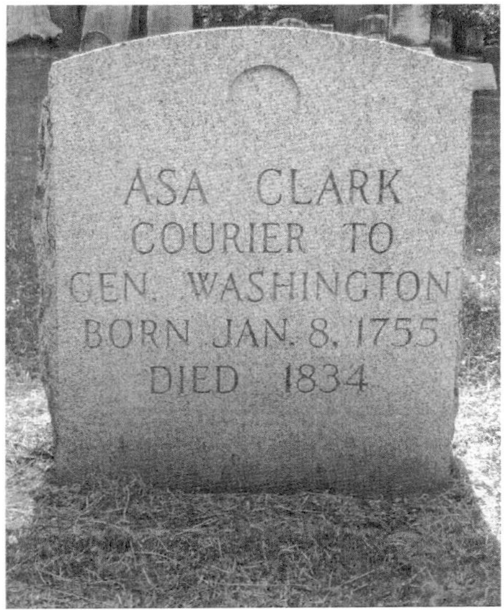

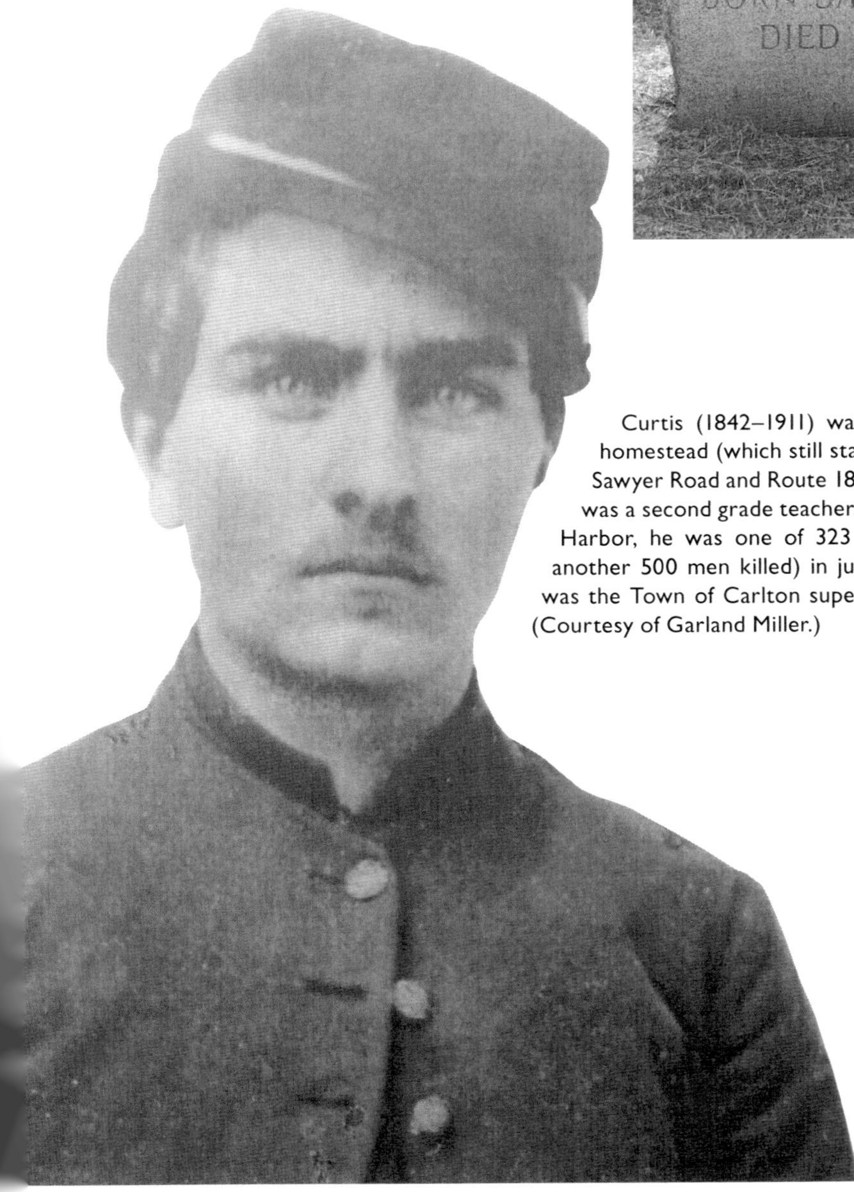

Curtis (1842–1911) was born at the Curtis homestead (which still stands) on the corner of Sawyer Road and Route 18 (Curtis Corners). He was a second grade teacher. At the Battle of Cold Harbor, he was one of 323 men wounded (with another 500 men killed) in just one charge. Curtis was the Town of Carlton supervisor for two terms. (Courtesy of Garland Miller.)

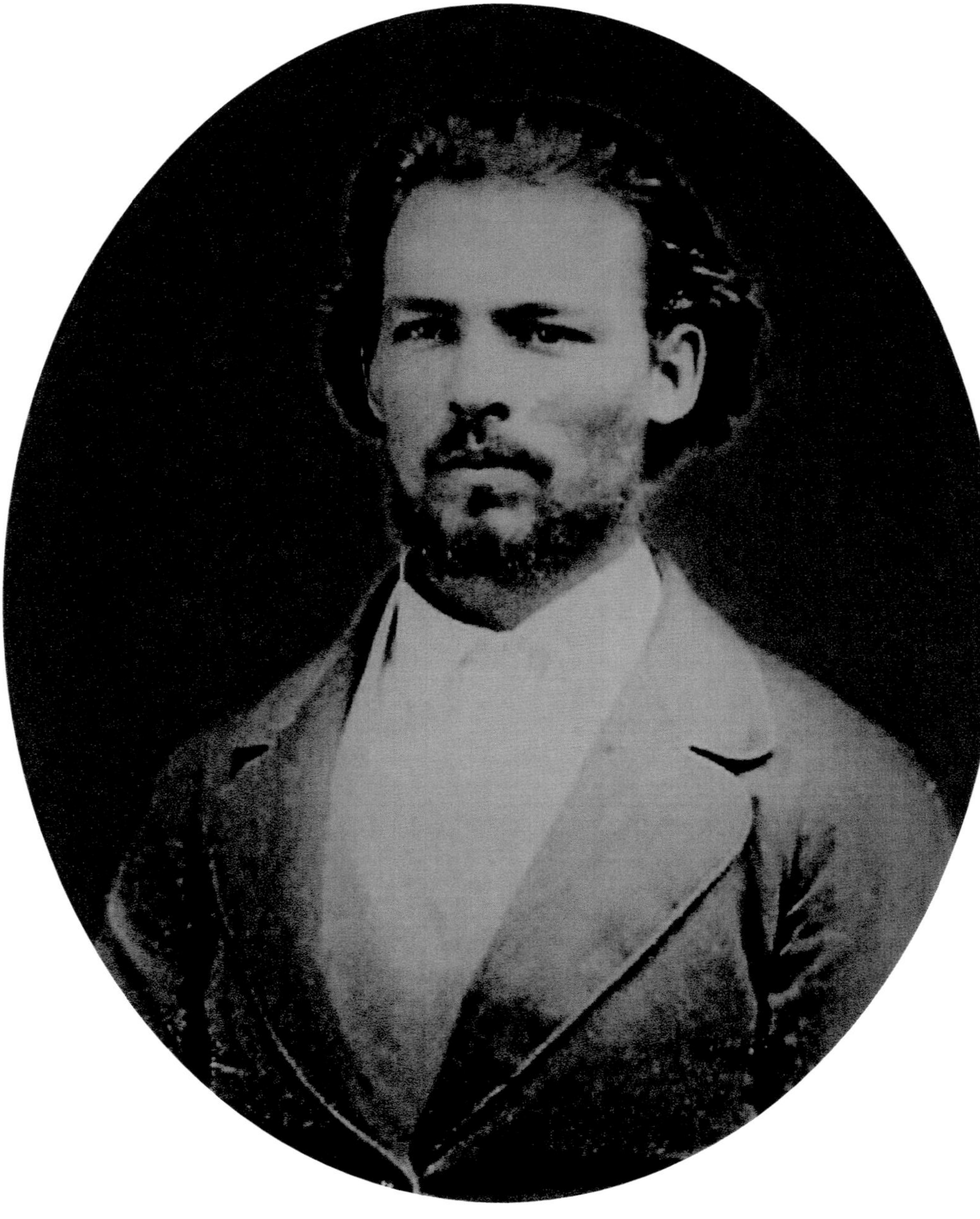

Born in Orleans County, Salisbury (1838–1913) enlisted in the 151st New York State Volunteers in 1862. By 1864, he earned the rank of captain and was appointed to the 26th US Colored Infantry's Company D. By 1865 he was stationed in South Carolina, where he served both during the end of the war and as part of the Union's occupation forces. After leaving the Union army, he relocated to Virginia and became well known for supporting freedmen; Salisbury provided jobs at fair wages and opportunities to own land. Captain Salisbury also donated a portion of his land to establish a cemetery for people of color. (Courtesy of Julie A. Lewis.)

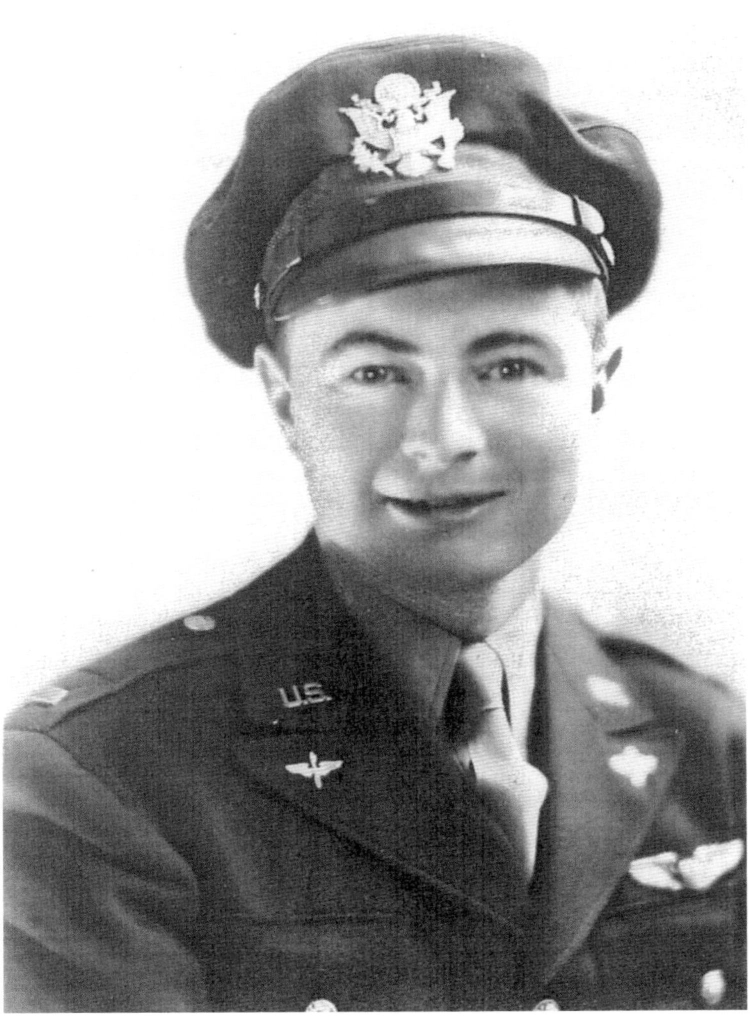

Bennett (1921–1997) was a soft-spoken gentleman who could tell war stories without graphic details, yet effectively convey what he had endured to preserve and protect our way of living. A P-51 Mustang pilot, Bennett told the story of how he had become a POW: "On February 5, 1945, a long, single-shot of German flack came up through the clouds as we were just clearing the Alps on our way home and found the Merlin engine of my P-51 Mustang. Parts flew and the glycol made a mist as it disappeared and I saw flames. I bailed out and the parachute worked." Bennett told this author (Holly Canham) he thought he was going to land in water and had his knife pulled to cut the chute cords, but realized at the last moment it was only fog, not water. "In the sweat box of isolation in Frankfurt, Germany, my first German POW camp, I underwent the usual one-week interrogation. Name, rank, and serial number only carried me through. On the walk from Nuremberg to Mooseburg, we received no food, but the German guards allowed us to go from house to house begging for food. After liberation, we reached Camp Lucky Strike at Le Havre, France, and were given a tin cup and eggnog. I know what it is to be hungry and the wonderful taste of eggnog." Despite his POW experience, Bennett treasured his time in the service. "I was given the best uniform in the world, a US serviceman's uniform." (Courtesy of Douglas Bennett.)

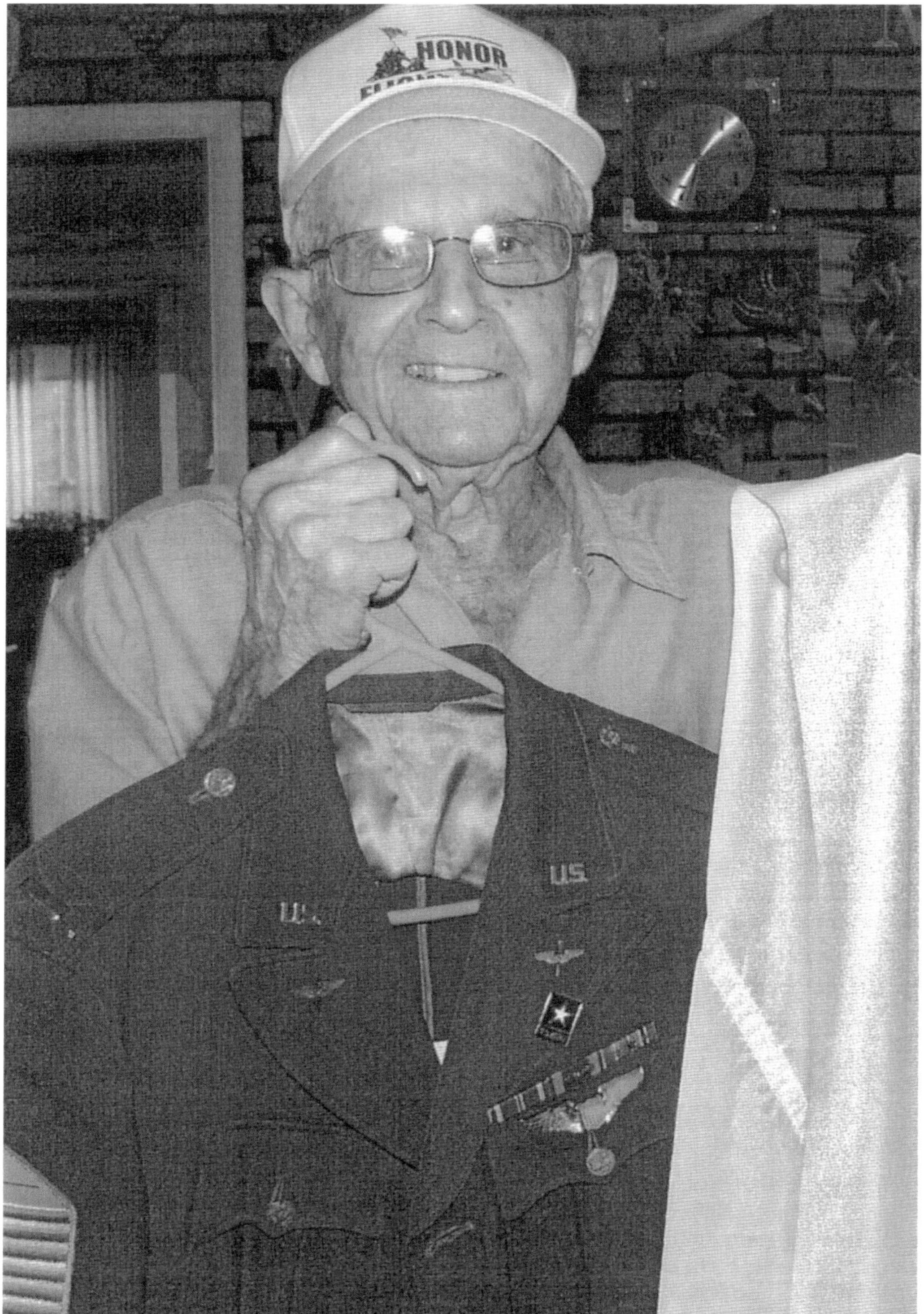
HONOR
U.S.

(LEFT)
Martin (1918–2011) spoke proudly of his 50 missions flown, the number of times his plane was shot up, and the times he disobeyed orders in an effort to land safely. On one occasion, he approached his base with one engine already out and his aircraft too low on fuel for the "go-around" the tower ordered. Notwithstanding the order, he took his chance and landed, coming to a rest just a few feet from the plane in front of him. The next day his radio operator awarded him the large piece of parachute (left), suggesting he could make a nice white scarf out of it; Bruce did just that. (Courtesy of Virginia Kropf.)

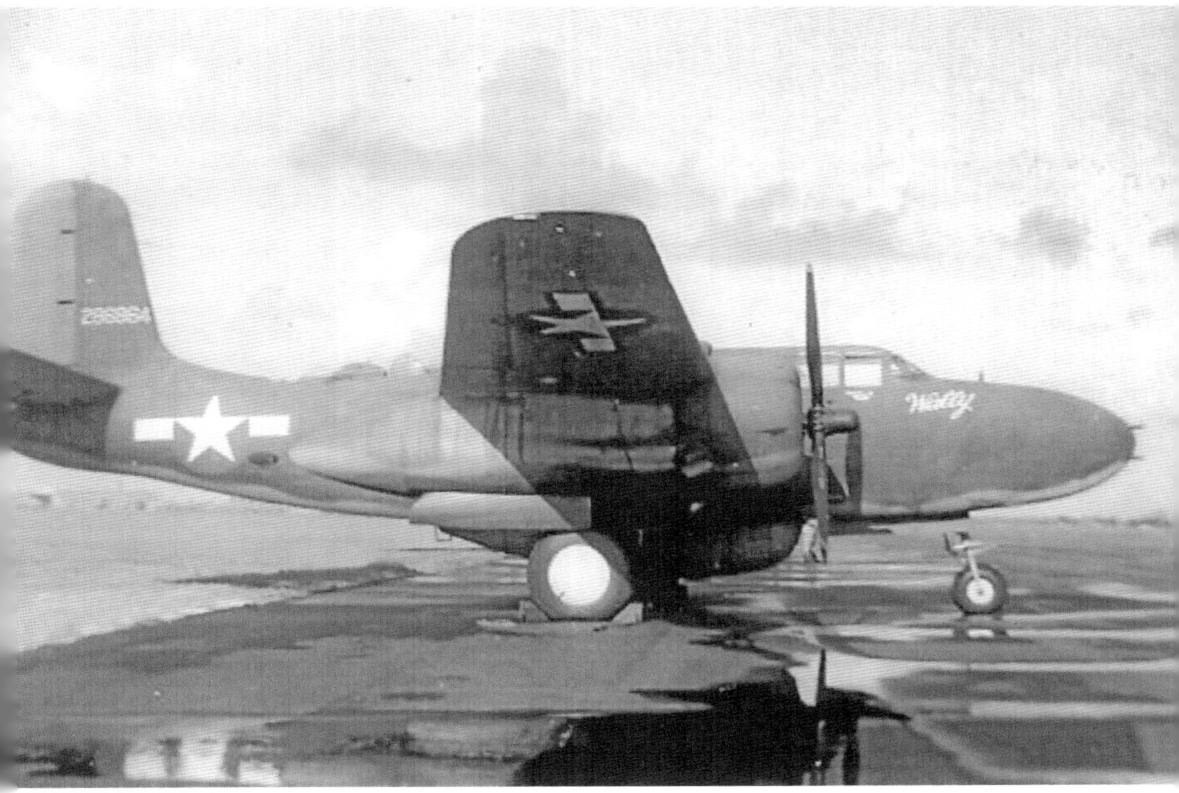

Pictured above is Newton's Douglas A-20 "Havoc" airplane inscribed with his bride's nickname. "Wally" was being ferried to northern India as part of the Lend-Lease Program to deliver aircraft for use by the Russians (then our allies) in early November 1943. On August 19, 1944, Newton was flying a C-47 cargo mission in Burma as a "Hump Pilot" when his aircraft was reported missing. The crash site has yet to be located. While still considered by his family to be Missing in Action, a year after the crash Lieutenant Newton was officially declared Killed in Action. The Department of Defense Joint POW/MIA Accounting Command has included locating his crash site as part of its current mission to account for missing Americans. (Courtesy of Claire Saxon.)

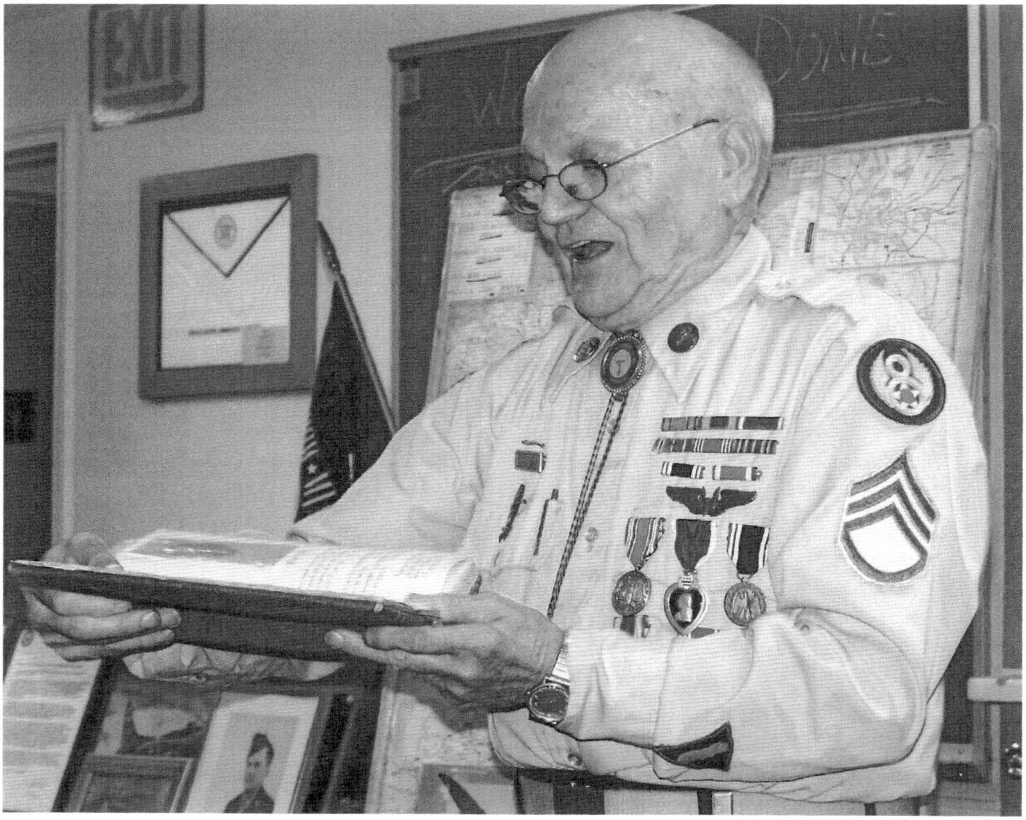

Owen traveled under special orders (first, on board the *Queen Mary* to Blackpool, England, and then by train to Le Wash) as an armament specialist to teach soldiers about ball turrets on B-17 Flying Fortresses and B-24 Liberators. He was assigned to the 306th Bomb Group (a division of the 369th Bomb Wing). Owen travelled with an acquaintance, Clark Gable the movie actor; Gable's military duties included the special assignment to make a combat movie specifically intended to recruit gunners. Owen was then sent to Thurleigh (northern England), where his aircraft was hit; with two engines on fire and about to blow up, he used his parachute. His next memory is that of lying in a deep ditch, where a young German Marine was poking him in the face with a bayonet. After being held in solitary confinement for 17 days, Owen was interrogated by an SS major who pulled a book off the shelf behind him and read Charlie's life story—from childhood and beyond—to him. Amazed, Owen asked how they got all that information; the major said, "your friends and neighbors in Medina." Ultimately, he was held prisoner in several locations, including 19 months in Stalag 17 among 4,000 American Air Force prisoners. "We did all kinds of things to pass the time. Some of the guys went berserk because they were just lying around thinking of home. Once, after the searchlight was shining in another direction, I went across the warning wire and picked this poppy and wrote about 'the Prison Poppy.' Later, I drew a picture of my 'church' and wrote a poem about it, 'The Kriege Temple.'" His group was placed on a forced march to a location above the Inns River in Bavaria. They were eventually freed by General Patton's 13th Armored Division; upon rescue, Owen weighed 85 pounds, substantially less than his original weight of 159 pounds when his plane was shot down. This past summer, at the age of 99, he attended the 4-H Fair. Owen was honored for his service during a ceremony held at the fairground's new memorial park. (Courtesy of Virginia Kropf.)

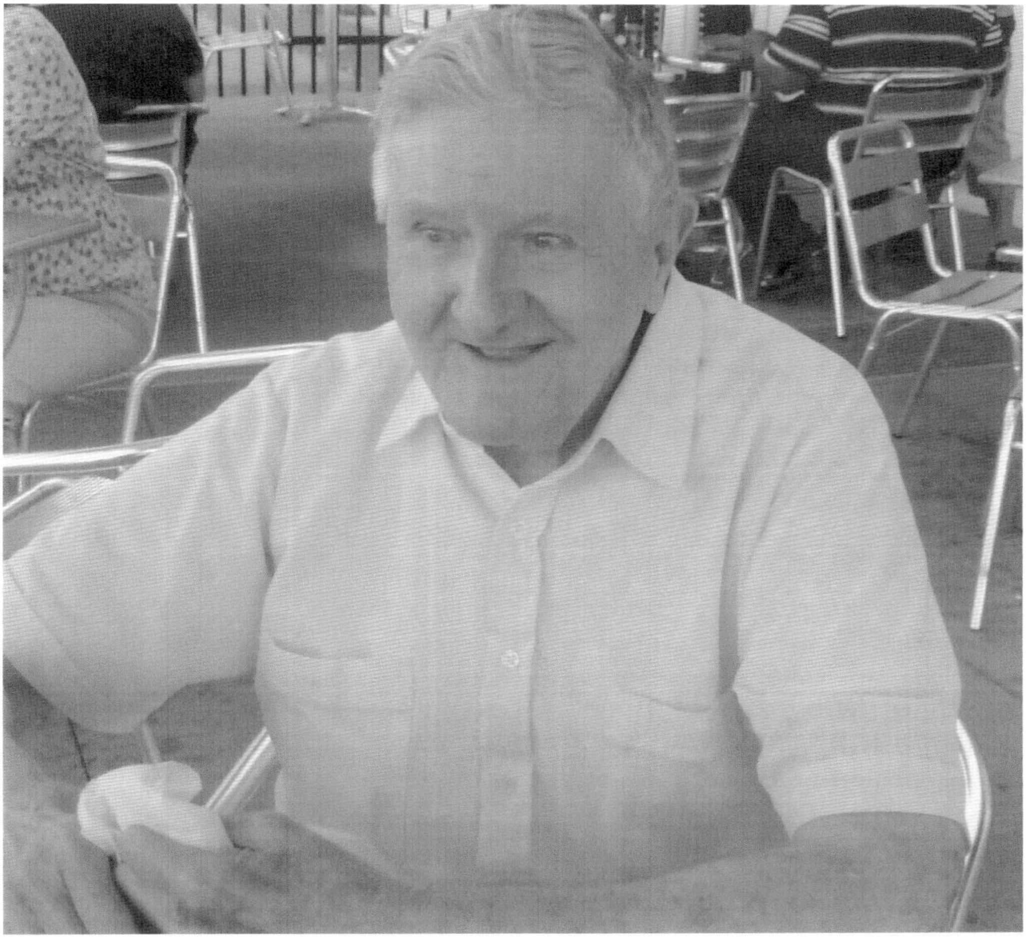

Bliss served on Merchant Marine ships in World War II. In 1944, he was with a convoy of 56 ships that were spotted by an observation plane—they knew they were in trouble. "Ice flow restricted our movement. Ships with explosives, fuel and ammunition were positioned mid-convoy; when the German Heinkles came they knew just where to attack." One bomb blast blew Bliss off his ship and onto ice, where a British vessel later picked him up. The blast took nearly all of Bliss's eyesight. Of 56 ships with 47 men on each, only four ships and 30 men survived. Returning to this area, Bliss and a good friend built the first marina on the Oak Orchard River. (Courtesy of Holly Canham.)

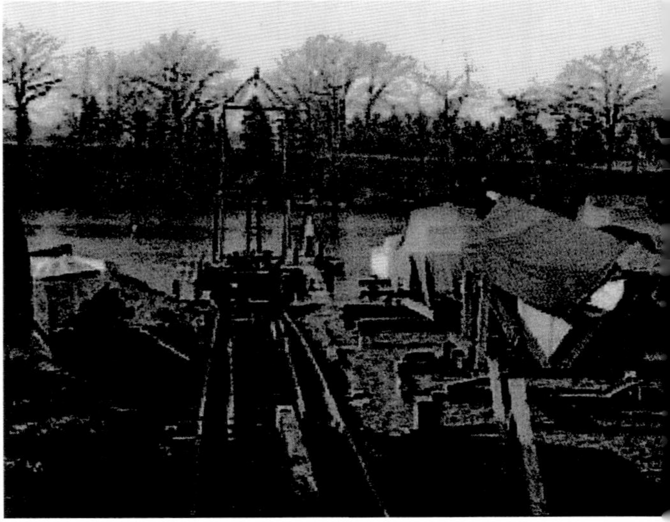

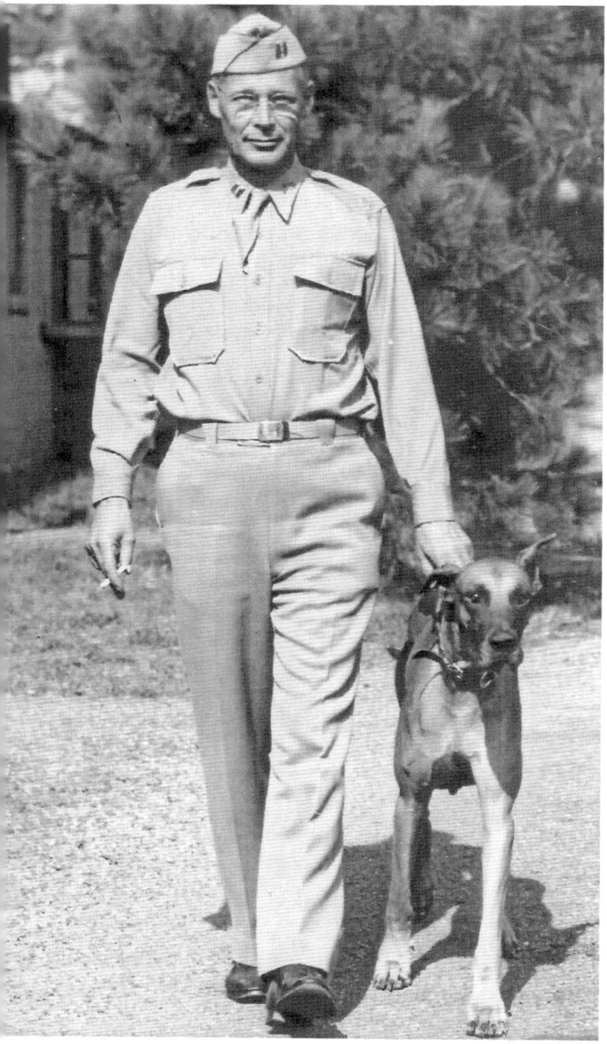

Clark (1898–1948), pictured at left, served in the US Marine Corps during World War II. He later received a commission in the US Army and served during the Korean Conflict. Major Clark received several citations and medals for his dedicated service. Clark was a state trooper, chief of police and Orleans County sheriff. While a sheriff, he introduced the county to the use of fingerprinting for evidence collection. (Courtesy of Julie Bennett and Eleanor Yungfleisch.)

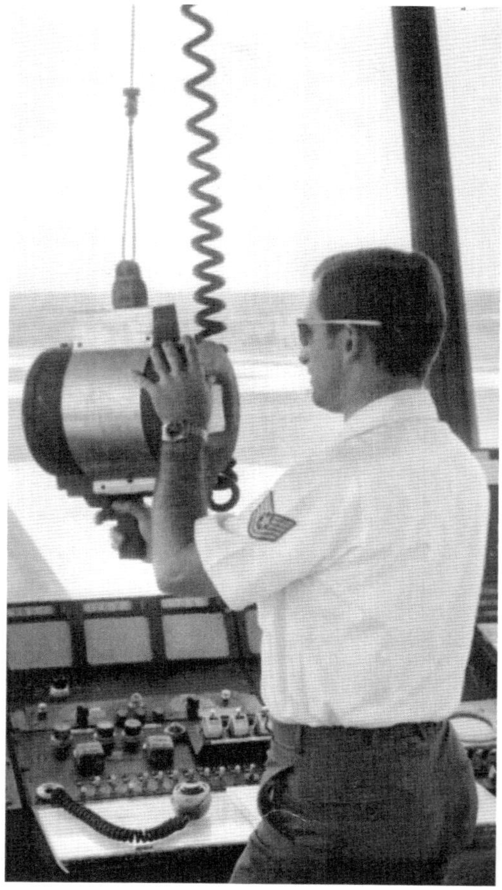

A US Air Force air traffic controller for 20 years, Bud Canham's duty assignments included seven and a half years in the Pacific and European theaters. Credited with saving the lives of all "souls on board" during dozens of in-flight emergencies, Canham was the subject of an *Airman Magazine* feature article. Canham received the Air Force Commendation Medal, awarded for "sustained acts of heroism or meritorious service." (Courtesy of Andrew Canham.)

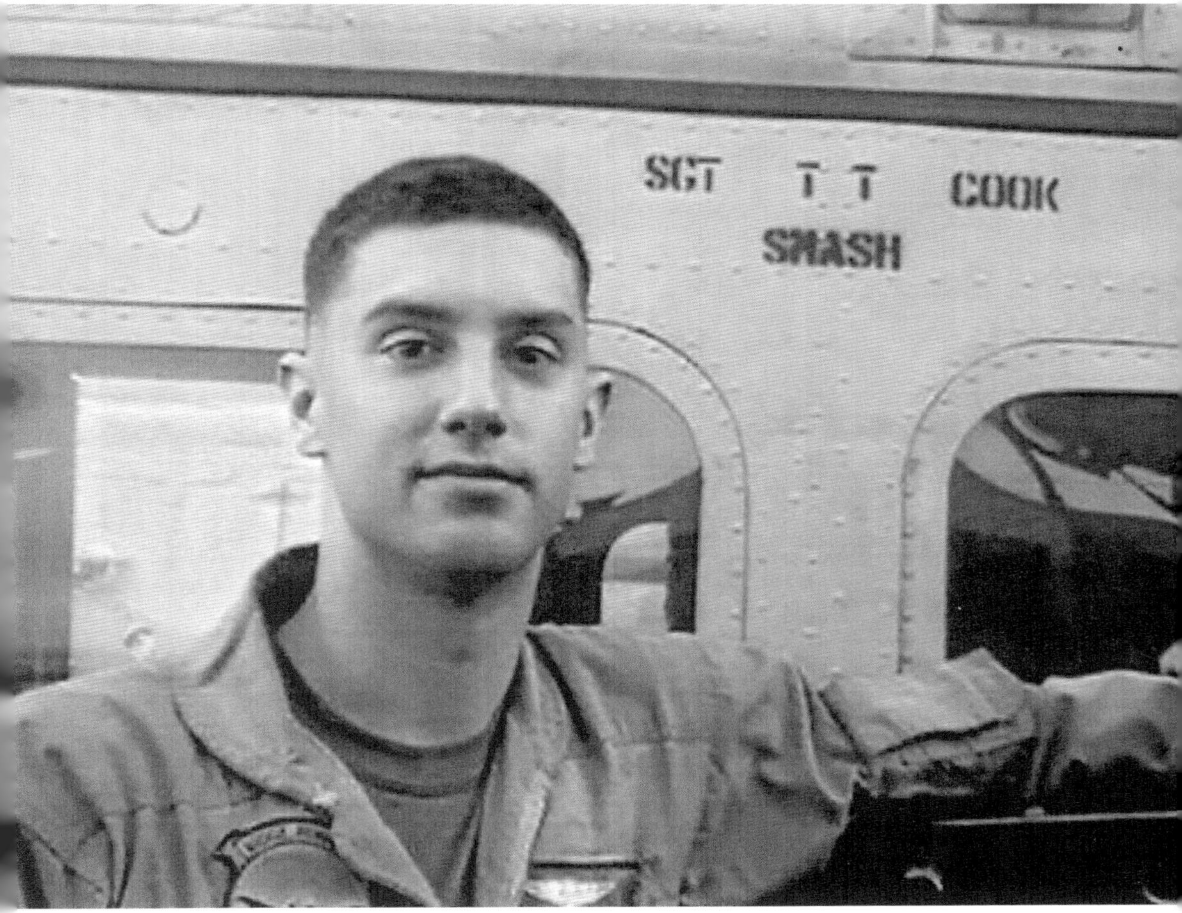

Twenty-five-year-old Sgt. Trevor Cook, of Lyndonville, was killed July 6, 2011, at Camp Pendleton in Southern California when a helicopter he was in crashed during a training operation. The death of Sergeant Cook was a loss felt throughout Orleans County, and hundreds of people attended his funeral. The Patriot Guard Riders, who escorted his body home, stood outside while long lines of mourners made their way to say good-bye. The US Marine Corps honored Sergeant Cook with a ceremonial gun salute. Cook (1986–2011) was one of six Marines involved in the UH-1Y helicopter accident; two other Marines were badly hurt and three others sustained minor injuries. He was a crew chief with Marine Light Attack Helicopter Squadron 369 of the 3rd Marine Aircraft Wing and had been in the Marines for 7 years. He spent time in the Gulf of Aden and the Pacific Theater and returned in November 2010 from his second tour of active duty in Afghanistan, where he served about eight months. Cook's military decorations include an Air Medal, Marine Corps Good Conduct Medal, Navy and Marine Corps Achievement Medal, Afghanistan Campaign Medal, Global War on Terrorism Expeditionary Medal, Global War on Terrorism Service Medal, National Defense Service Medal, and NATO Medal. It was Cook's personality and goodness that won him many friends at Camp Pendleton. Lt. Col. Ian Clark is quoted as saying, "Trevor was one of the kindest and most giving Marines in the unit; he stood out for his skill and courage during his tour in Afghanistan." Sgt. Matt Cummings commented, "Trevor was one of the most honest and genuine people I've ever met. Cook handled the stress of the Marines and his job, knowing he was helping to make the country safe." (Courtesy of David Cook.)

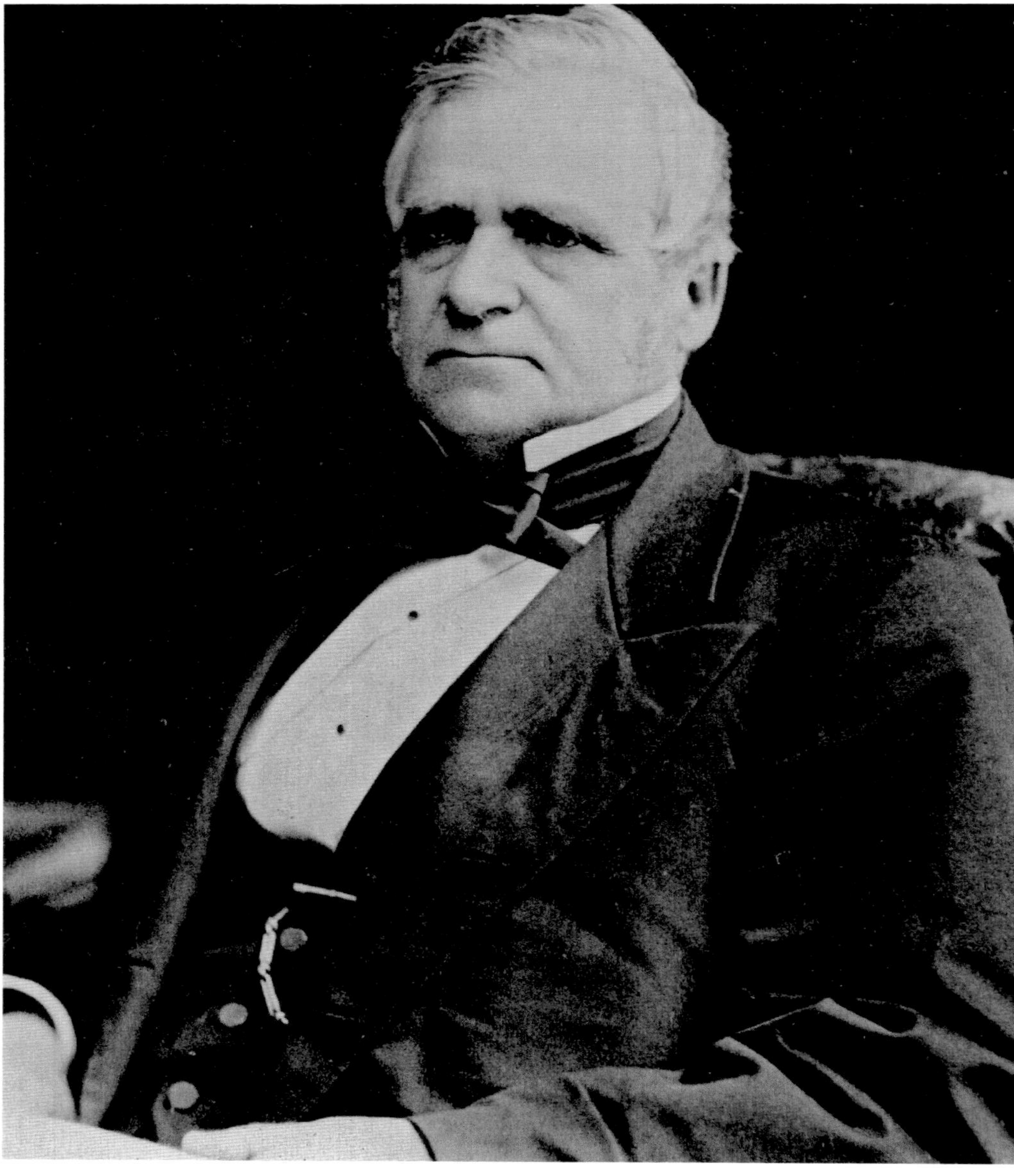

Church (1815–1880) moved to Albion in 1835 with his parents. He became an attorney, and had numerous legal partnerships such as Church & Sawyer, and Church, Munger and Cooke; perhaps most notable was his partnership with Noah Davis (who was later elected to the 41st US Congress as a Republican). Church (a Democrat) held numerous positions in the county and state, including Orleans County district attorney, New York state comptroller, lieutenant governor, and finance committee chairman of the 1867 New York State Constitutional Convention. In 1868, at the Democratic National Convention, he was New York's nominee for the presidency for several ballots (other candidates were later chosen). Church later served as chief judge of the Court of Appeals. He is buried in Mt. Albion Cemetery. (Courtesy of Orleans County Department of History.)

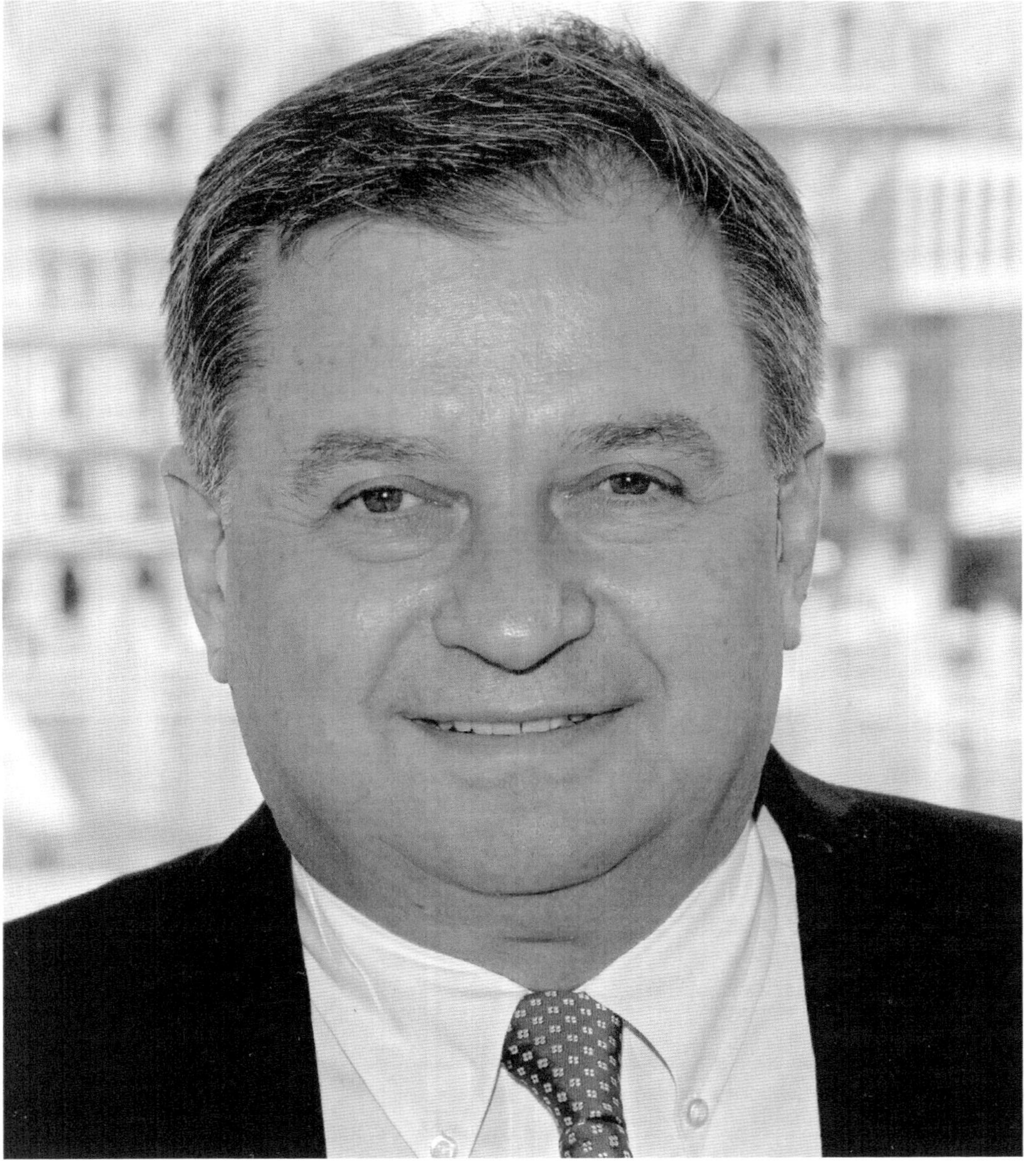

Appointed to serve as president and commissioner of the New York State Tax Appeals Tribunal in 2005, Nesbitt had served as minority leader of the New York State Assembly, and for 13 years as an assemblyman. In 2003, Mr. Nesbitt helped create the historic Patriot Plan, a benefits package that assists New Yorkers serving their nation in the Reserve components of the Armed Forces. Signed into law, this became the most comprehensive assistance package extended to members of the National Guard and Reserve since the GI Bill and has become a model for other states. For this effort, The National Guard Association of the United States presented Charlie with the highest award a state legislator is eligible to receive. He is a decorated helicopter pilot, having served with the 57th Assault Helicopter Co. during the Vietnam War. (Courtesy of Charles H. Nesbitt.)

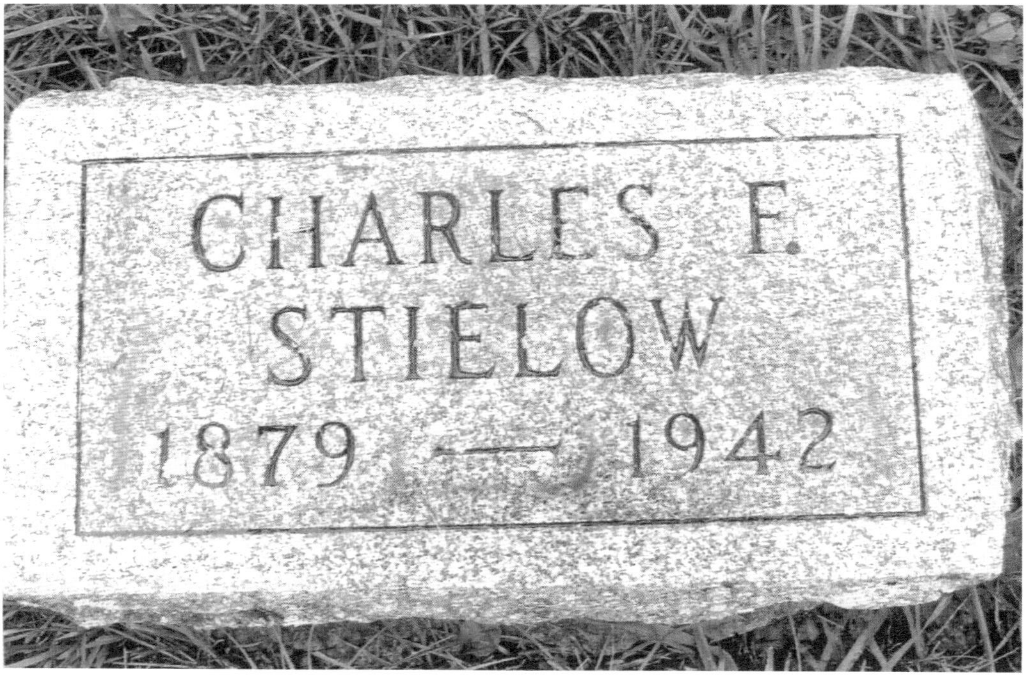

A sweet and gentle giant of a man, Stielow (1879–1942) was easy prey for corrupt Orleans County politicians and authorities in 1915. Having grown up in the German speaking community of Wolcottsville, in neighboring Niagara County, Stielow never learned to read and could barely write his own name. His English was less than perfect. Nature's equalizer came into play providing Stielow with extraordinary physical strength and a command of all aspects of farm work. He could work the land, tend crops, make repairs, raise livestock, and butcher, as well. These skills led him to be hired on by a cantankerous, but prosperous, elderly farmer by the name of Charles B. Phelps of the Salt Works Road, just inside the Orleans County line. A little over a week after moving into Phelps's tenant house, Stielow discovered his employer's housekeeper's dead body in the snow outside his house, and subsequently, his employer's near dead body. Stielow went for help and was all too quickly accused of the crimes. The few people who realized the investigation was based more on politics than sound police work were silenced. Four months later, Stielow was on death row, but not forgotten by his court appointed lawyer, David White. White accomplished the impossible more than a few times, including enlisting the help of Grace Humiston, then America's greatest detective, who happened to live and work out of New York City. The two were able to root out new evidence, expose falsified testimony and coercion—literally in the nick of time. Later, for the fourth time, the farmhand was minutes away from death in Sing Sing's electric chair for a double-murder he did not commit when justice finally prevailed. America's most famous wrongful conviction case, this tragic event is still discussed in American law schools today. (Courtesy of Bud Canham.)

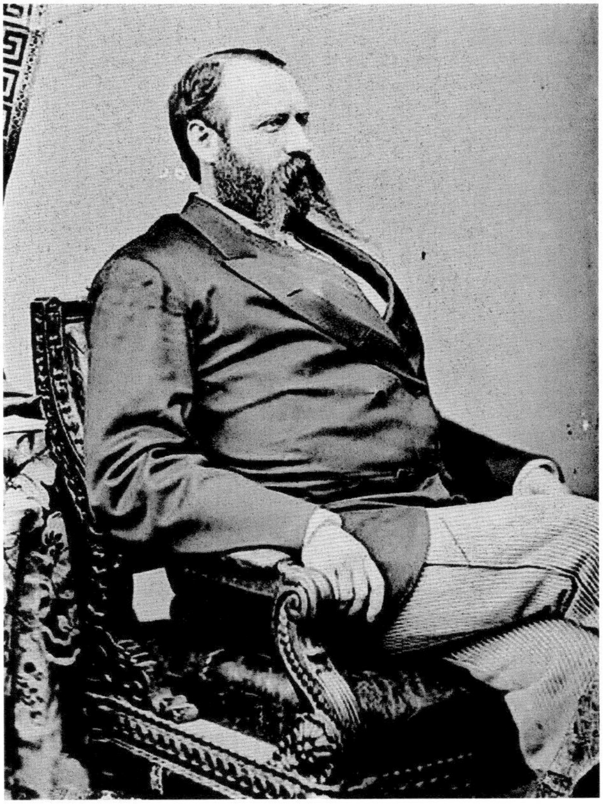

Bullock (1834–1907) graduated from the old Albion Academy in 1850 and subsequently mastered the art of telegraphy. His father, Volker Veeder Bullock, brought telegraphy to Albion. Bullock later invented a combination printing telegraph system. He worked all over the northeastern area of the United States, constructing telegraph lines in cities. His work eventually led him to form the Southern Express Co., headquartered in Atlanta, Georgia. He continued his businesses under the Confederate government's direction when the Civil War broke out. He was assistant quartermaster general, and surrendered with Gen. Robert E. Lee at Appomattox. In 1868, he was elected as the first Republican governor in Georgia, and the last until 2002. He was threatened by the Ku Klux Klan, which allegedly forced him from office. He resigned from office in 1871 amid scandal. In 1876, he stood trial on embezzlement charges and was found not guilty—twice. Bullock remained in Atlanta and became one of the city's most prominent citizens. He was president of Atlanta's first cotton mill, president of the English-American Loan Company, an elder of St. Philip's Episcopal Church, president of the Atlanta Chamber of Commerce, president of the Commercial Club, vice president of the Capital City Club, and a member of the Piedmont Driving Club. Governor Bullock's advocacy of black rights made him very unpopular, which led to much personal abuse. The novel, *Gone with the Wind*, by native Georgian Margaret Mitchell, references the election of Rufus Bullock at the end of Part Four, calling it the end of a process of Northern subjugation of Georgia that had begun with Sherman's March to the Sea in 1864. From *Gone with the Wind*: "If the capture of Georgia by Sherman had caused bitterness, the final capture of the state's capitol by the Carpetbaggers, Yankees, and negroes caused an intensity of bitterness . . . Atlanta and Georgia seethed and raged. And Rhett Butler was a friend of the hated Bullock!" Note: The photograph was taken by none other than legendary Civil War era photographer Mathew Brady. (Courtesy of Orleans County Department of History.)

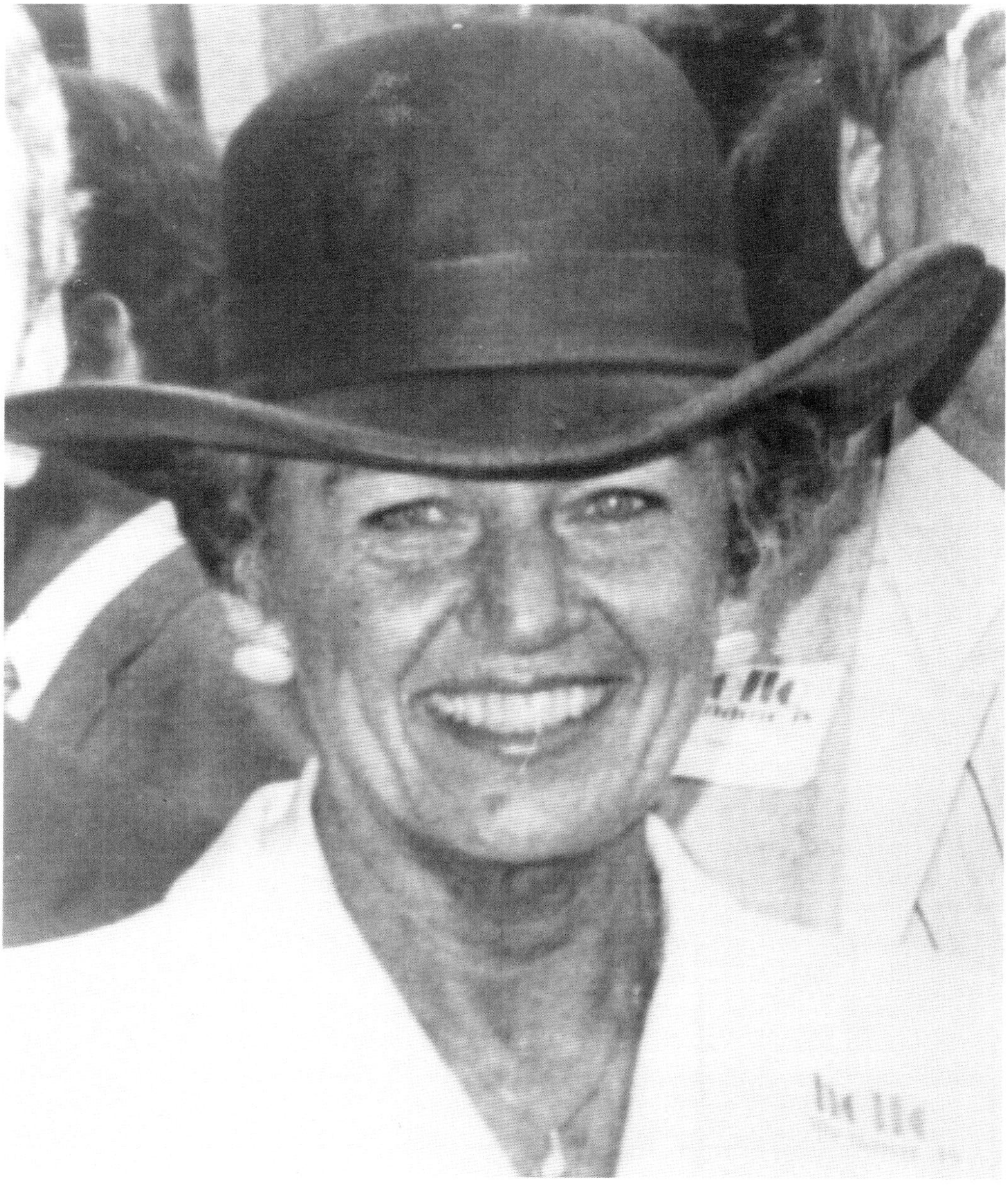

Born in Medina, Tuohey began her political career on the Shelby Town Assessment and Review Board. Elected as Medina Village trustee in 1979, she became the first woman mayor in 1982, serving until 1990 when she became the county's first female legislator. She served the first 10 years of her 16-year tenure as the first woman chairman. Among her visible accomplishments are the renovation of the courthouse and County Legislature buildings, an addition to the County Nursing Home, creation of a new Public Safety Center, and a new Fire Training Facility. Tuohey has been the recipient of numerous awards and has contributed hundreds of community service hours. Her legacy will consist of blazing a political and business trail for the women of this county. (Courtesy of Marcia Tuohey.)

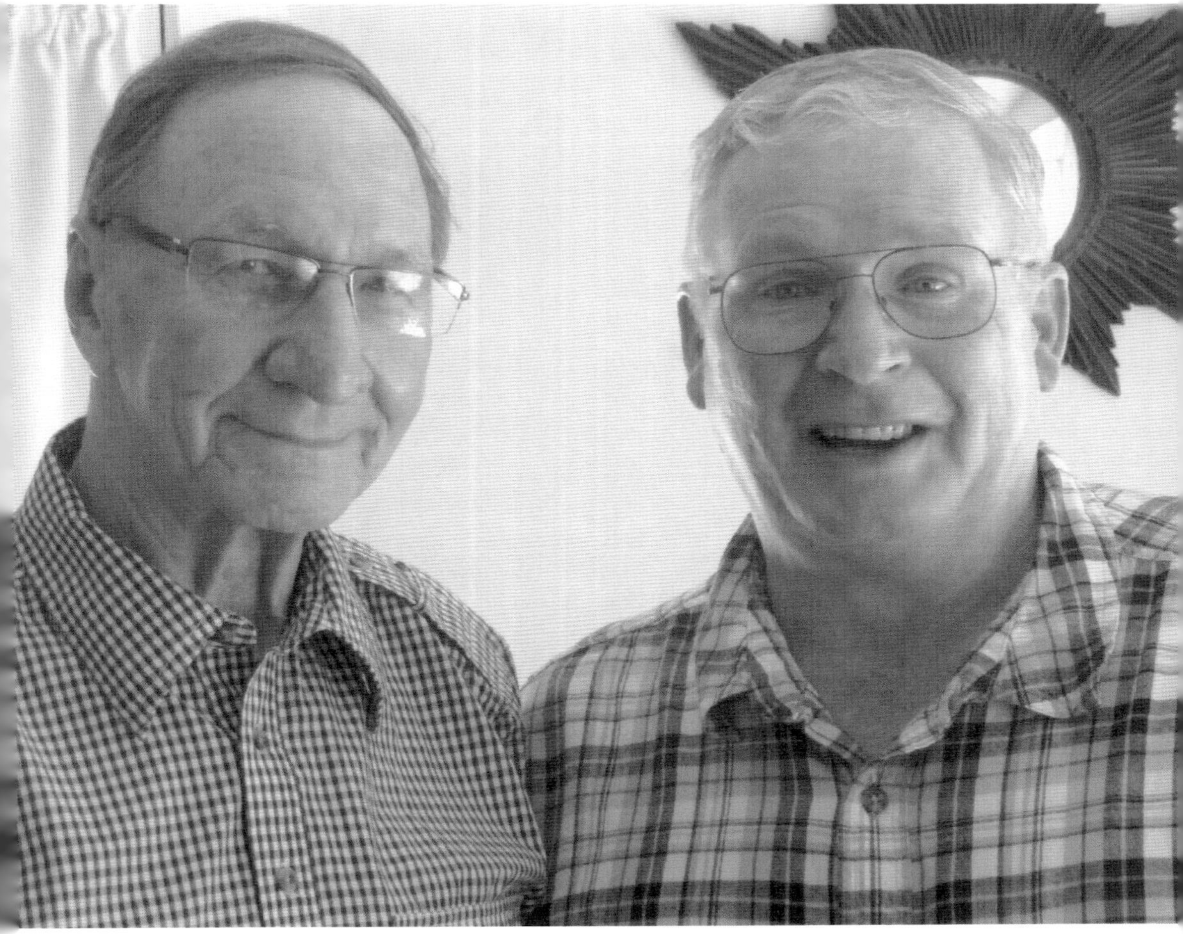

Besides being great friends to each other, these men are great friends of the citizens of Orleans County. Both having served as town supervisors, they also served as county legislators. Together they submitted a resolution to allow the construction of a second state correctional facility in Orleans County. This new facility was of such great importance to the county that ground breaking took place just 60 days later. Their action solved several problems, including bringing badly needed jobs to county residents. Additionally, Swierczynski worked toward establishing the area's Industrial Development Agency, bringing Bayex/Saint-Gobain, Anchor Bank and its many successors, and BernzOmatic to the area, all contributing to the general prosperity and economic welfare of the local population. Swierczynski also served on the first Board for Off Track Betting in 1976. (Courtesy of Holly Canham.)

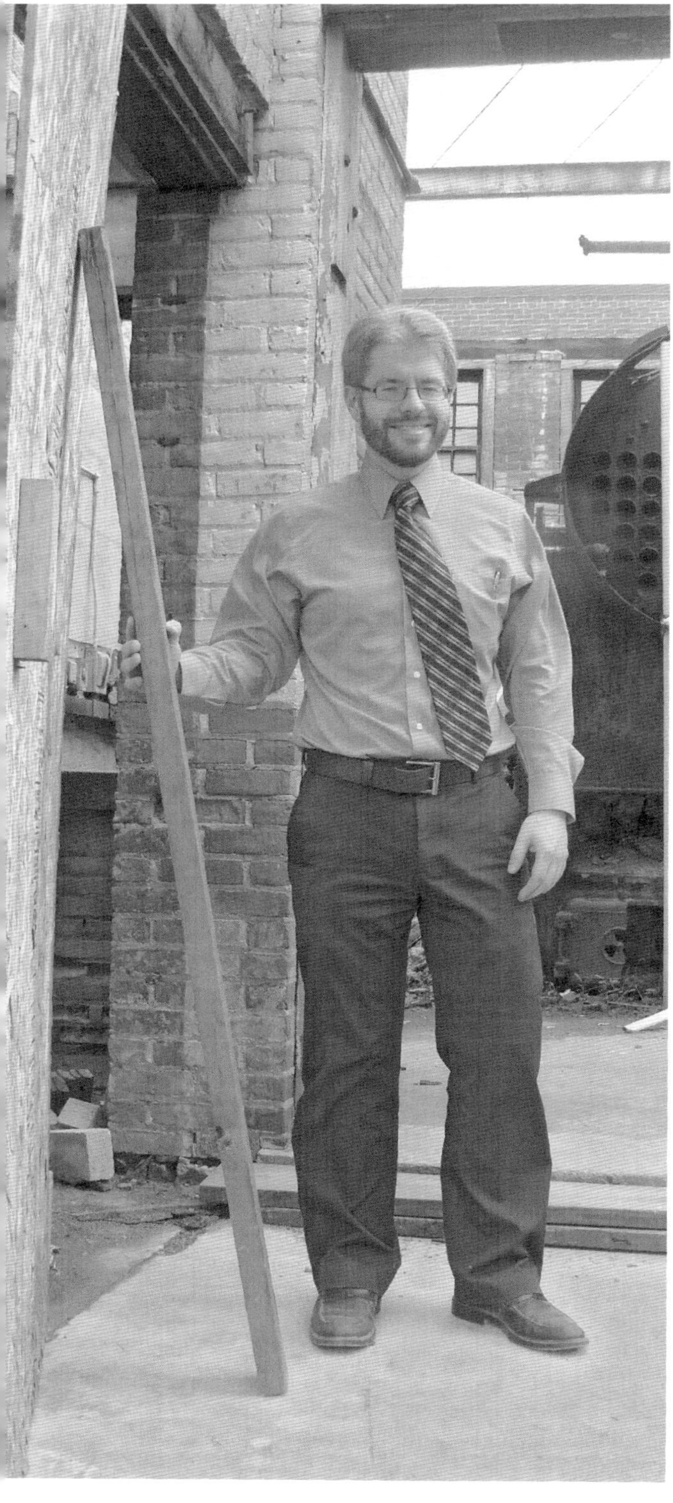

Meier is not only a "local boy who made good," but he came back to share his talents with his native Medina. Meier, 32, loves architecture and historic buildings. A 1997 graduate of Medina High School, Meier graduated from the University of Rochester in 2001, and earned his law degree from Syracuse University in 2004. He returned to Medina to practice law, joining the firm of Webster and Schubel, now Webster, Schubel and Meier. Meier purchased the former Newell Shirt Factory when it came up for sale. "Working on this project has been a source of joy and something I am very passionate about," he said. "I have always been up for a challenge, and this was about the biggest challenge you could get, to restore a building for the community which most people considered functionally obsolete. Upon acquisition, I saw huge possibilities and started complete engineering and architectural studies." He obtained funding from the National Trust for Historic Preservation and started work. Hardly a day would go by when he wasn't physically working there himself. The first floor was converted into a coffeehouse, which also offers space for local artists to display their work and a meeting or event room that can accommodate 50 people, themed after the shirt factory. The second floor is partially complete and now houses his firm's law offices. The third floor is a work in progress, and will eventually provide unique, loft-style apartments, something not currently available in Orleans County. A patio has also been built for outdoor dining. When completed, the project will have cost in excess of $1 million. In 2008, after serving the Village of Medina as its attorney, Meier was elected to the village board. Meier is now Medina's mayor. Musically inclined, he plays organ every Sunday for both the Lutheran and Presbyterian churches in Medina. As time allows, he sings in a trio with his friends, former mayor Adam Tabelski and Aaron Grabowski. (Courtesy of Virginia Kropf.)

Agriculture and 4-H— Growing Community

From the time early settlers cleared away forests and drained swampland in order to grow their food, the people of Orleans County have known a close relationship with the earth. Some excerpts from Arad Thomas's *Pioneer History of Orleans County* tell the story: "My last feat in chopping was in 1832, when I walked three miles morning and evening, and chopped over three acres, leaving it fitted for logging in ten and a half days" (Samuel Salisbury of Eagle Harbor); "But the sound of the axman was heard at his toil through the forest, hurling the old trees headlong. The worlds and the heavens were lit up with the lurid glare of the fire by night, and the heavy forest soon melted away. Those little holes in the old woods soon became enlarged to broad fields of waving grain that glistened in the sun light" (George E. Mix). Betty Genter, a local teacher, writer, and artist, discusses farm life in her books: "as children of muck farmers we learned at an early age how to drive a tractor and truck, how to fill the baskets or crates on a potato or onion picker, how to pick three to five rows of plants at a time, and how to mix chemicals with water for spraying plants." Farming equipment and methods have changed tremendously, which is demonstrated in this chapter's modern-day farm stories. One thing that has not changed is the value and importance of the 4-H Fair to area families. Based on European trade fairs and later seasonal trade fairs, these country fairs were important social and educational events. New ideas and inventions to improve production of both livestock and crops were, and still are, freely exchanged. Though deep-fried pickles have been added to the treats offered, the educational exchange remains the same.

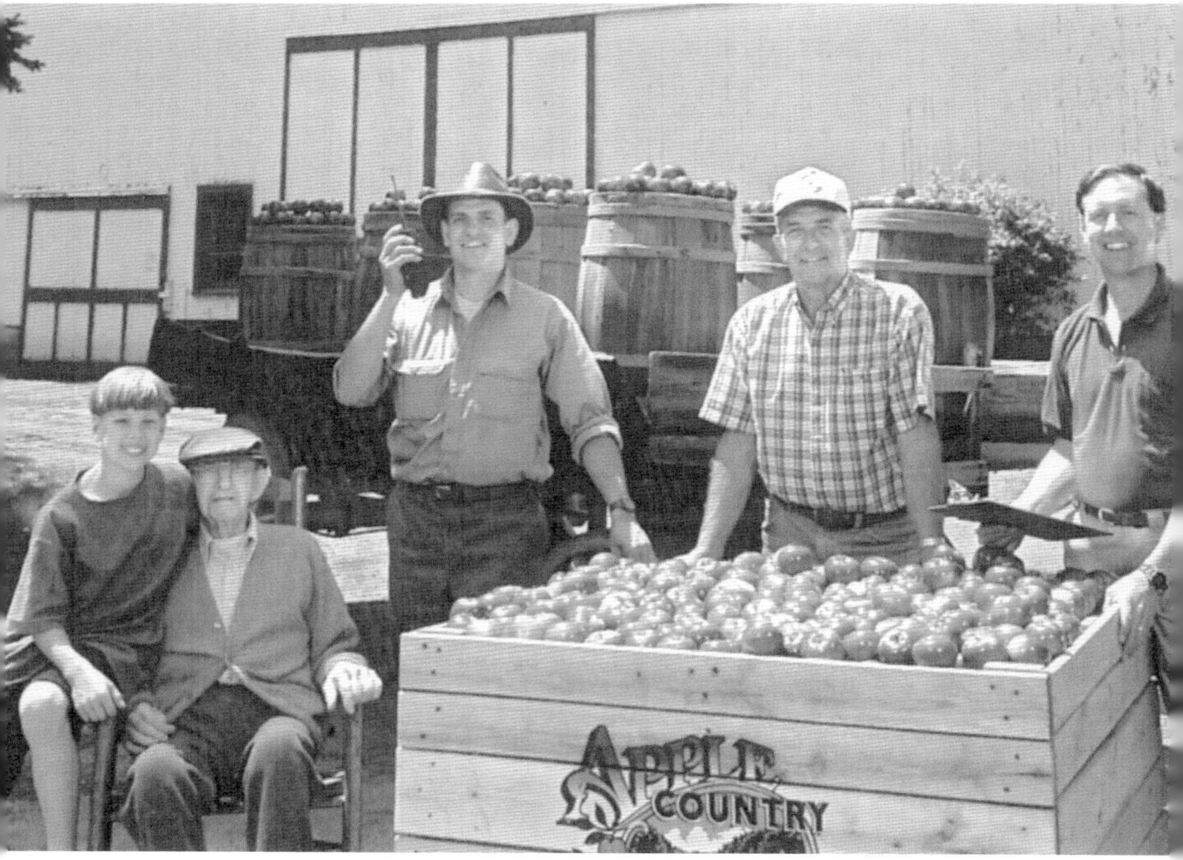

The Brown family includes a unique legend of their own. The family matriarch Bathshua was a young bride living on Fishers Island during the early years of the Revolutionary War. Bathshua confronted a British officer, who was conducting a raid, provoking him to order their animals to be confiscated and their household belongings to be removed from the home and destroyed. The Browns moved to the mainland and by the turn of the century decided to take advantage of the Holland Land Office sales, purchasing the area where Brown's Berry Patch and Orchard Dale Farms are now. While relocating his family to what is now Carlton via boat on Lake Ontario, Elijah, aged 56, became ill and died. Bathshua, 49 years of age at the time, buried her husband as the first settler buried in Orleans County. Nine years later, during the War of 1812, a British warship deployed a boat of armed troops to make their way up the Oak Orchard River to pursue settlers. Their captain was captured while pausing to enjoy some ripe plums and was taken to the nearest house—Bathshua's. The widow recognized the captain as the same person she had confronted back on Fishers Island! Knowing the captain would likely be executed if turned over to the American forces, and not wanting to be responsible for that, she decided he should be returned to his ship with the agreement he would never set foot on land via the Oak Orchard River again. Bathshua lived to be 71. In 1895, the farm was being run by Harry L. Brown, who sold his flock of sheep to buy trees to plant their first quince orchard; it developed into the largest quince orchard in the world at 60 acres. The seventh generation operates the farm now, which has become an agritourism destination with ice cream, sandwiches, a bakery, and a large country gift shop. The Brown family has added a children's amusement park called Barnyard Adventure, which offers a playground in the midst of farm animals. (Courtesy of the Brown Family.)

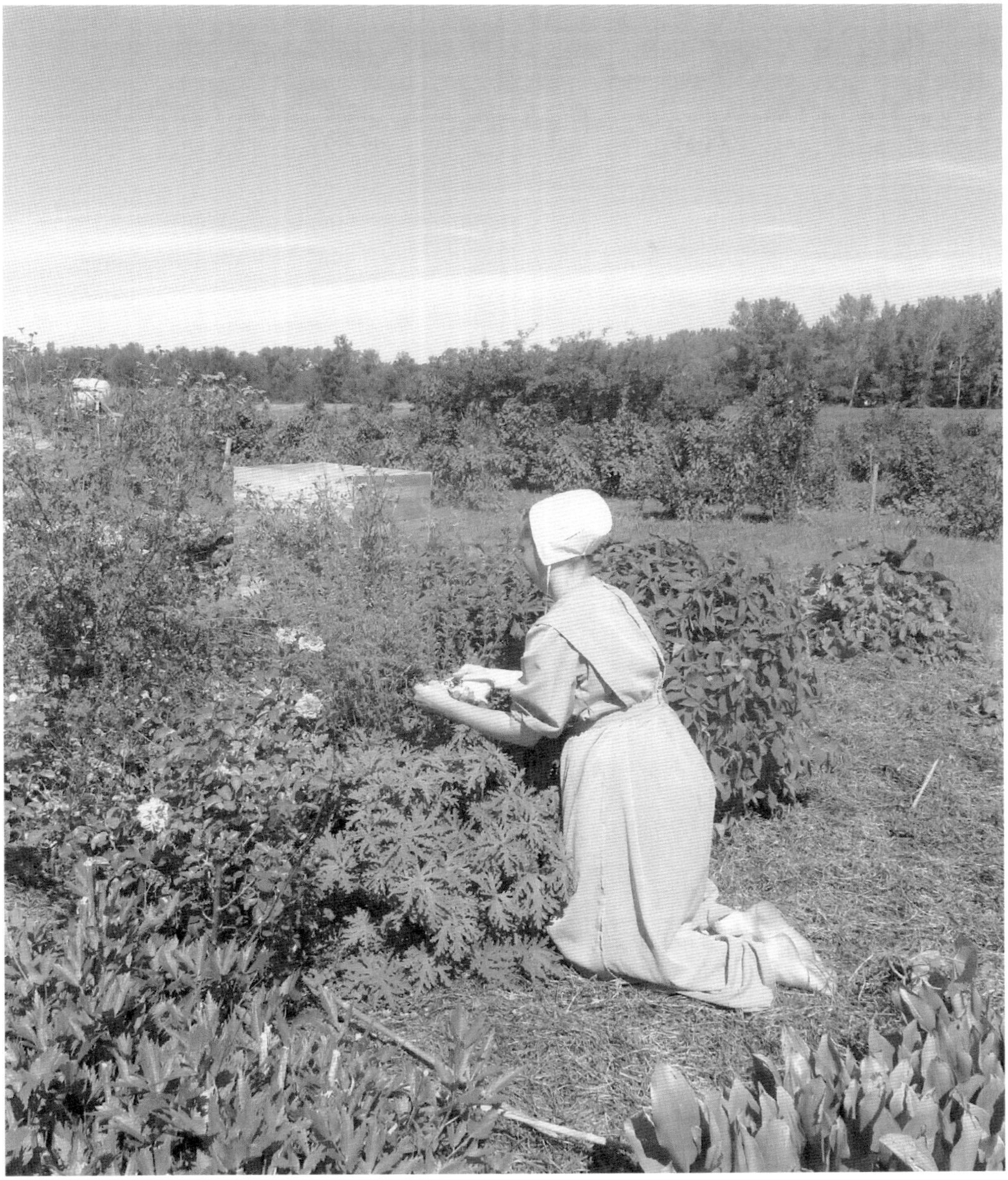

Schlabach began sharing her vast experience growing and using herbs in the early 1990s and now has a regular column, "Gracia's Garden." She often focuses on a single herb, explaining how to grow, harvest, and use it. Aside from their important use in cooking, many herbs have medicinal value—she explains how to make salves in her column. "People can learn by reading," she says. "Working with herbs is very hands-on and people can grow into it." Schlabach has a strong second interest in music and has self-published a book, *Now Thank We All Our God*, an overview of German hymns still sung today by over 300,000 Amish, Old Order Mennonites, and Amish Mennonites in the United States and Canada. (Courtesy of Holly Canham.)

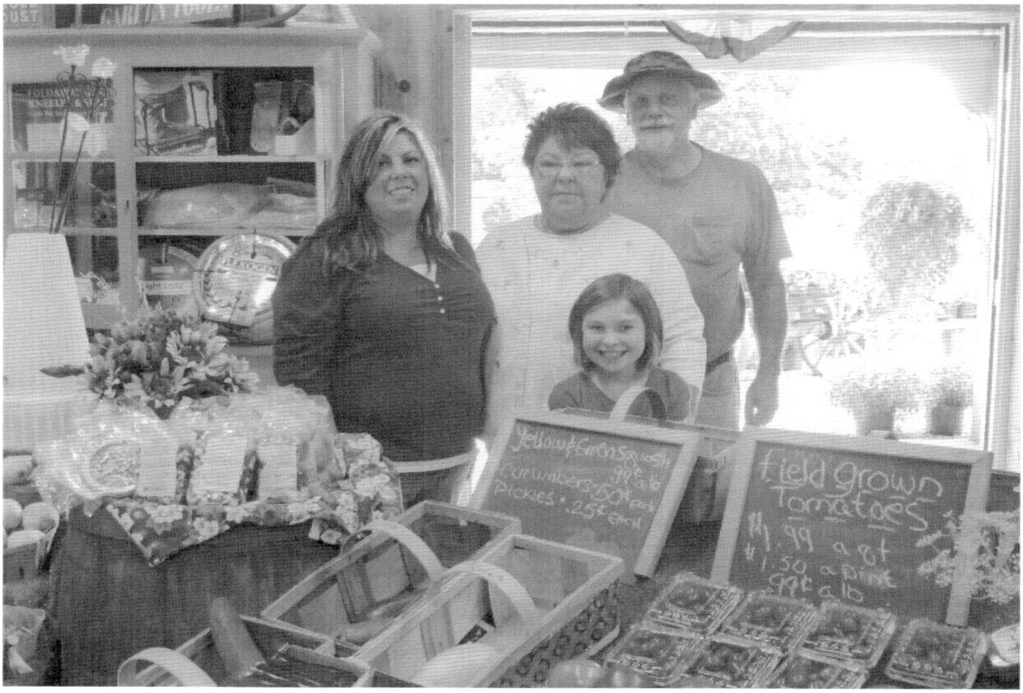

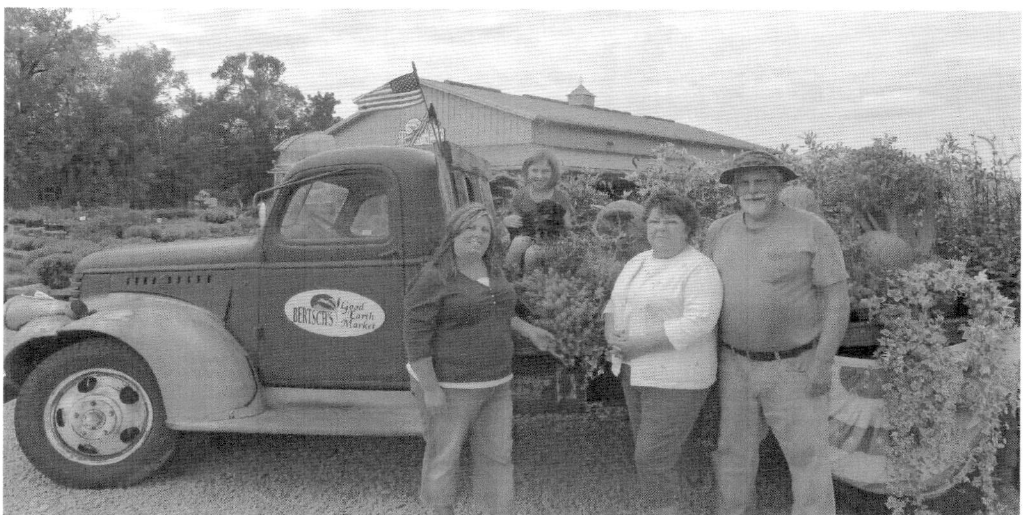

The Bertsches have been local farmers since the 1920s and established their farm market in 1999 at the corner of Route 98 and Route 18 in Carlton, New York. Long before the market existed, the neighborhood community enjoyed going to Bertsch's roadside stand to purchase seasonal items, such as strawberries in the summer and pumpkins for Halloween. Today, they not only provide fresh produce and nursery stock, but also consult on landscaping. In the images are Heather Bertsch Tabor, daughter Madeline, and her parents, David and Sharon Bertsch; absent from the photos is Heather's husband Jim Tabor, a hands-on owner. (Courtesy of Holly Canham.)

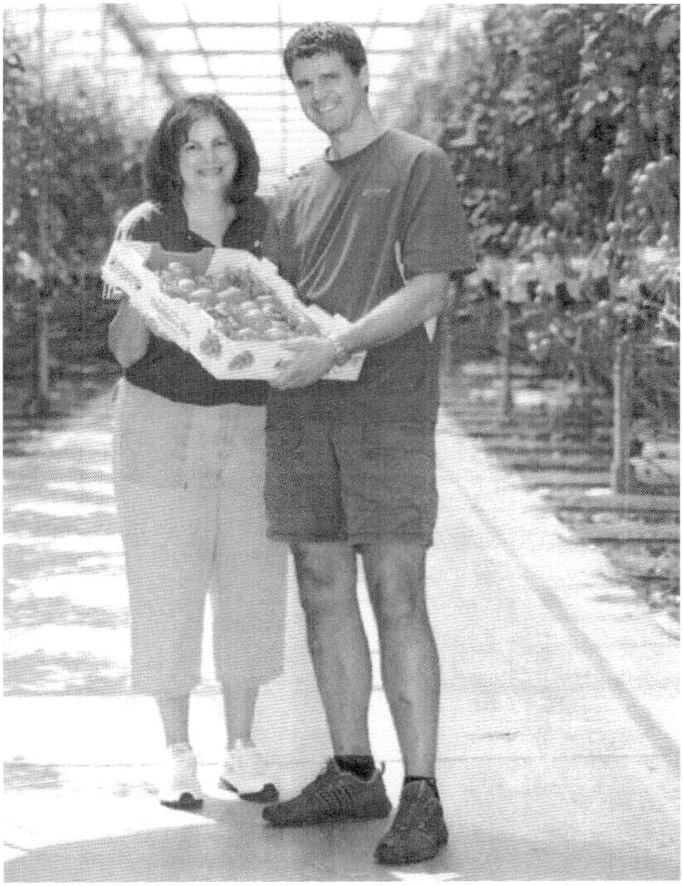

Principles of conservation and preservation were built into the Biemans' growing process. Diane explains that "from the flower stage right through shipping, we take into consideration our environmental impact. Whether its recycled paper in our packing boxes or minimizing our food miles so our carbon footprint is smaller, there's no step too small to take." Forty-eight acres under glass makes Intergrow the most advanced county farm. Twenty percent of their crop is sold to Wegmans stores in the Northeast and Mid-Atlantic; the rest is sold to stores throughout the eastern half of the country. (Top courtesy of Diane Bieman; bottom courtesy of Eugene Haines.)

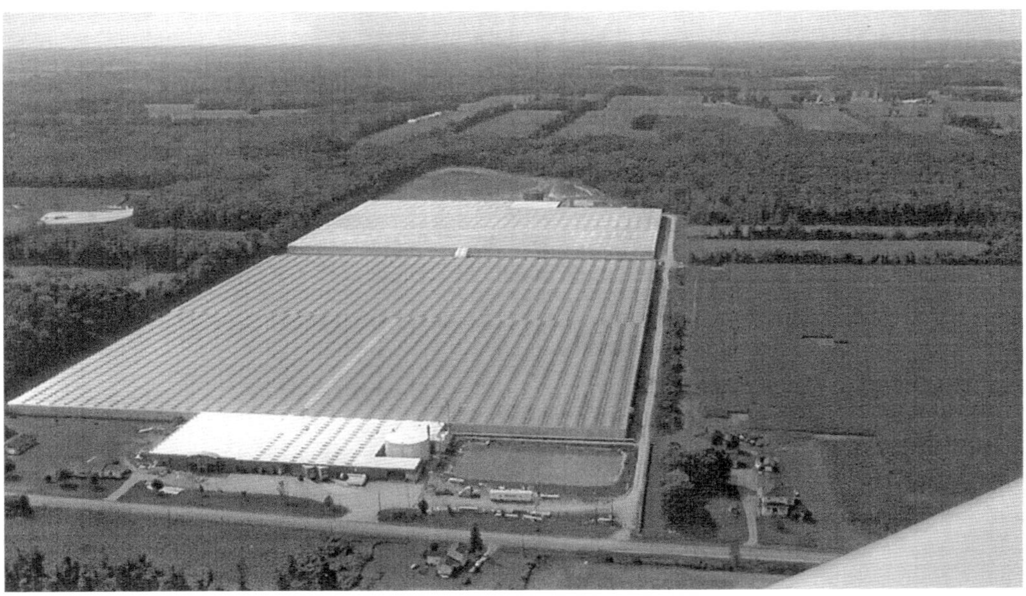

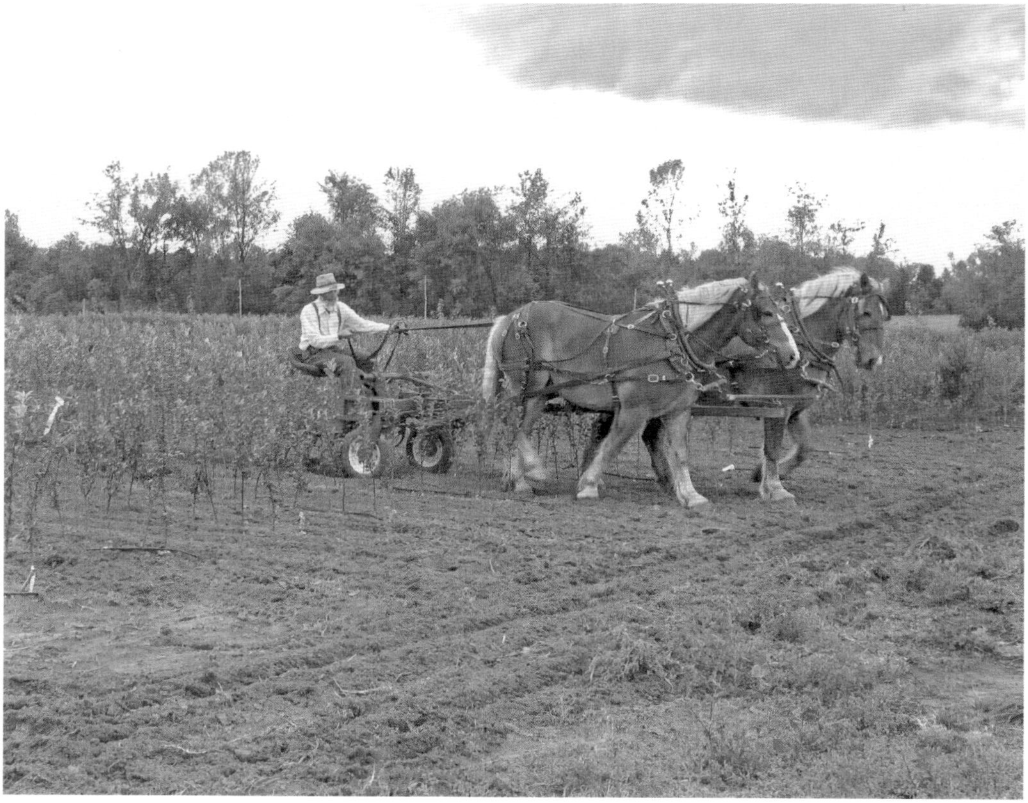

Schlabach came to Orleans County from Holmes County, Ohio, to join several other Amish families here. Schlabach, a nurseryman before arriving, reports it did not take long before he found himself working with Cornell, on matters relating to propagation and custom grafting. He supplies larger nurseries and operates a substantial mail-order business. Upon arrival here, nurseries were using mechanized ice, but have turned now to using pond ice to hold the trees from fall until spring—a change he helped foster. Regarding his success, he reports, "It's a matter of stewardship . . . it doesn't get any greener than the way we do it." In fact, they make efficient use of work horses. Schlabach teamed up with Darrel Oakes (see next page) to create a living museum of antique apples, 20 acres of pre-1800 varietals. He tells us the oldest-known named apple is from the 1200s, the "Winter White Permaine," and they also have a Civil War era apple, the Ben Davis. "It was the most popular apple through the early 1900s—it is attractive, yet rugged, dense and juicy. Hardy and productive, they were a real mortgage lifter that could be socked in barrels and bags, then carted, railed or floated almost anywhere and still arrive with dignity." Schlabach tells about the Lady Apple, a tiny, aromatic apple that takes its name from being carried in the small handbags of ladies in Europe. "They used them as perfume. Today they are popular along the Hudson River in ornamental decoration on wreaths." The Lady Apples are a nice-sized apple for children. Schlabach published *Backyard Fruit Production*, an illustrated fruit-growing guide. With proper planning Orleans County, with its zone five climate, can enjoy freshly picked fruit from the later part of May until mid-October. He also includes information and advice on fruit preservation and offers suggestions for drying, canning, or freezing. He adds, "If you have enough land to justify owning a lawn mower, you can grow some kind of fruit! Begin with the basics. Learn as you go, and discover the fulfillment of utilizing your property to become more productive and useful." (Courtesy of Haines Printing Company.)

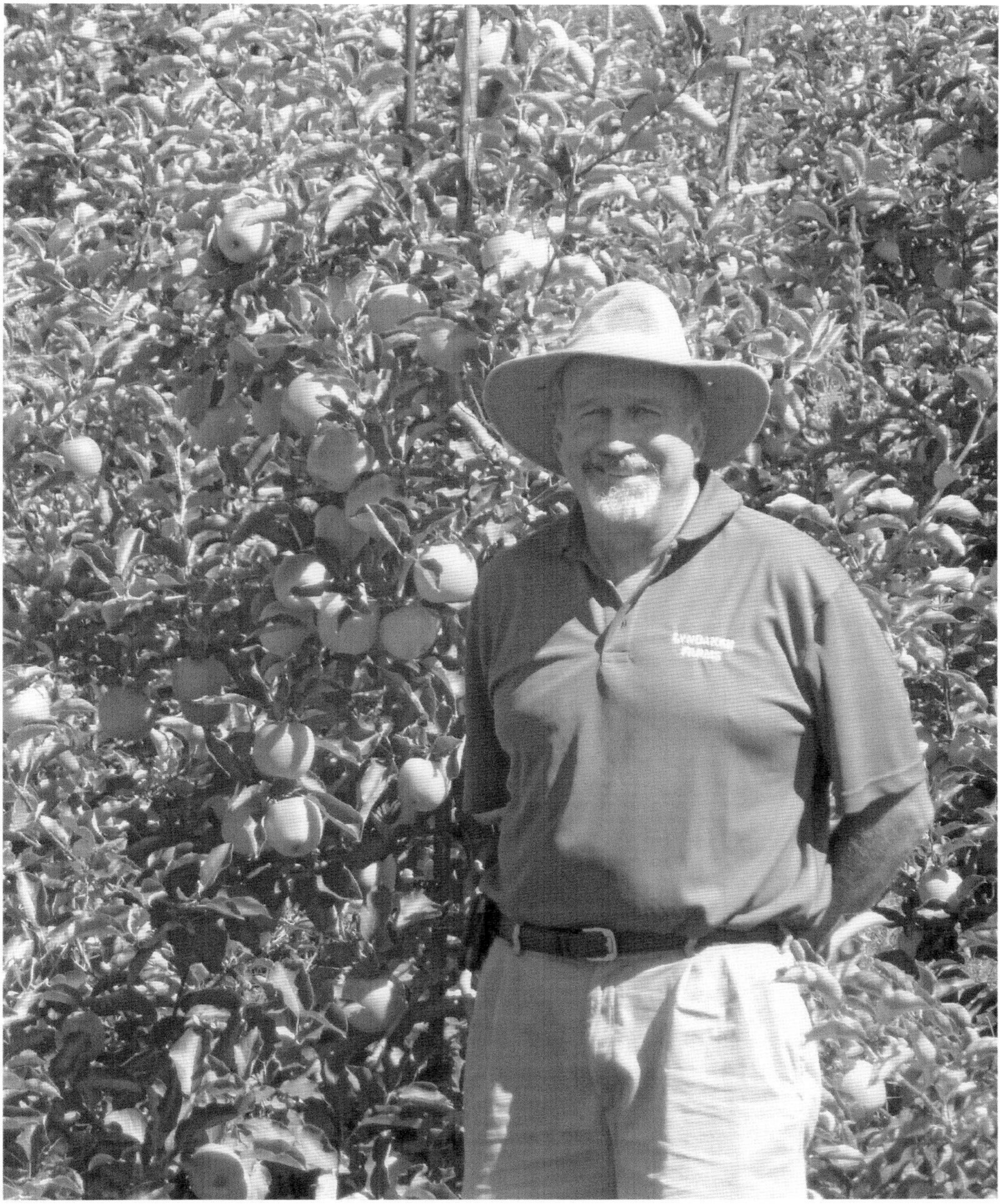

"The apple growing tradition of the Oakes family and LynOaken Farms dates back to 1918 when our grandfather purchased land in rural Orleans County to grow the best apples possible," Oakes says. He also loves to discuss his upbringing, stating that, "growing up, our parents and grandparents taught us to learn from the past to build our future. This principle guides us in every aspect of our orchard operations and has helped us continue to grow apples recognized as world-class in quality." Oakes's progressive approach, examples of efficient production methods, and leadership in fruit associations at both the state and international level have earned him recognition. (Courtesy of Holly Canham.)

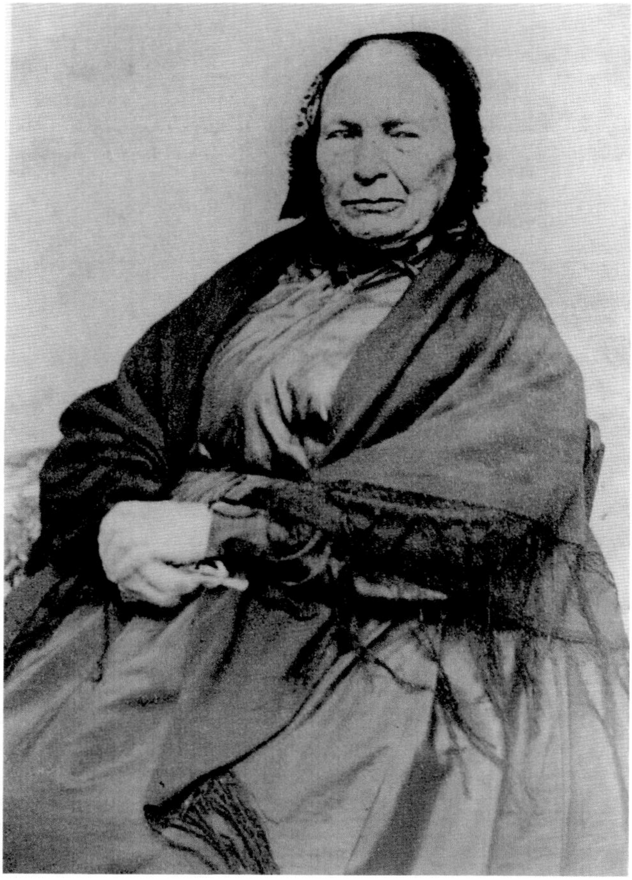

Western New York is second only to the State of Washington for apple production in the United States—and no small part of that claim belongs to Orleans County. It all began with Lovewell (1795–1875). The Lovewell family endured the intensely cold winter of 1803 as one of only seven families in the pioneer community of Manilla, now Point Breeze, on the mouth of the Oak Orchard River. Conversations often focused on the promise of a supply boat arriving from Canada as soon as ice left the harbor. The children, including eight-year-old Rachel, watched for days and excitement ran high at the sight of Sailor Jack's sail. The morning after his arrival, Sailor Jack gave Rachel a large yellow apple. Soon after, she overheard that the Brown family was going to plant an apple orchard; she immediately buried her apple. Two years later, she remembered the apple; running to the bluff, she located a spindly green shoot growing where the core had been placed. Her father verified this was indeed an apple tree, and it is believed to be the first one planted in Orleans County north of the Ridge Road. Apples from that tree were small and tart, but very good for cooking and baking. When she shared the apples with the local women, it was discovered that cooking with a piece of the apple in any kind of jelly made the jelly firm (pectin). Unfortunately, waves from Lake Ontario undermined the sandy soil bank where the tree grew and uprooted the tree in 1871. When the waves finally claimed the tree, legend holds that pieces of wood from the tree were made into trinkets, canes, picture frames, and more. A gavel from this wood is in the possession of the Knights of Good Templars and kept at their State Lodge. The Carlton Town Hall currently displays the last portion of Rachel's tree alongside a photo of Rachel taken when she was 66 (see above). (Courtesy of Town of Carlton.)

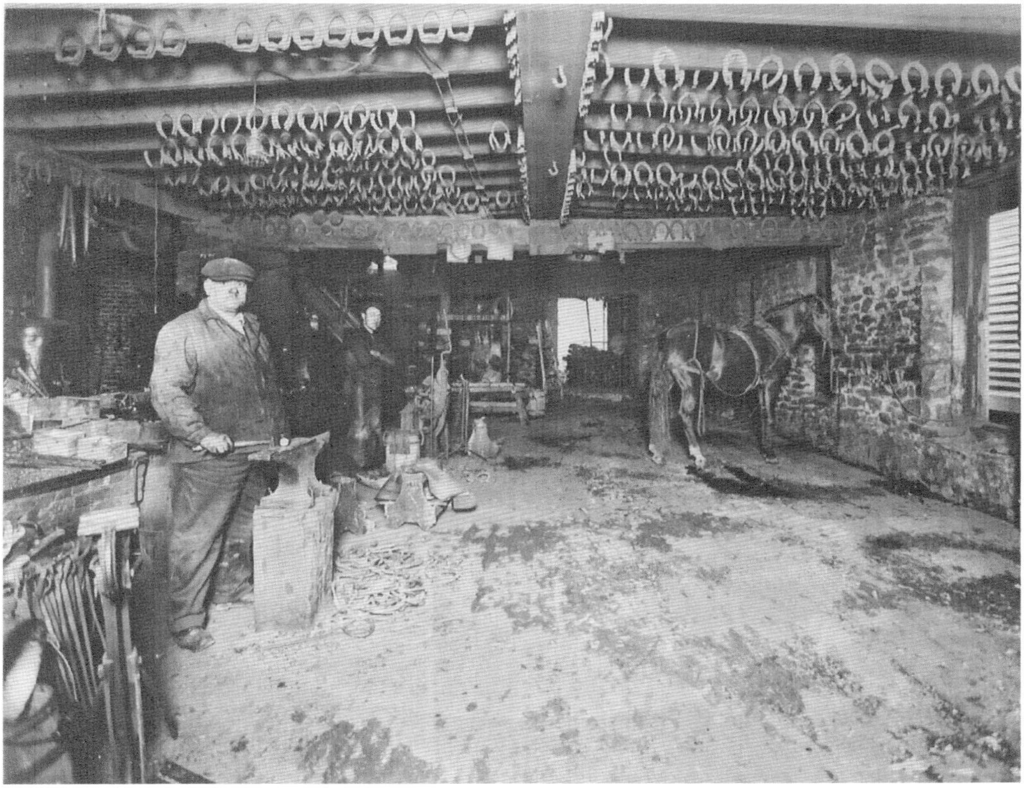

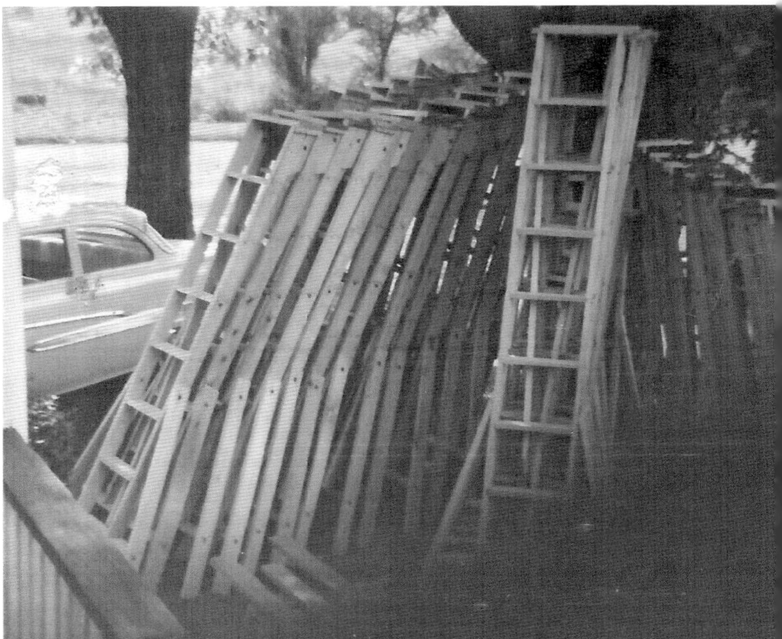

Dibley lived from 1857 to 1941, witnessing many changes in the lifestyle of Orleans County people. His blacksmith services, once a crucial community need, were less in demand with the advent of motorized transportation. Realizing he needed to offer additional services, Dibley began making ladders, also important to a farming community with orchards of fruit to be picked and barns to maintain. A man dedicated to his community, he fashioned the giant rolling pin (see page 118) used to roll crust for the world's largest apple pie displayed at the 1929 County Fair. (Courtesy of Lorraine Dibley.)

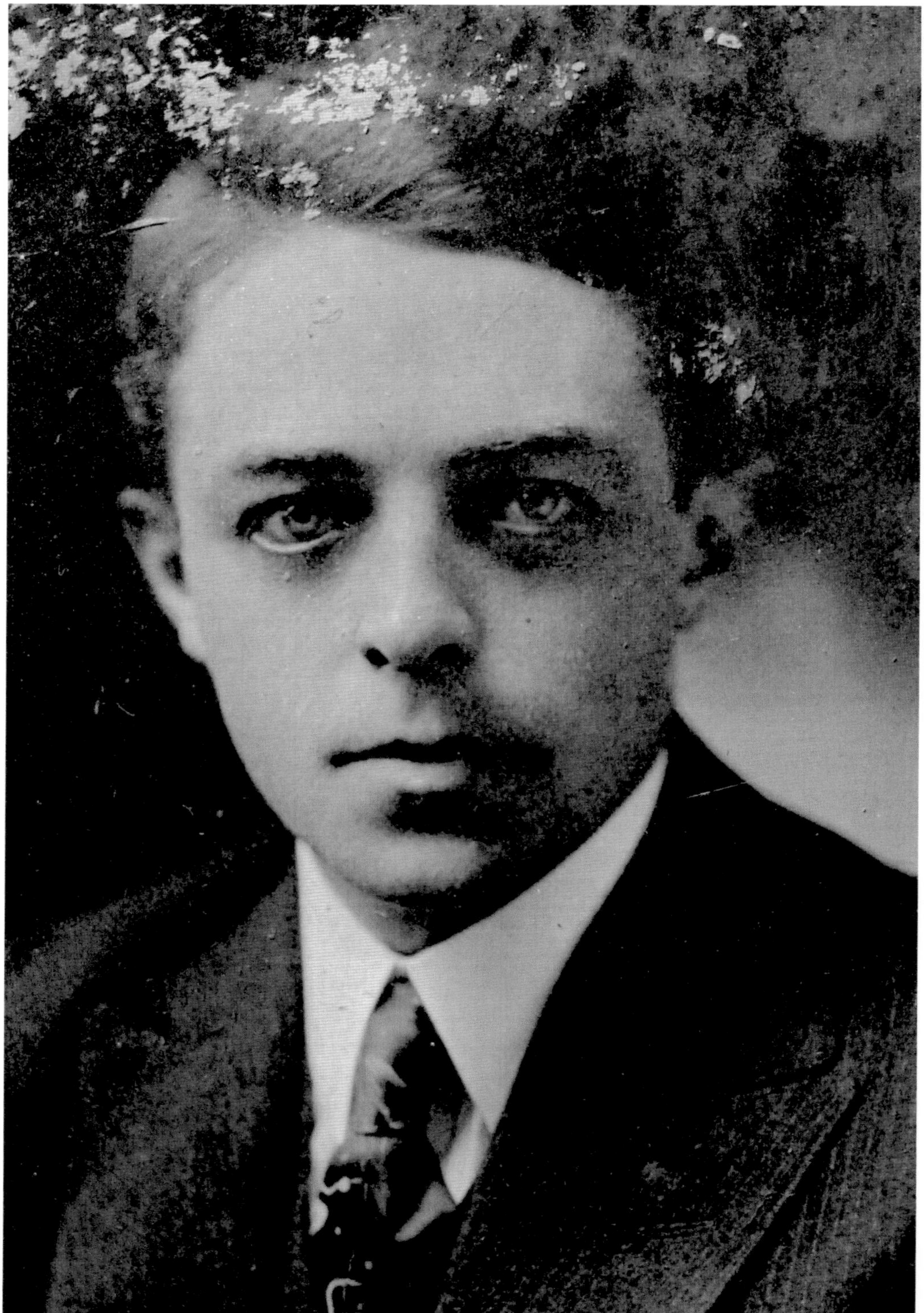

(LEFT)
Eugene Peter Forrestel acquired the property for the camp during the Depression. It is now operated by Mary Keppler Hebert (Eugene's granddaughter)—making it a fifth-generation working farm. Hebert started the Forrestel Riding and Sports Camp in 1980, and 31 years later, believes they are one of the finest riding camps in the country. Instructors and campers come from across the United States and abroad. Hebert considers the farm a "treasure," and finds it interesting that while the farm was agriculturally based in the past, recreational use is what sustains the property today. The farm has had its share of champion horses. Roscoe Peel was a national champion Belgian, bred, raised and trained by Eugene Forrestel, and Morey (produced by Persian Slipper) became one of the nation's top five "conformation hunters." (Conformation hunter relates to a horse's build and jumping ability.) (Courtesy of Mary Keppler Hebert.)

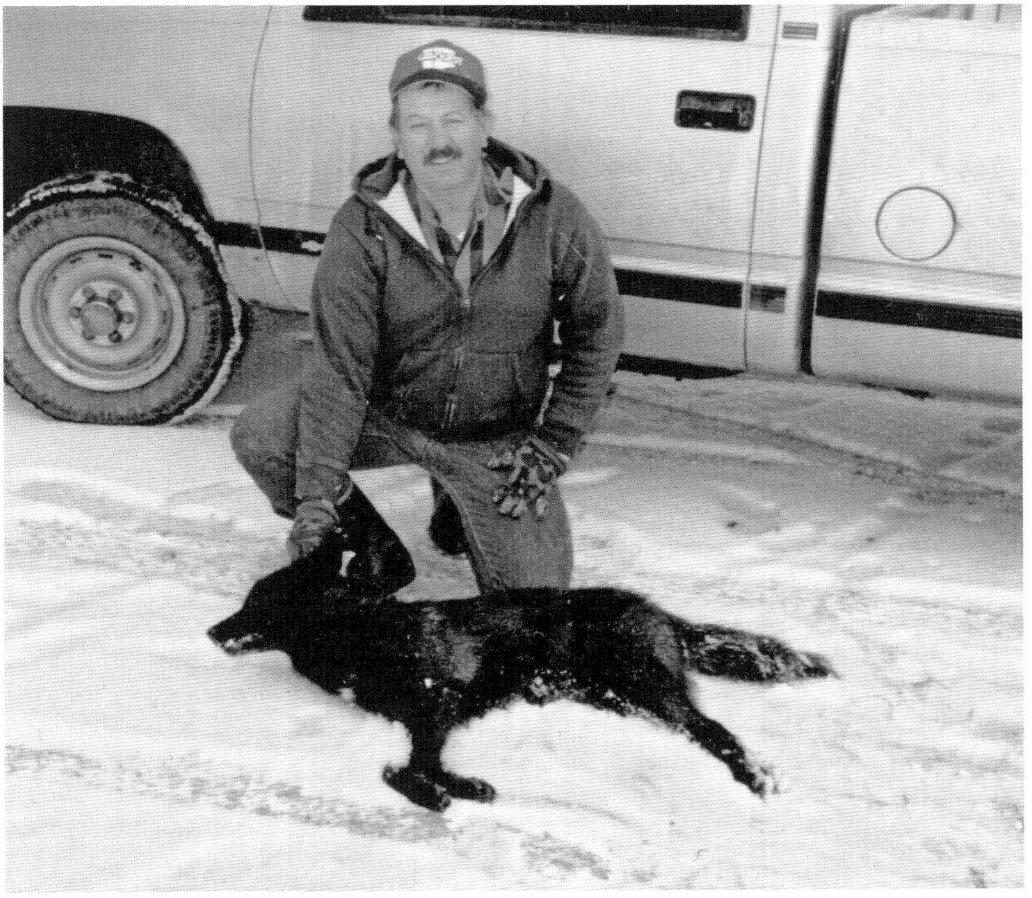

An avid hunter, Bennett has many trophies to show for it. He killed both a record 42-pound coyote and the rare black one (shown above) locally. The DEC reports coyotes normally run 20 to 25 pounds in this area. Early history books reported a high presence of wolves here (coyotes' natural predator), which settlers killed off, giving coyote a chance to populate. Over time, the small "Mom and Pop" farms have gone by and their former pastures and barnyards have become wooded. Orleans County currently has more woodland than it did 100 years ago, providing a better natural habitat for coyotes, which are now prevalent in the area. (Courtesy of Holly Canham.)

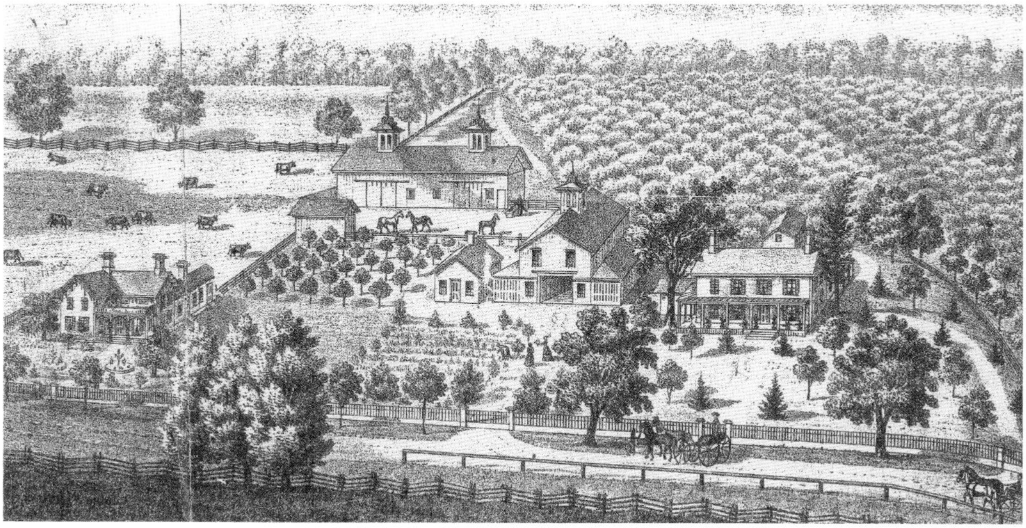

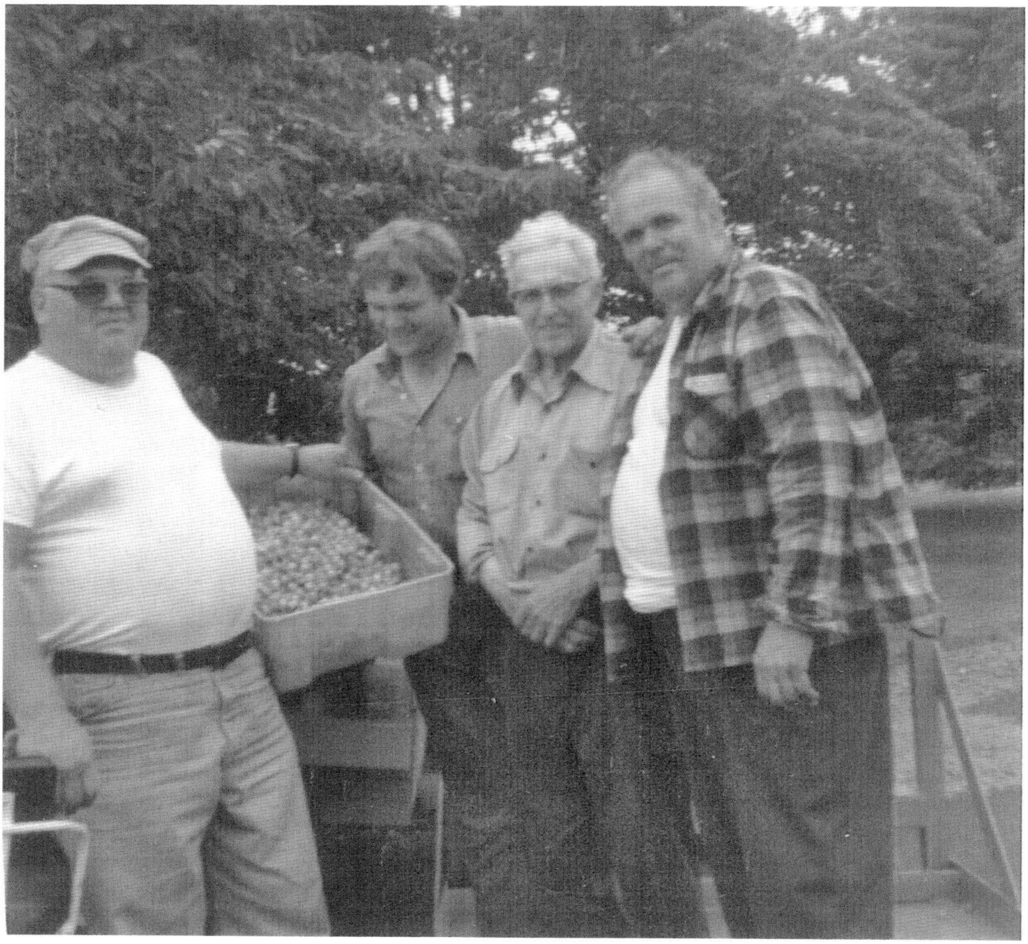

(LEFT)
The Smith Farm is located south of Medina (formerly the Sumner Farm; see photograph left). Jeff Smith is a fourth-generation farmer. He remembers selling tomatoes to H.J. Heinz Co., and tells of German POWs housed on the Heinz property, offloading trucks. "If you happened to have cigarettes, your truck would get offloaded faster." African Americans came from Buffalo, and Native Americans from Akron, to pick the harvest. In those days, the family was so grateful for the help that Smith's grandmother fed everyone breakfast and lunch. Now, the fifth generation has joined, and farming practices have changed. Where the orchards once supported 40 apple trees, we now find 1,100 trees per acre. The family also grows cherries; below left, pictured left to right are Roger Thiel, Jeff Smith, Floyd Smith, and Garra Smith. (Courtesy of Smith Family.)

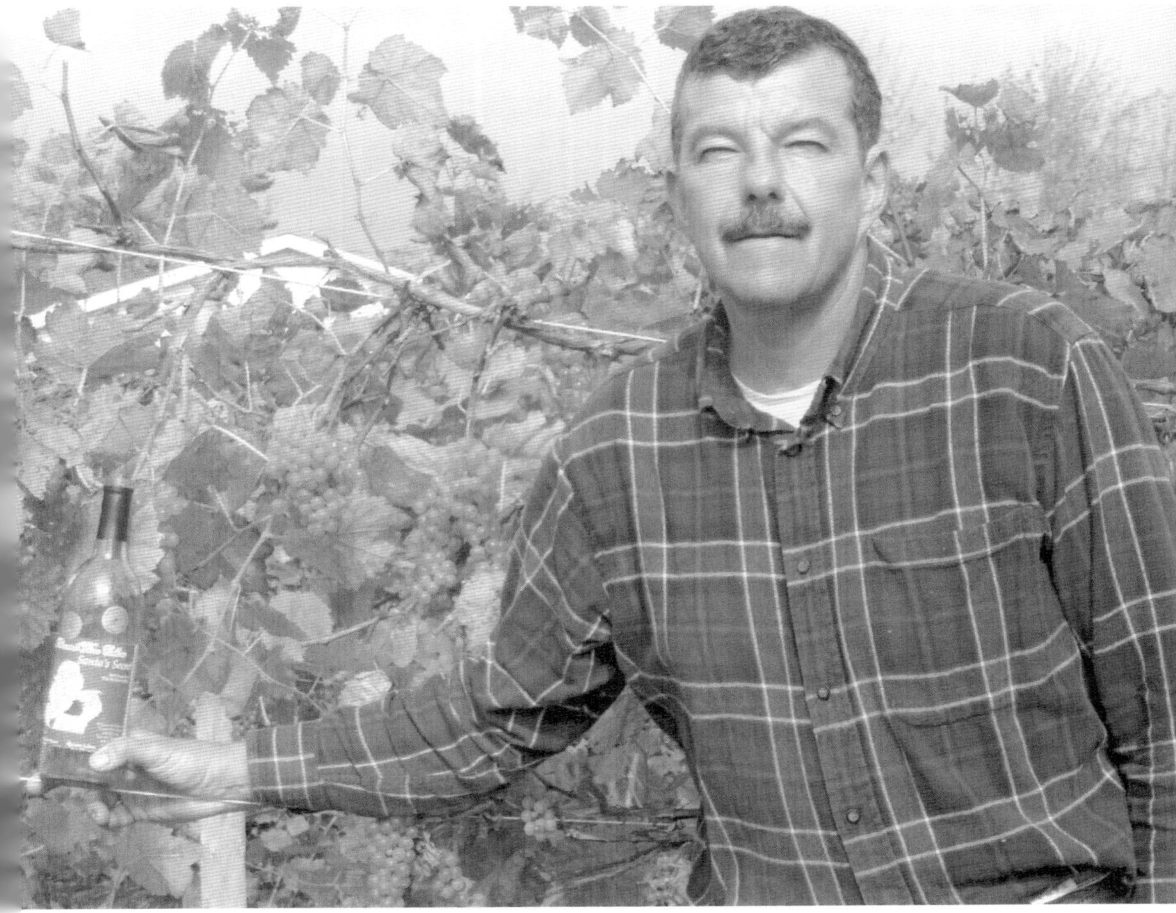

Descended from maternal and paternal winemaking grandparents from Germany and Austria, perhaps it was inevitable that Schwenk would become a winemaker too. A graduate of Cornell, where he studied viniculture and ecology, and having raised grapes most of his life, Schwenk planted his Orleans County Mallard Point Vineyards in 1990. As Orleans County's first person to apply for a "Registered Winery," he continues to expand his vineyard and wine production. Schwenk is known for his award-winning wines, such as Rieslings, Santa's Secret, and many other sweet and dry wines. (Courtesy of Andrew Canham.)

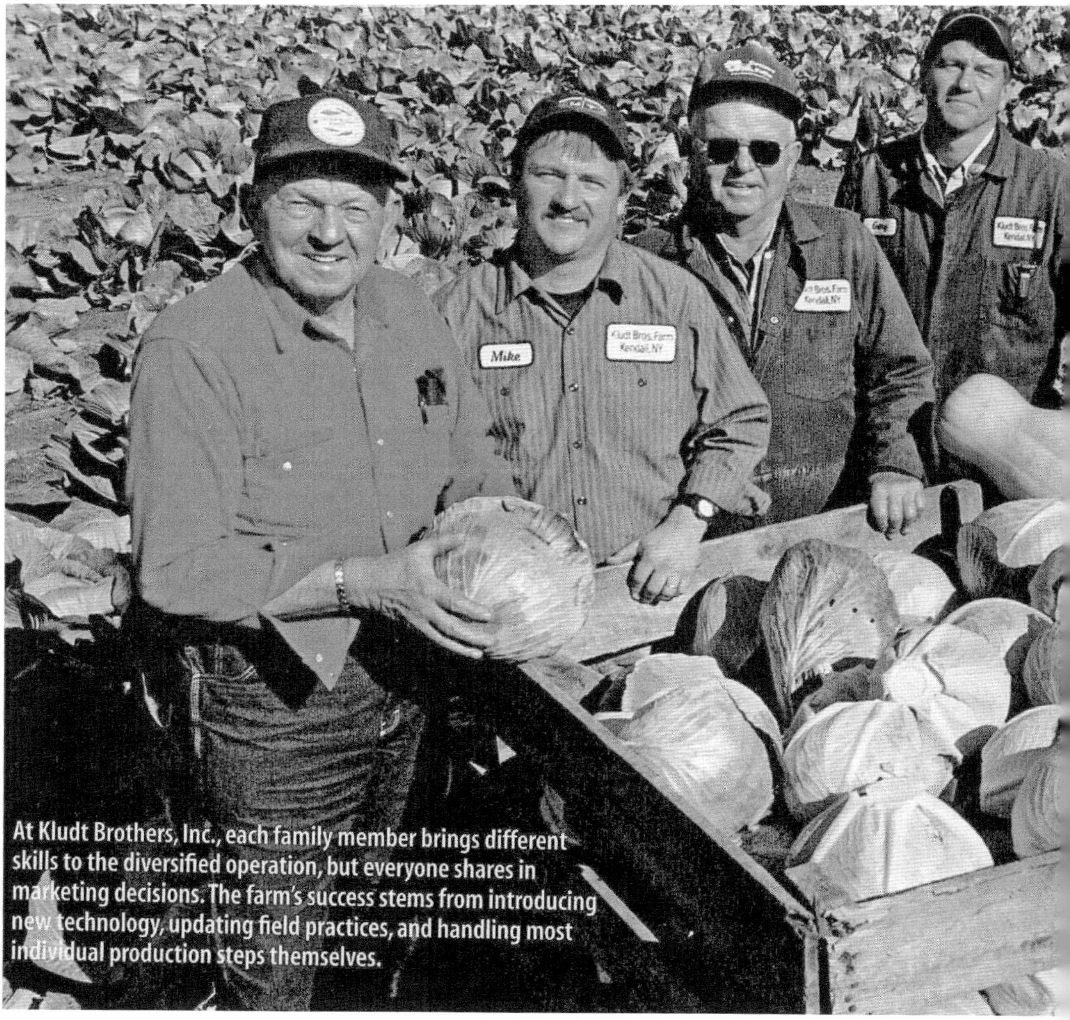

The Kludt Brothers' 7,500-acre farm is one of New York's largest and most progressive vegetable and grain operations. German immigrants Otto and Marie Kludt started farming on the south shore of Lake Ontario in 1929. Their descendants inherited their strong work ethic. The award-winning fourth-generation farm is managed by Gary, Mike, and Matt Kludt. Kludt Farms is actively involved in several agricultural organizations and has received many awards for its outstanding production of vegetables. They currently produce sweet corn, peas, snap beans, beets, carrots, cabbage, butternut squash, field corn, wheat, and hay. Pictured left to right are Rudy, Mike, Harold, Gary, and Matt Kludt, and Russ Levett. (Courtesy of *Revolution Magazine* and Barbara Kludt.)

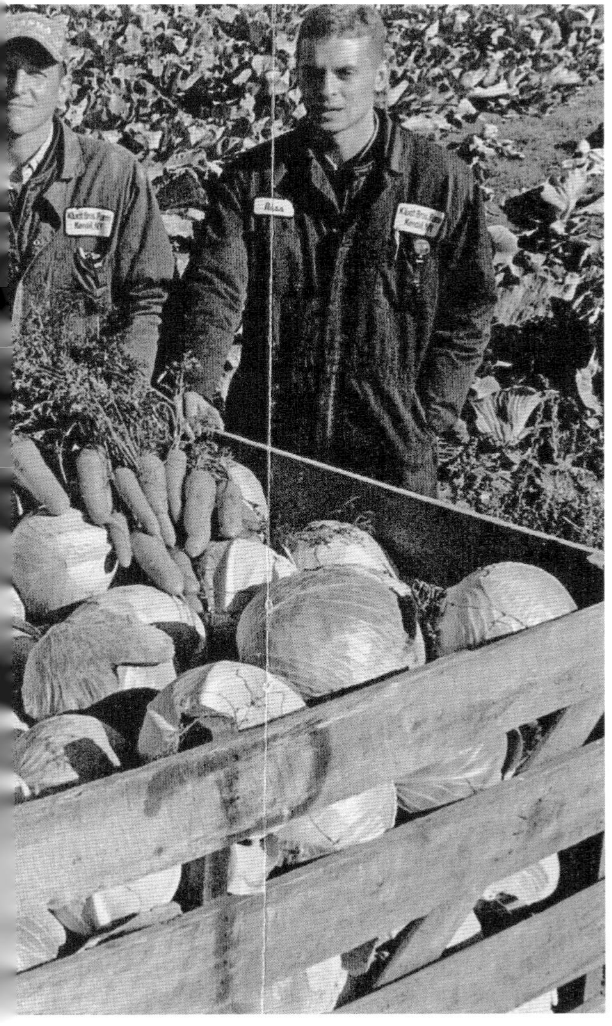

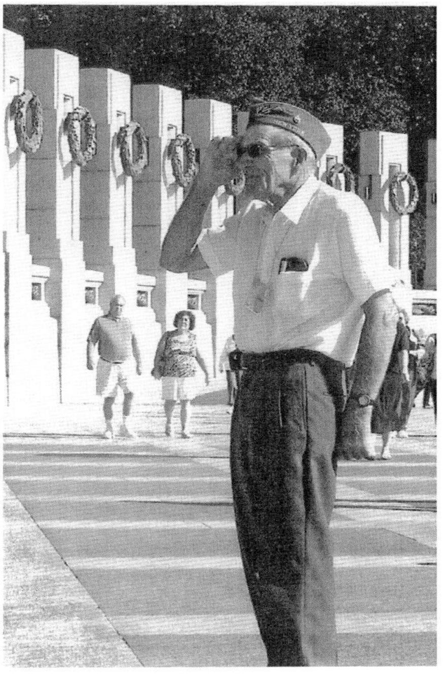

Paduchak was born to a farm family and, at age 85, continues to farm the same 200 acres in Kendall. He earned many military honors, including the Bronze Star. Civic-minded, he served as the Town of Kendall supervisor for 32 years. He also continues over 30 years of service on the Orleans County Board of Supervisors and the Soil and Water Conservation Board. (Courtesy of Nadine Hanlon.)

In the 1930s, Ross N. Wilson (left) and Irving Weet (center) ran a fox ranch located west of Albion on Route 31. They are pictured with an employee displaying racks of fox pelts ready for shipment to a furrier. (Courtesy of Orleans County Department of History.)

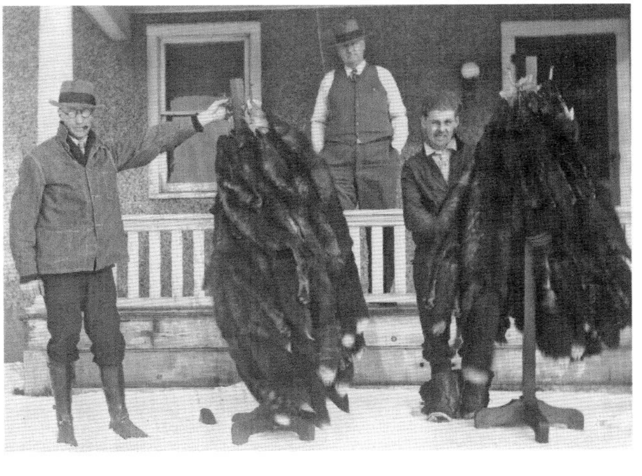

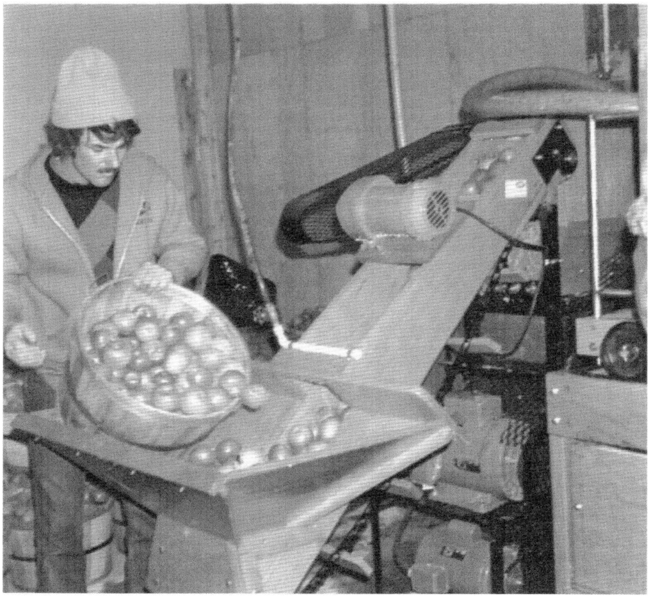

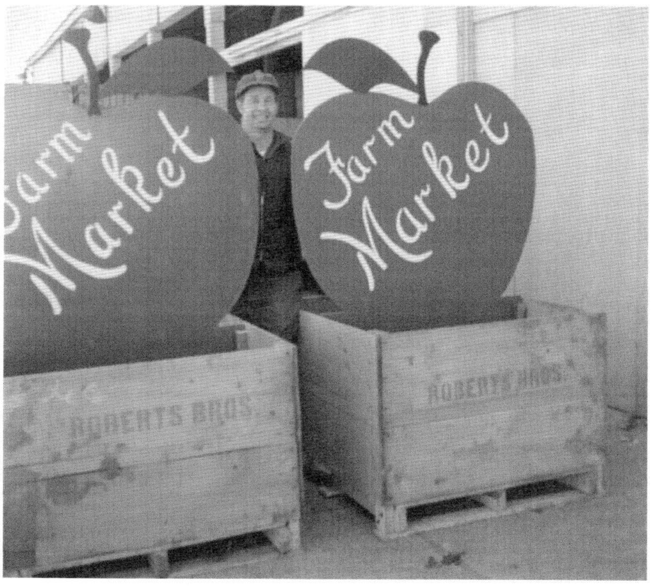

The Roberts Farm Market sits on the site of the former H.J. Heinz pea vinery in Medina; the farm now has its third generation of owner-operators. Their 75-year-old farm generates both produce and cider, which is made from a 35-year-old cider press. Alan Kodzy is pictured above filling the hopper of the cider press. The peak selling season for their cider is the week before Thanksgiving, when sales reach 500 gallons for the week. The business was started in 1931 by Justin Roberts, who has held several important positions: supervisor of the Town of Shelby for 22 years; director of the Orleans County Farmers Mutual Insurance Co. for 16 years; director of the GLF Marketing Board; and a member of the Western New York Apple Association. (Courtesy of the Roberts Family.)

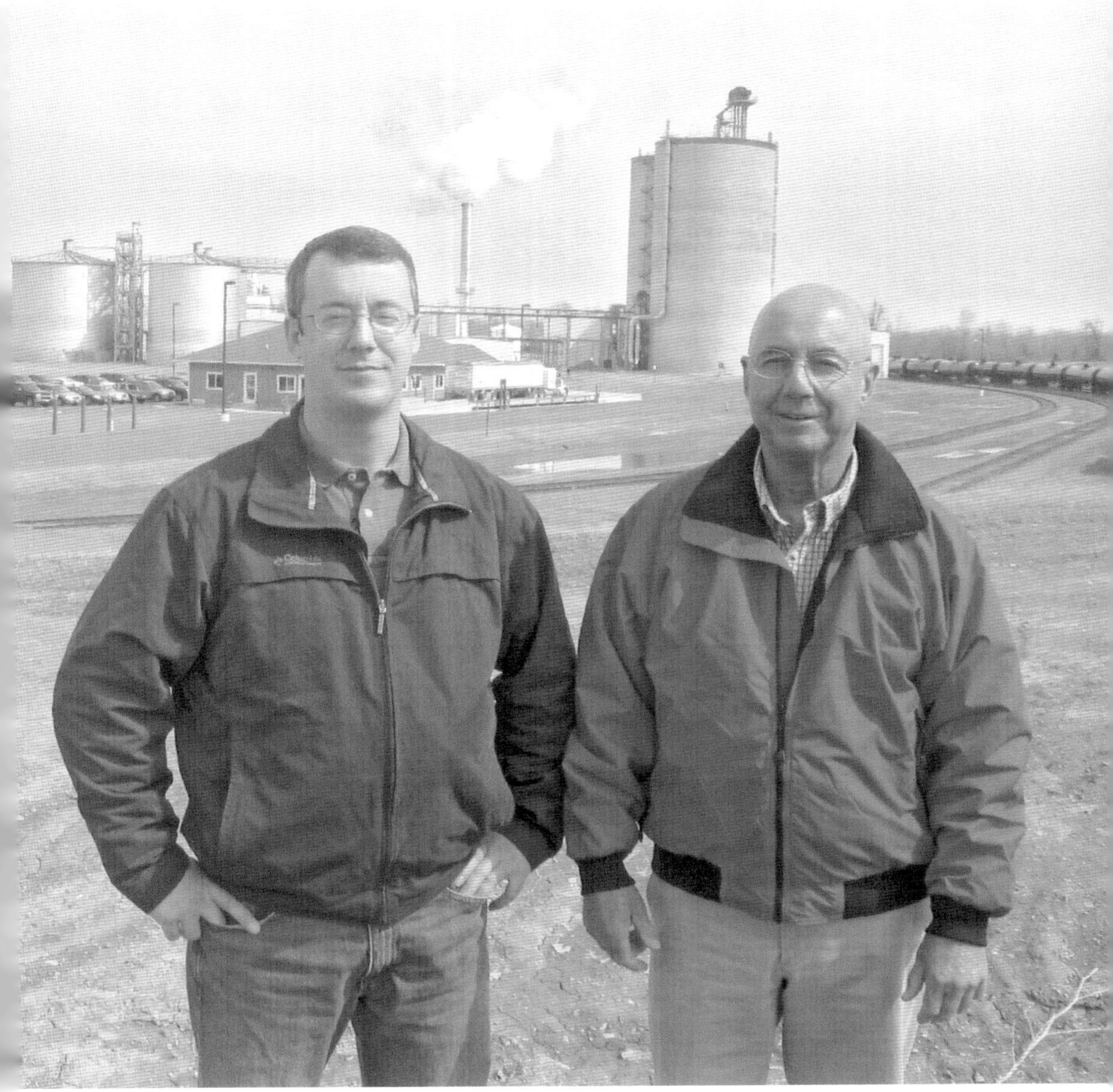

Western New York Energy, LLC, CEO John Sawyer, and his son Mike Sawyer (the CFO), run this "locally owned company committed to developing the full potential of Western New York's renewable energy resources." Opened in 2007, the plant runs nonstop 365 days a year, producing ethanol, and three by-products: distiller's grain for livestock feed, corn oil, and carbon dioxide. One environmental benefit associated with this plant is the retention of carbon dioxide released when making ethanol, reducing the plant's carbon footprint; Mike Sawyer has called the plant "waste free." The plant, the first of its kind in the northeastern United States, consumes about 20 million bushels of corn to produce over 55 million gallons of fuel-grade ethanol. The plant supports the community by purchasing much of its corn locally. (Courtesy of the *Daily News* in Batavia.)

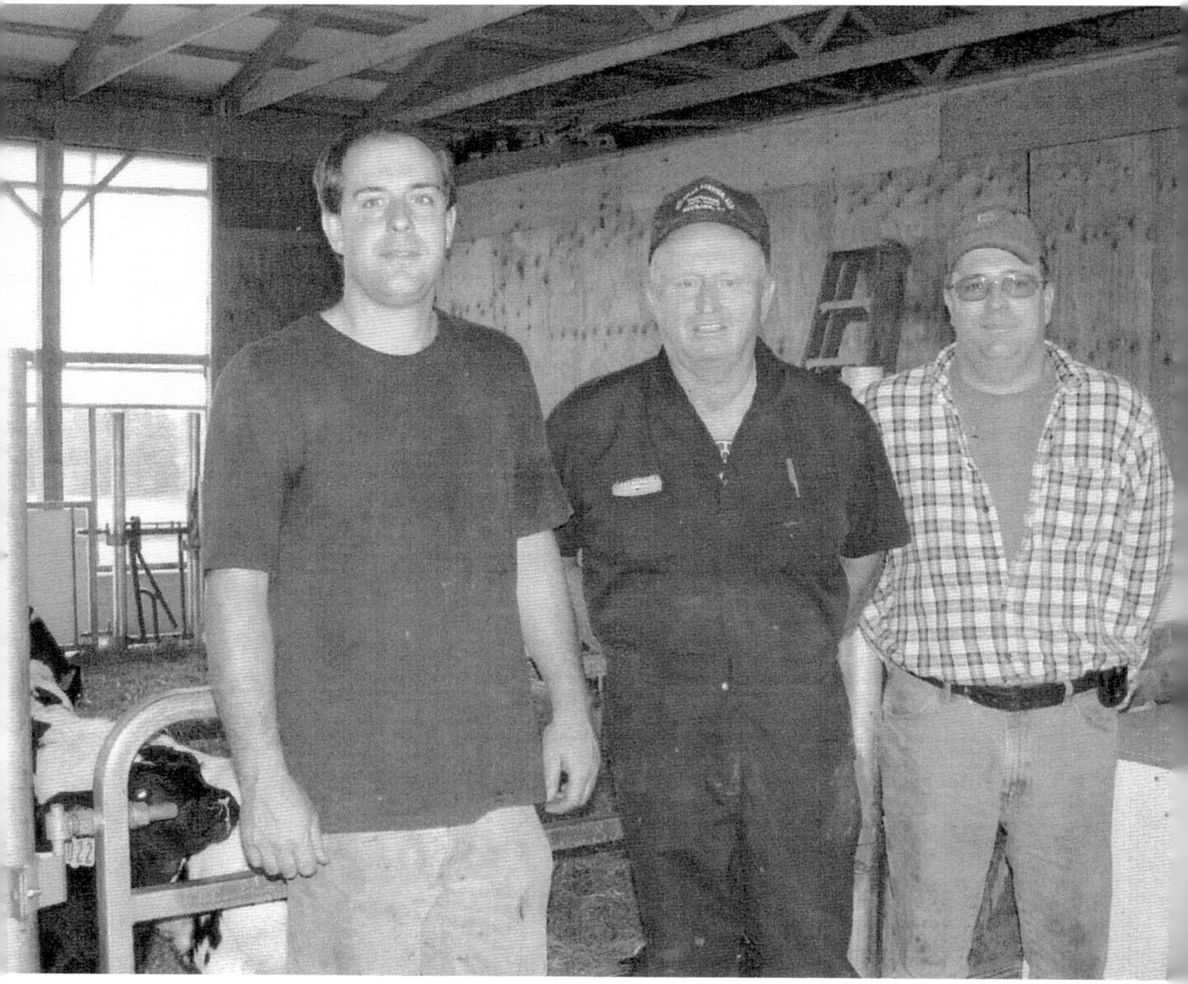

The Neal brothers and their father, Ed, run a dairy farm and are important behind-the-scenes workers for the Orleans County 4-H Fair. Jamie (not pictured) is a member of the Fair Board, which plans the week-long fair. The Neals showed pigs and dairy animals at the fair when they were younger and have never stopped being directly involved. The whole family helps out in various ways. They send a tractor and operator to assist in setting up and tearing down amusement rides, and a forklift to keep the pole slathered for the greased pole event. Volunteers for the Cornell Cooperative Extension of Orleans County, the Neals were presented a "Friends of the Extension" award in 2010 for their consistent help. (Courtesy of Jody Neal.)

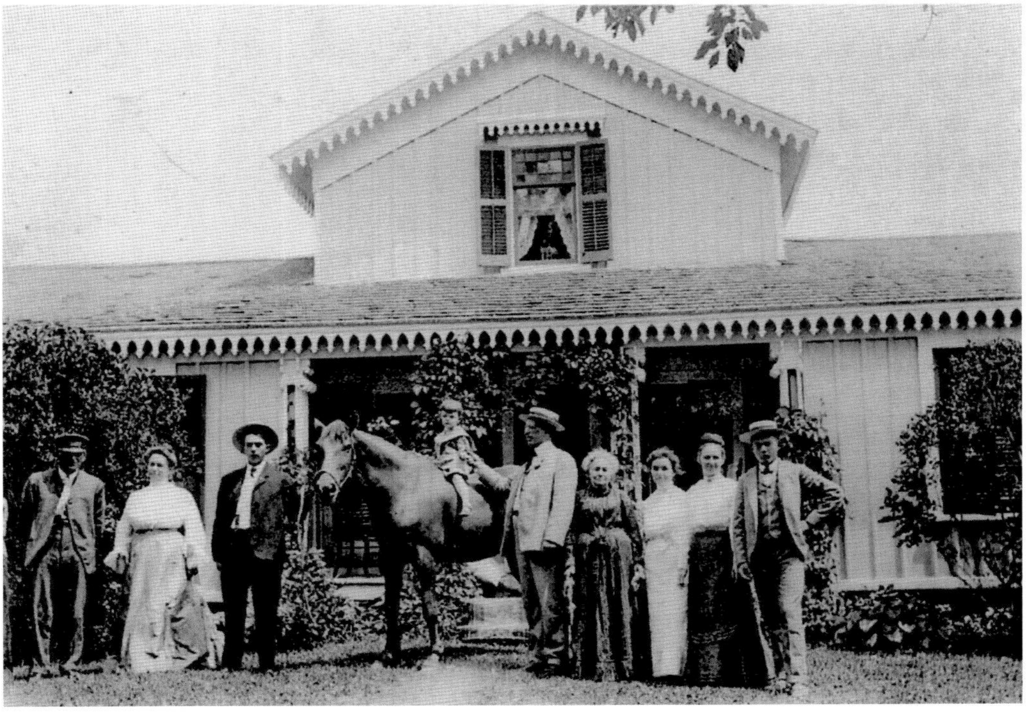

Baker (1852–1933) knew how to grow potatoes and developed a variety all his own, the Early Orleans. Naturally, he also sold the Baker Potato! The Baker homestead pictured below still stands in Carlton at the corner of Oak Orchard Road and Baker Road (named after his family). John's grandfather Calvin arrived in Carlton in 1849. (Courtesy of Helen Baker Bachellor.)

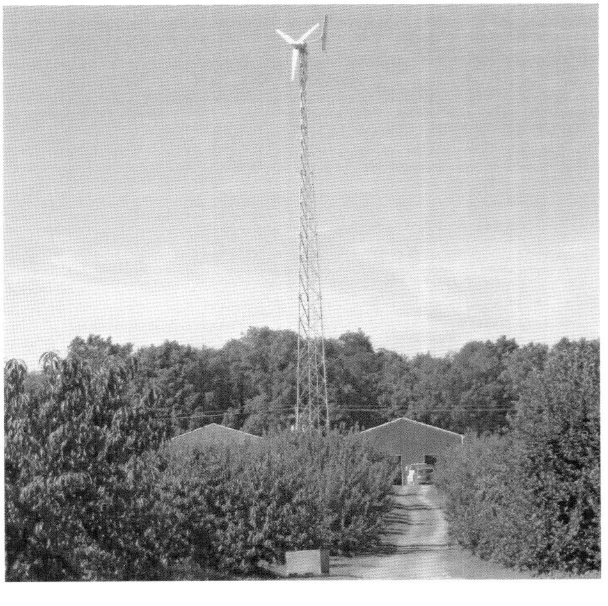

The Watts believe farming technology is always changing, and they were the first in Orleans County to put up a 140-foot-tall wind tower. Being innovative can cause controversy, but patrons are supportive and enjoy the modern version of yesterday's windmill. Karen and Chris have raised over $125,000 for breast cancer research by sponsoring "Orchard Walks." (Courtesy of Holly Canham.)

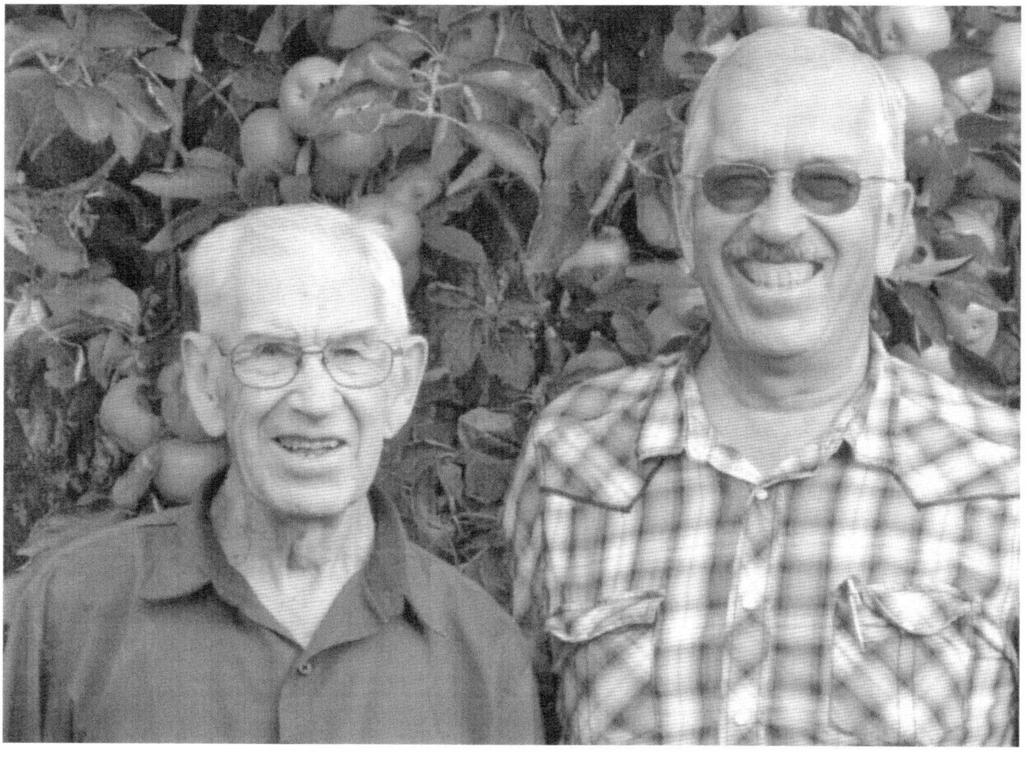

The Kast family are successful farmers and proudly shared with their community by generously donating to help build the new Albion library and the new Cornell Cooperative Extension building at the fairgrounds. Their farm was established in 1885 and they have earned recognition over the years in many ways, including the 2009 Conservation Farmer of the Year award, and the 2006 I Love My NY Farmer award. (Courtesy of Kathy Kast.)

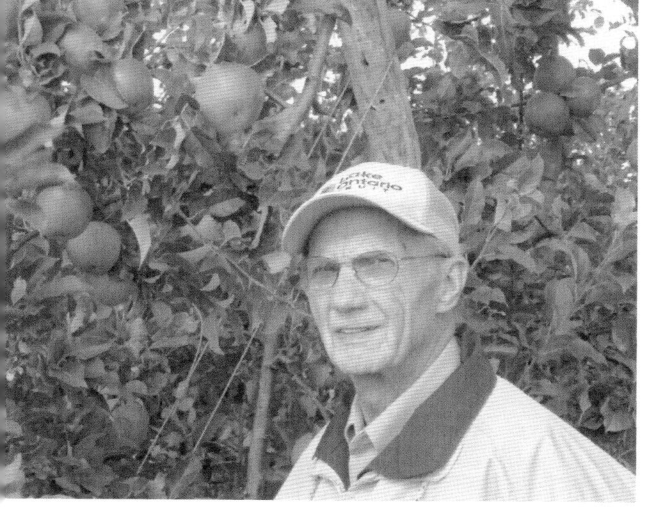

Lamont graduated from Cornell in 1957. His many accomplishments include being named Apple Man of the Year and Apple Grower of the Year by two different national publications, and Outstanding Alumnus at Cornell. A sixth-generation farmer, he followed in his father's footsteps as the executive director of the New York State Horticultural Society. The farm was established in 1815 by George's great-great-great-grandfather, Josias Lamont. George operated Lamont Fruit Farms, Inc. with his brother Roger and a third partner, Rod Farrow. Roger has served as chairman of the grower group NYAG since 2009. Roger and his wife Ingrid have provided instrumental support for Albion's new library. (Courtesy of Andrew Canham.)

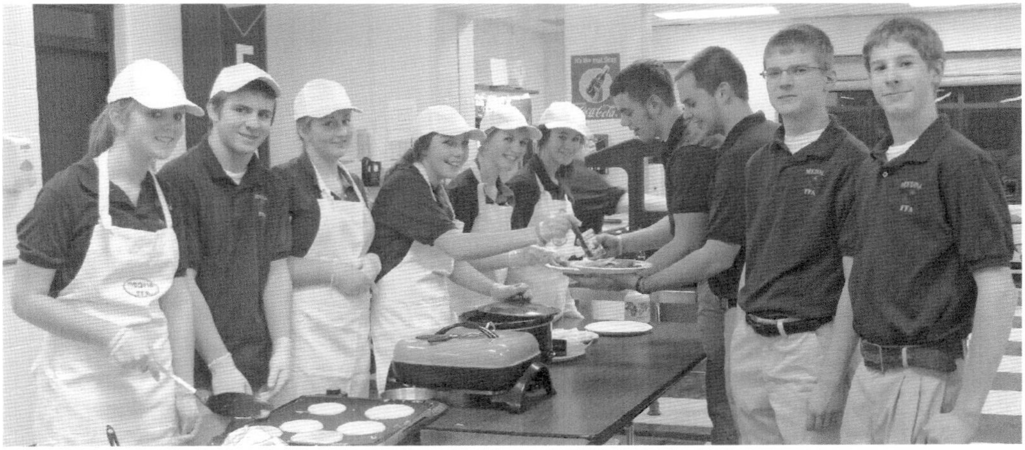

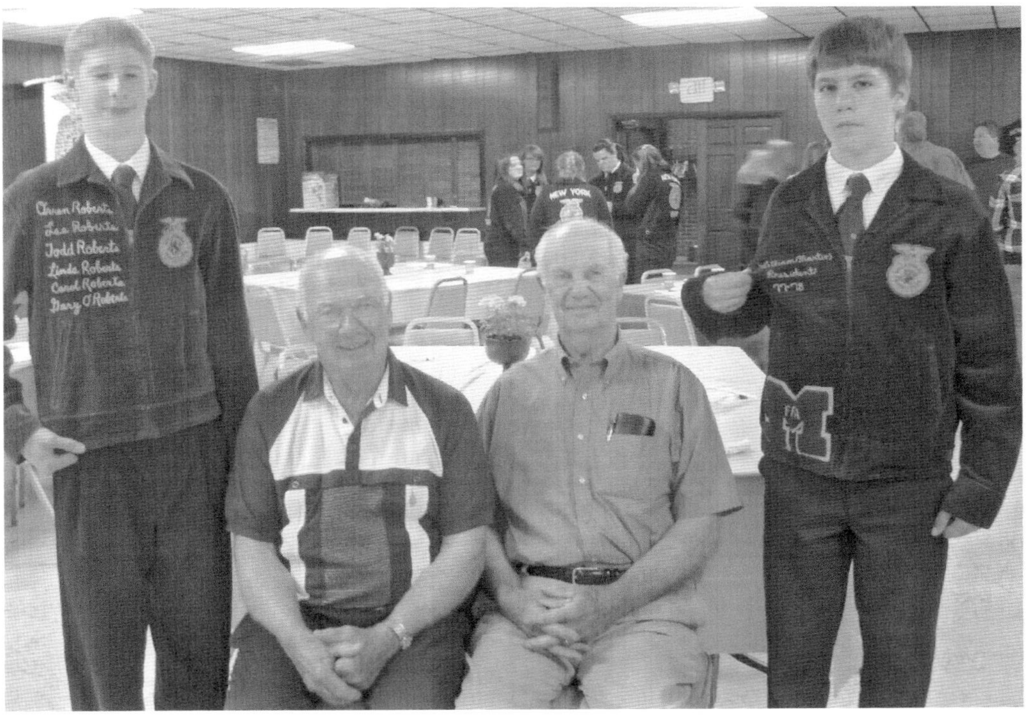

The Albion chapter marked its 100th Anniversary in 2010, making it New York's oldest chapter. Nationally, FFA serves as an American youth organization that promotes and supports agricultural education. With over 520,000 members, its motto is "Learning to Do, Doing to Learn, Earning to Live, Living to Serve." The Medina chapter marked its 75th Anniversary in 2011. Originally, girls were not allowed membership; that has changed. Today, 42 percent of FFA members are girls. Pictured above, students of both genders host the successful pancake supper. Pictured below, Mason Roberts (left) wears the FFA jacket his uncle Orren Roberts (second from left) and grandfather Lee Roberts (second from right) also wore. On the right, Benjamin Martin shows off the jacket worn by his father, William Martin. They are all from Medina. (Courtesy of Virginia Kropf.)

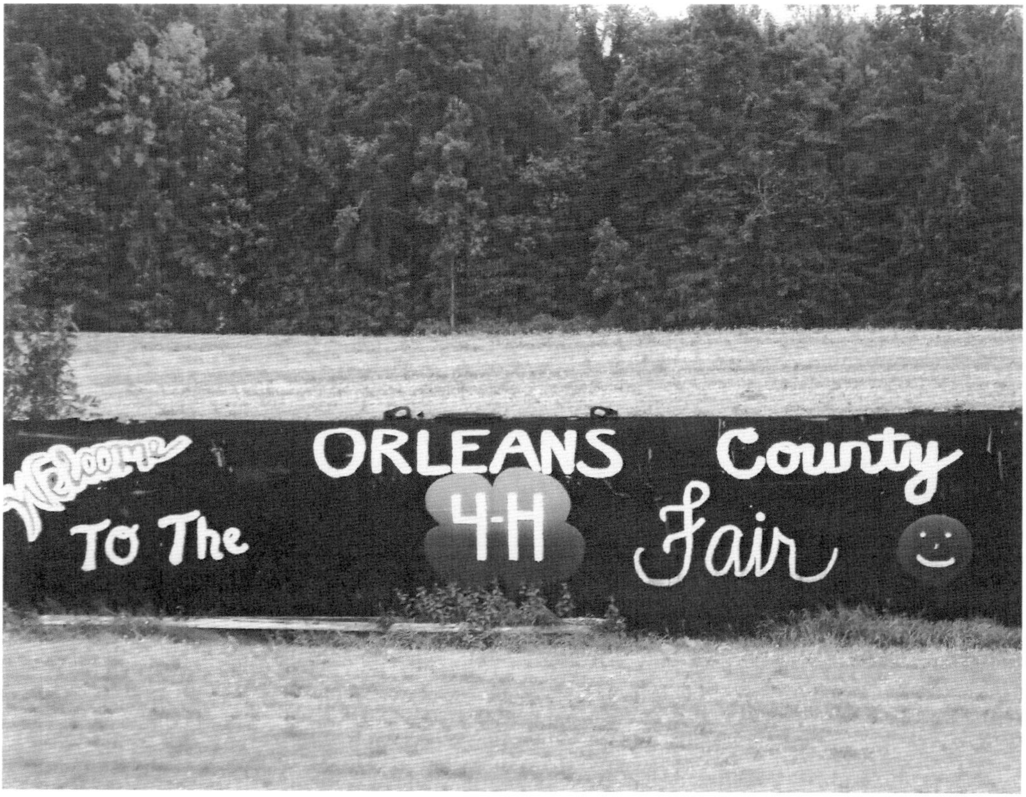

The Orleans County Agricultural Society formed in 1856 and the following year purchased 26 acres on West State Street in Albion for a fairgrounds (an agricultural society likely existed before 1850, but records no longer exist). Fair activities and admission prices have varied over time. By 1871, admission was 25 cents per person; a double-carriage team and driver paid 75 cents, and a horse and rider 40 cents. Today's admission fee is $5 per car. World War II caused the fair to be put on hold, but thankfully the fair resumed in 1946. Community support was tremendous, and the event became an organized youth fair. Several farmers helped the organization financially by allowing the use of their property, such as Peter Dan Ricci II, who shared his barns for cattle auctions, and Mike Bowman, who in 1963 allowed the fair to be hosted on his farm (corner of Route 31 and Long Bridge Road). A wide variety of animals are displayed today, including cats, dogs, rabbits, sheep, beef and dairy cattle, meat and dairy goats, horses, llamas, guinea pigs (cavies), and poultry. Youth participating in the fair must tend to their animals daily and learn the art of showmanship. Other activities showcase family and consumer science (formerly home economics) projects, such as conservation, citizenship, engineering, sewing, scrapbooking, photography, childcare, cooking, woodworking, and food science. A popular fair pastime is the 4-H bake sale. Notable events each year include the Greased Pole Climbing Contest, the Tractor Pull, and the Famous Brown's Berry Patch Pie Eating Contest. The fair has also featured the World's Largest Wedding Cake and World's Largest Apple Pie. The fair's current location was purchased in 1965 and, with the assistance of the 4-H Leaders Association and the County Livestock Club, a building was erected. Successful programming, such as the 4-H Walk-a-Thon, raised enough funding to build the livestock arena. A public address system was put in by way of grant funding from the Curtis Foundation. Generous community support continues to foster improvements and sustain the wonderful fair, which currently attracts about 25,000 patrons each year. (Courtesy of Holly Canham.)

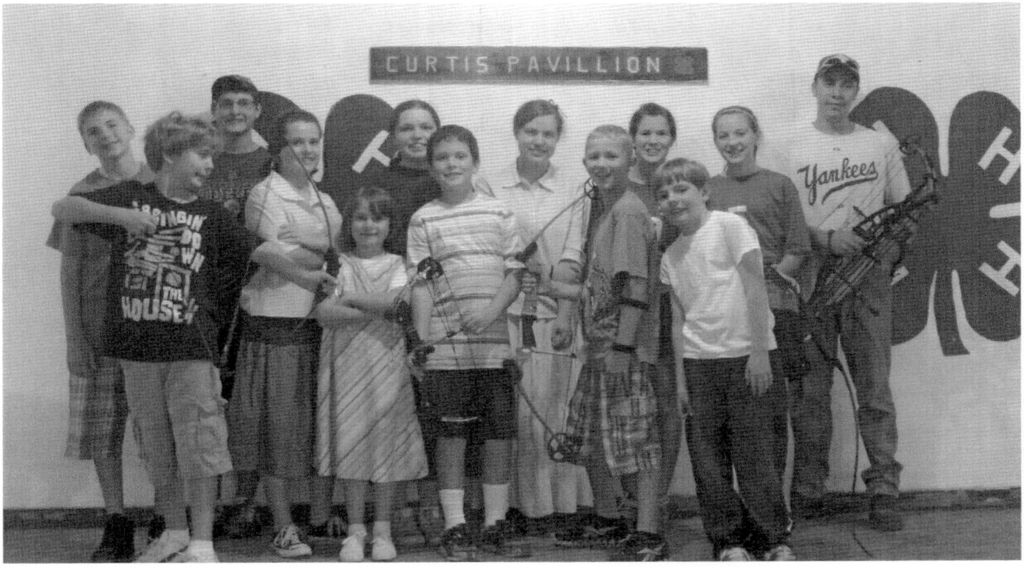

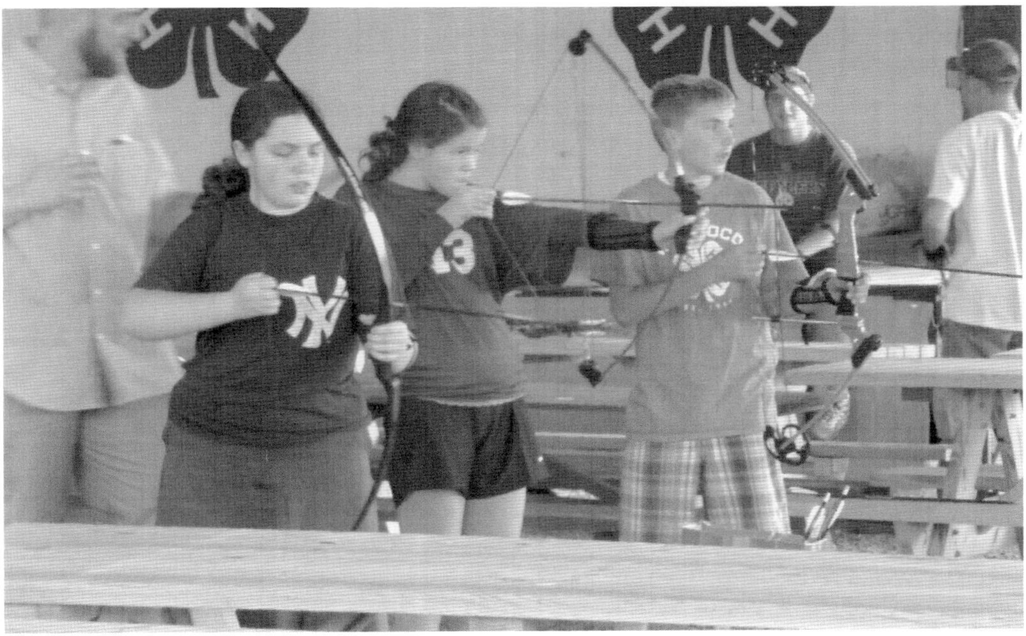

Formed in 2008, this club has about 15 members who love the outdoors. They study and practice archery, foraging, camping, rowing, hunting, and more. Their studies include ecological concepts and population control, and they one day hope to be able to offer hunter safety training classes. The group leaders are Robert Batt and Joe McCracken. Students in the photograph above, from left to right are (front row) Zach Moore, Maggie Gabalski, Joan Gabalski, John Gabalski, Kohl Morgan, and Andrew Drechsel; (back row) Andrew Moore, Zach Chiro, Peggy Gabalski, Mary Grace Gabalski, Katie Morgan, Claudia Drechsel, and Adam Hazel. In the image below are (left to right) Joan Gabalski, Katie Morgan, and Andrew Moore. (Courtesy of Bud Canham.)

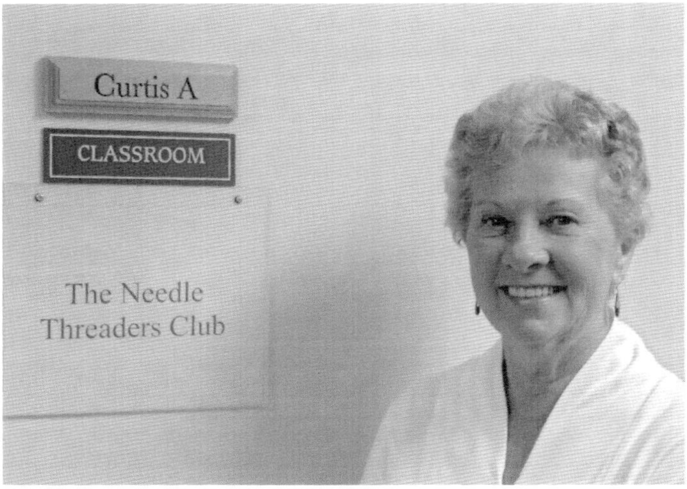

Following in her mother's footsteps as a 4-H leader, Lanning currently heads the Needle Threaders. She is advisor of the Senior Council at the 4-H Fairgrounds, a member of the Fair Committee, the 4-H Leader's Association, and the Property Committee. She will celebrate her 80th birthday next July and, thankfully, will continue her 4-H and fair work. (Courtesy of Holly Canham.)

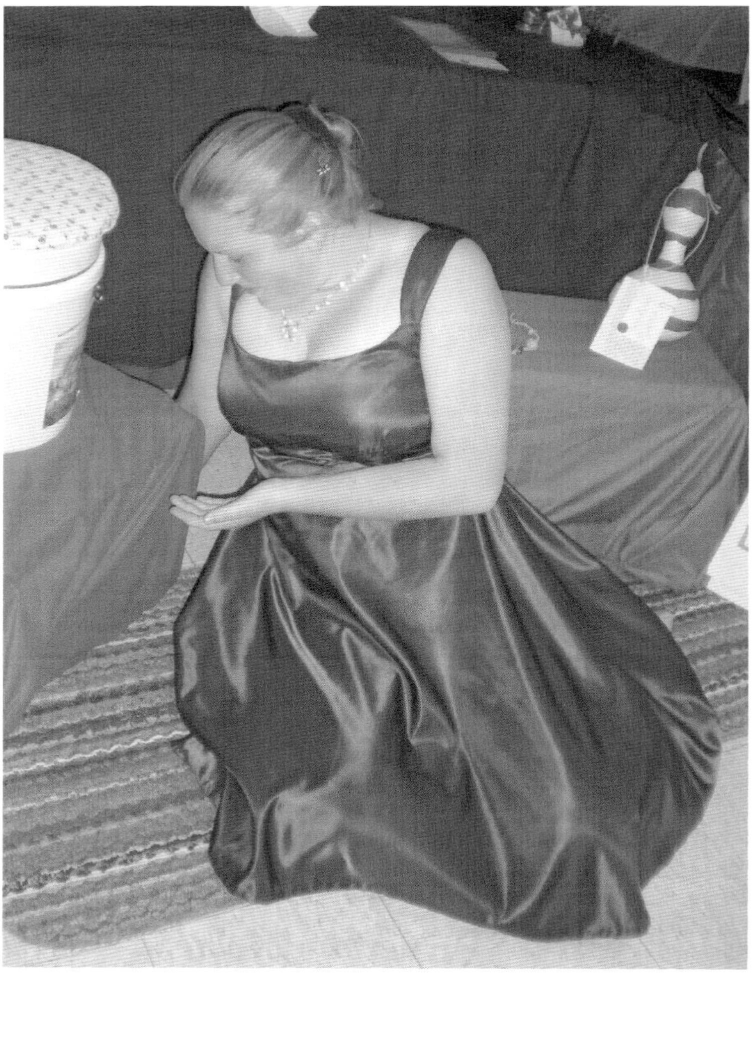

Nicole Sands (2011 Fair Queen) "mannequin models" at the 2010 Orleans County 4-H Fair. This type of modeling requires a person to "freeze" for five minutes, pretending as if he or she is a mannequin, which proves to be a fun way to show off a member's sewing while modeling clothing or holding handmade items. Sands has been in 4-H for nine years. (Courtesy of 4-H Fair Archives.)

A master showman is the best at showing his breed in competition. Smith's family raises beef; he is also an expert beef showman and has competed at the national level. He is currently attending Cornell University's College of Veterinary Medicine. Dr. Cynthia Shelley (presenting the award) is an associate professor of animal science at SUNY Cobleskill. (Courtesy of 4-H Archives.)

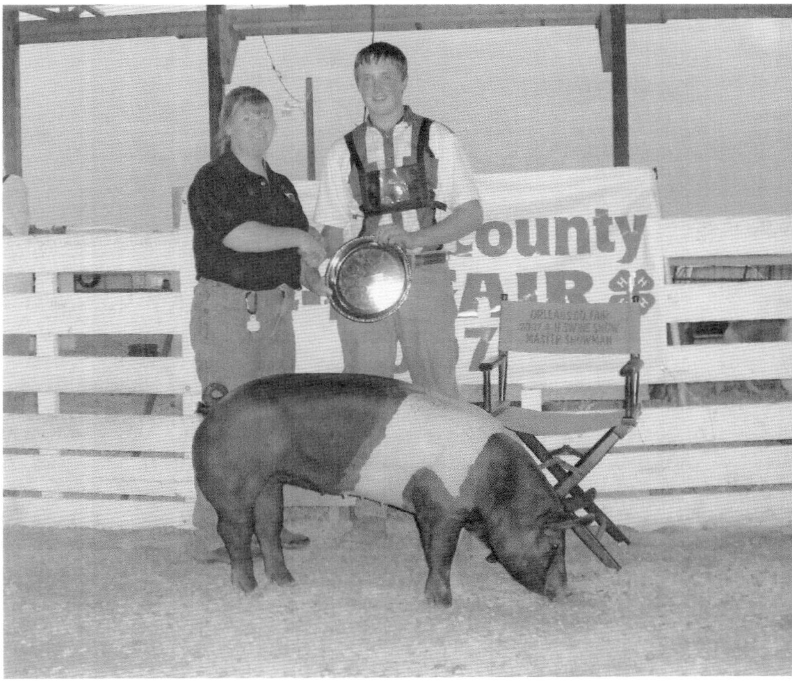

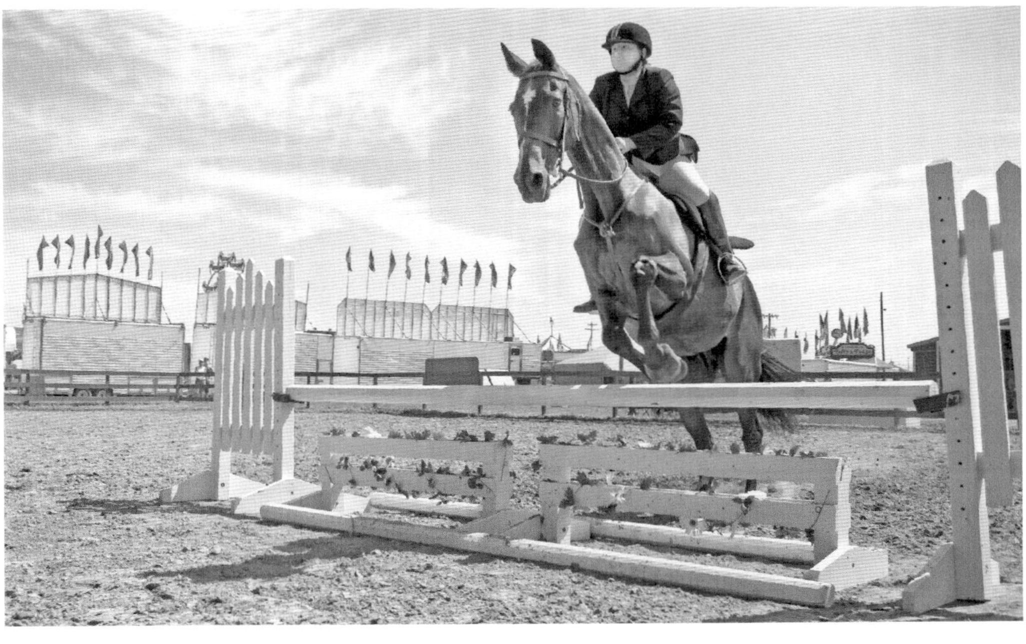

Zink rides her horse, Shadow, in the English discipline. The Orleans County 4-H Horse Program teaches English, western, gymkhana, and driving disciplines. Zink was the only Orleans County 4-Her at the junior level to go to the 2011 New York State Fair. It was her first time competing there, and she won second place in showmanship! (Courtesy of George Lama Photography.)

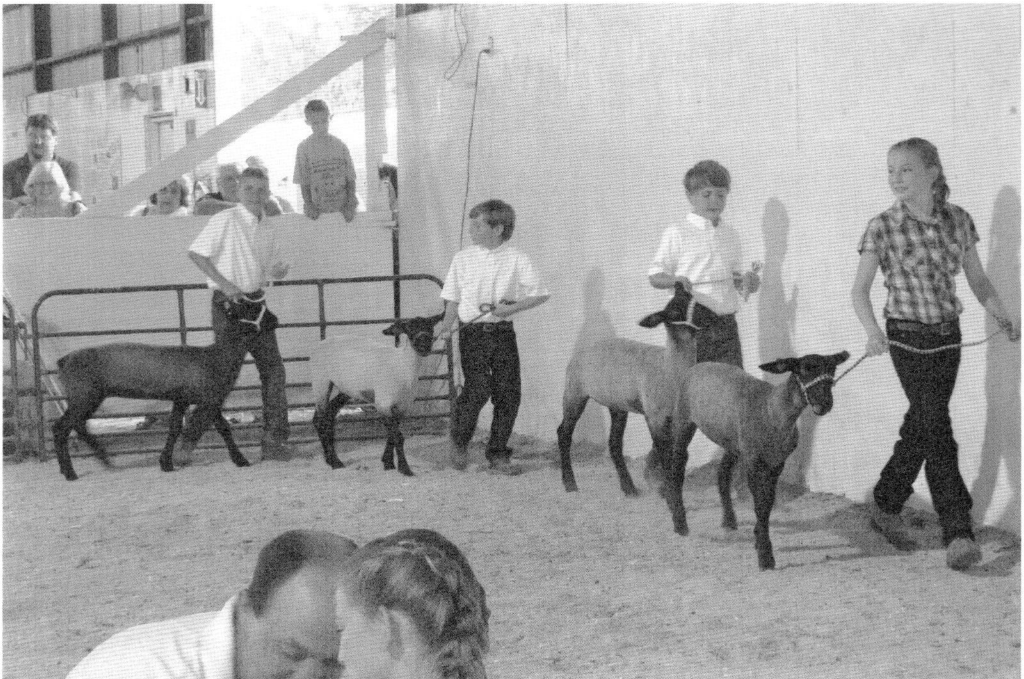

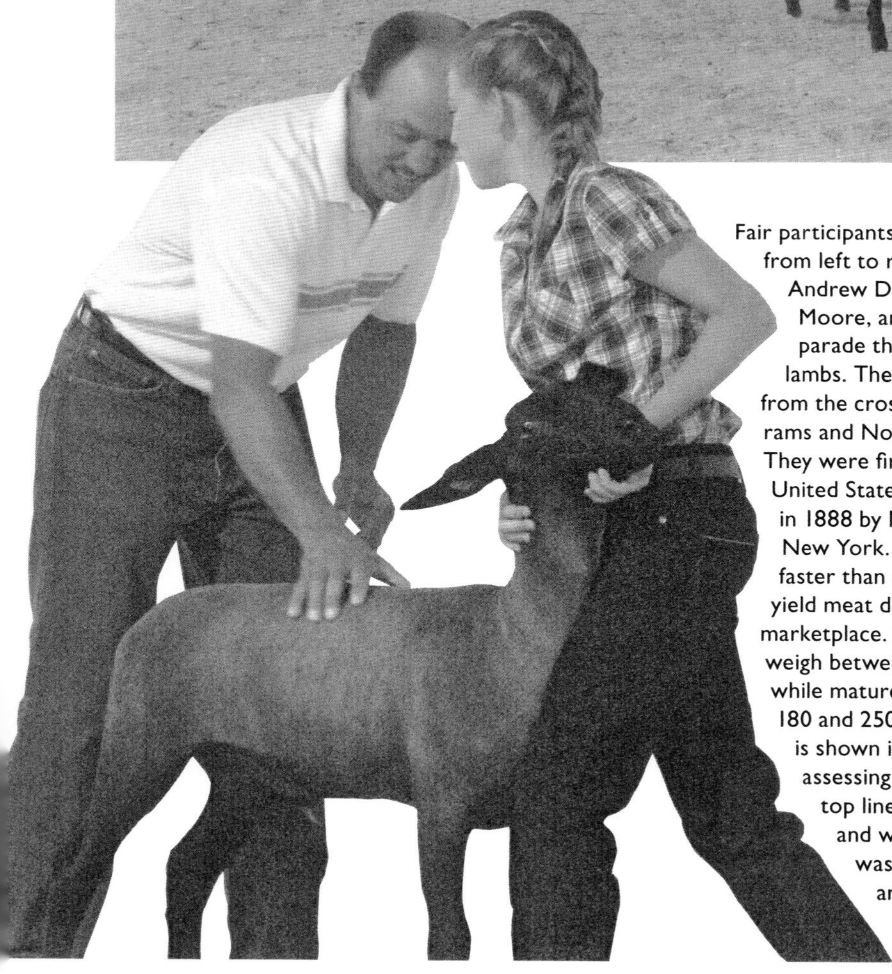

Fair participants, pictured above from left to right, Andrew Moore, Andrew Drechsel, Zachary Moore, and Claudia Drechsel, parade their Suffolk market lambs. These sheep originated from the crossing of Southdown rams and Norfolk Horned ewes. They were first brought to the United States from Suffolk, England, in 1888 by Mr. Streeter of Chazy, New York. Suffolk lambs grow faster than any other breed and yield meat desired in today's marketplace. Typical mature rams weigh between 250 and 350 pounds, while mature ewes weigh between 180 and 250 pounds. Kevin Kron is shown in the photograph (left) assessing a lamb for a straight top line, good length of loin, and weight; this market lamb was awarded first place and belongs to Claudia Drechsel. (Courtesy of Linda Rosenthal.)

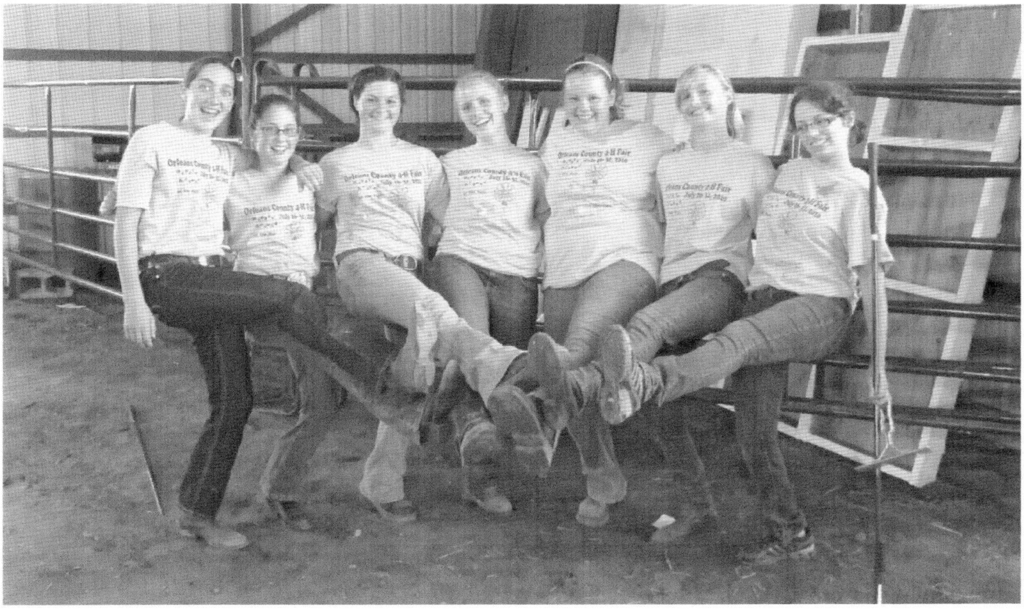

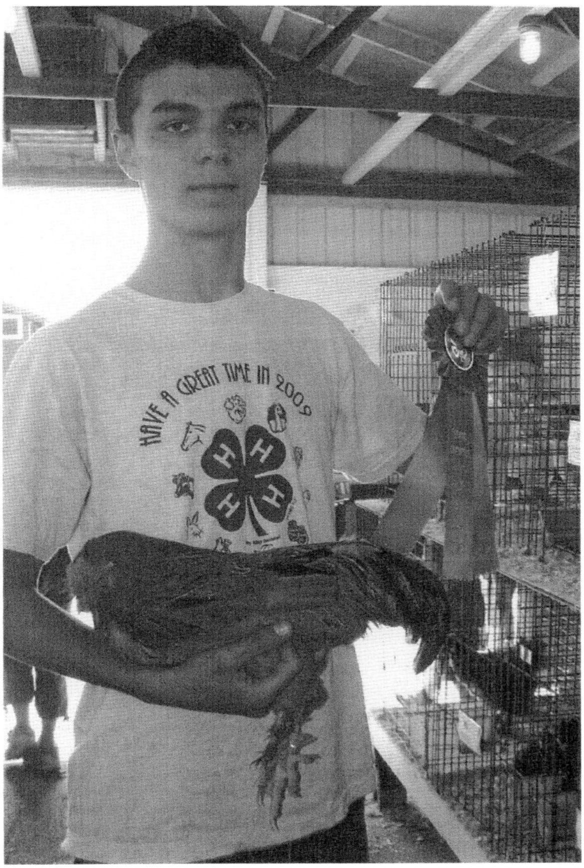

The girls in this photograph are 2010 Grand Master Showman Competition participants. These master showmen, winners within their particular breed category, then compete for Grand Master Showman, showing eight different animals, all with different standards. Pictured left to right are Emily Bannister, Beef; Jayne Bannister, Swine; Star Graning, Meat Goat; Betsey McKenna, Dairy Cow and Dairy Goat; Sarah Metzler, Sheep; Raquel Roberts, Horse; and Antonia Garcia-Codori, Llama. (Courtesy of 4-H Fair Archives.)

Wachob is pictured with his award-winning Buff Brahma Rooster at the 2009 4-H Fair. Poultry and the 4-H fair are second nature to Wachob and his family; the Poultry Building was dedicated to David Wachob Sr. in 1978. Anthony's grandmother Claire, his father Jim, and his seven siblings represent a long line of 4-H Poultry Wachobs. (Courtesy of 4-H Fair Archives.)

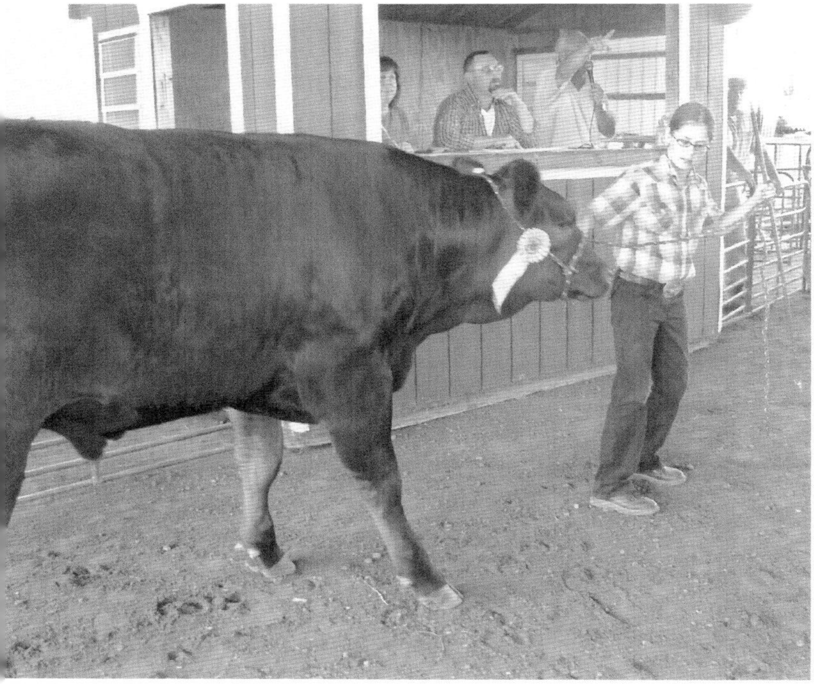

The meat auction at the Orleans County 4-H Fair is the culmination of a year-long project where members learn the skill of raising and marketing meat animals. They determine the total cost of the project, find their own bidders, and write thank you letters. This year Kast Farms in Albion was the biggest spender, paying $4,446 for the steer Bannister raised. (Courtesy of 4-H Fair Archives.)

Theodore Swiercznski, father of seven, enlisted his own crew of kids to help plant cabbage. Swiercznski was a knowledgeable farmer and served on the Agricultural Resources Commission, which continues to review and administer farming practices to ensure communities have viable farmland. Pictured from left to right are John Stirk; Colleen, Maureen, Cathleen, and Christine Swiercznski; Tom Stirk; and Patrick and Todd Swiercznski. Ted is driving. (Courtesy of Swiercznski Family.)

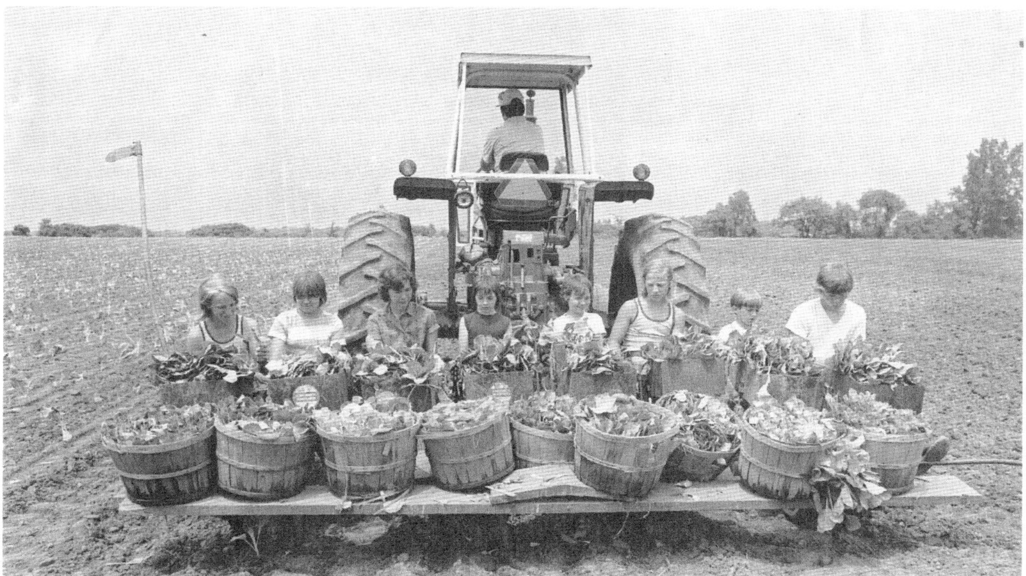

Artists, Educators, Entertainers, and Writers

In his book *Memories of Life on the Ridge*, J. Howard Pratt recalls that Orleans County's first school "was a little log cabin on Ridge Road near the Eagle Harbor corners. Here, a dozen children gathered in winter to learn to read and cipher under the instruction of Orin Gleason, a neighboring farmer." Orleans County citizens have held education in high regard from the beginning. As resources allowed, they continued building these country schools and located them approximately every three miles in an effort to make schooling accessible. Today, children continue to receive quality instruction from dedicated teachers. Thankfully, that education extends beyond the classroom. It may take place in a field on the County House Road or in Mt. Albion Cemetery. And, it may be the long, snowy winters, but for some reason Orleans County seems to offer a great number of talented artists, writers, and entertainers. Learn about Kim Martilotta's art gallery, which showcases many local artists. From George Stebbins's hymns to Larry Weed's "Wipe Out," local composers' work transcends generations. The multitalented Patrick Riviere delights his audiences as actor, singer, and author. This chapter presents folks of varying backgrounds, all of whom contribute to the arts.

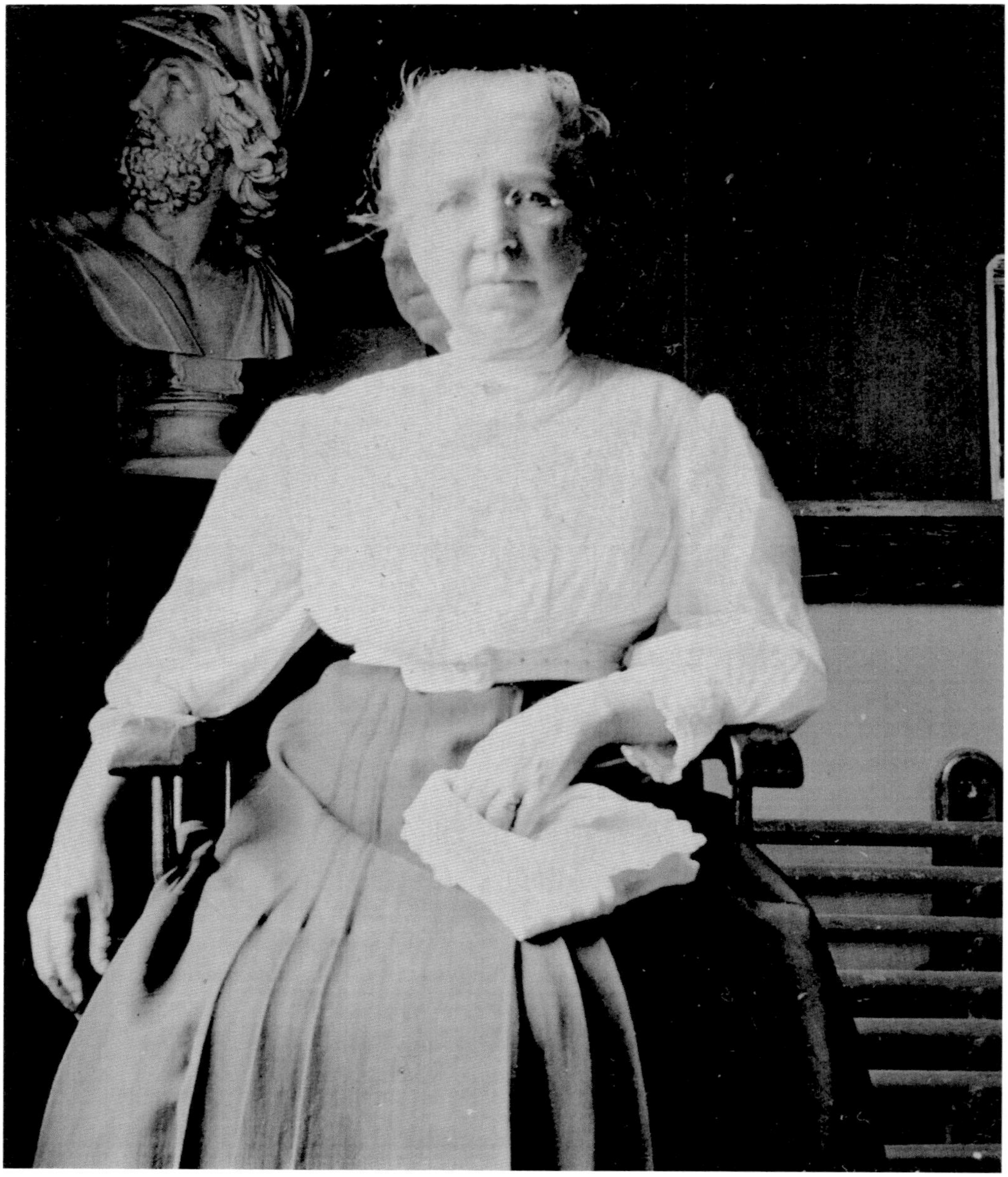

Denio (1842–1922) was born to an Albion family able to support her independence. Highly educated, she taught at Vassar, and was a professor of German and art history for 20 years at Wellesley College. She later studied in Europe, earning her PhD at age 56. Returning to the United States in 1902, she accepted a position teaching art history, a job she retained until retiring in 1917 at age 75. She helped organize the Memorial Art Gallery and served on its board of directors. She was killed when struck by a car. Dr. Rush Rees, University of Rochester president, officiating at her funeral remarked, "here was a noble life, well lived, which leaves a fragrant memory." (Courtesy Rush Rees Library, University of Rochester.)

Riviere has been a performer, playwright, director, producer, teacher, and arts administrator since he began "clowning around" at the age of 10. He has performed over 100 roles in theater, film, and television. Patrick most recently starred in the 2011 Stephen King short film *A Very Tight Place*. Last fall he received kudos for his portrayal of Sancho Panza in the Merry-Go-Round Playhouse production of *Man of La Mancha,* co-starring David M. Lutken and Esther Stillwell. Prior to that, he was seen in the world premiere of Michele Willen's *Family Dinner,* off-Broadway. Currently, he can be heard as the voices of Dr. Einkopf and Jimmy the Cabin Boy in the animated series *Captain Stargood*. He has earned critical acclaim, highlighted by performances as Manos in the new musical *OPA!* (nominated for MITF 2008 Outstanding Supporting Actor in a Musical), the Purser in the Broadway on the Boardwalk production of *Anything Goes* at the Trump Plaza in Atlantic City, Che in *Evita* at ArtPark, Stewpot in *South Pacific* at Candlewood, and Snoopy in *You're a Good Man, Charlie Brown* at ECST. He is proud of his play *The House of Nunzio,* which earned semifinalist recognition twice. Riviere is particularly fond of his first acting role in third grade, when he played Sir Desmond Decay in a play honoring teeth! Riviere founded the All Seasons Theatre Company (ASTC), co-founded The Emerging Artists Project, Inc., was a founding member of Sonnet Repertory Theatre, and was industry/professional liaison and a member of the adjunct faculty for the Drama Department at NYU's Tisch School of the Arts. He has worked for Second Stage Theatre, Arts Horizons, and The Hudson Riverfront Performing Arts Center. He is a proud member of AEA, AFTRA, and SAG. (Courtesy of Glen Gaston.)

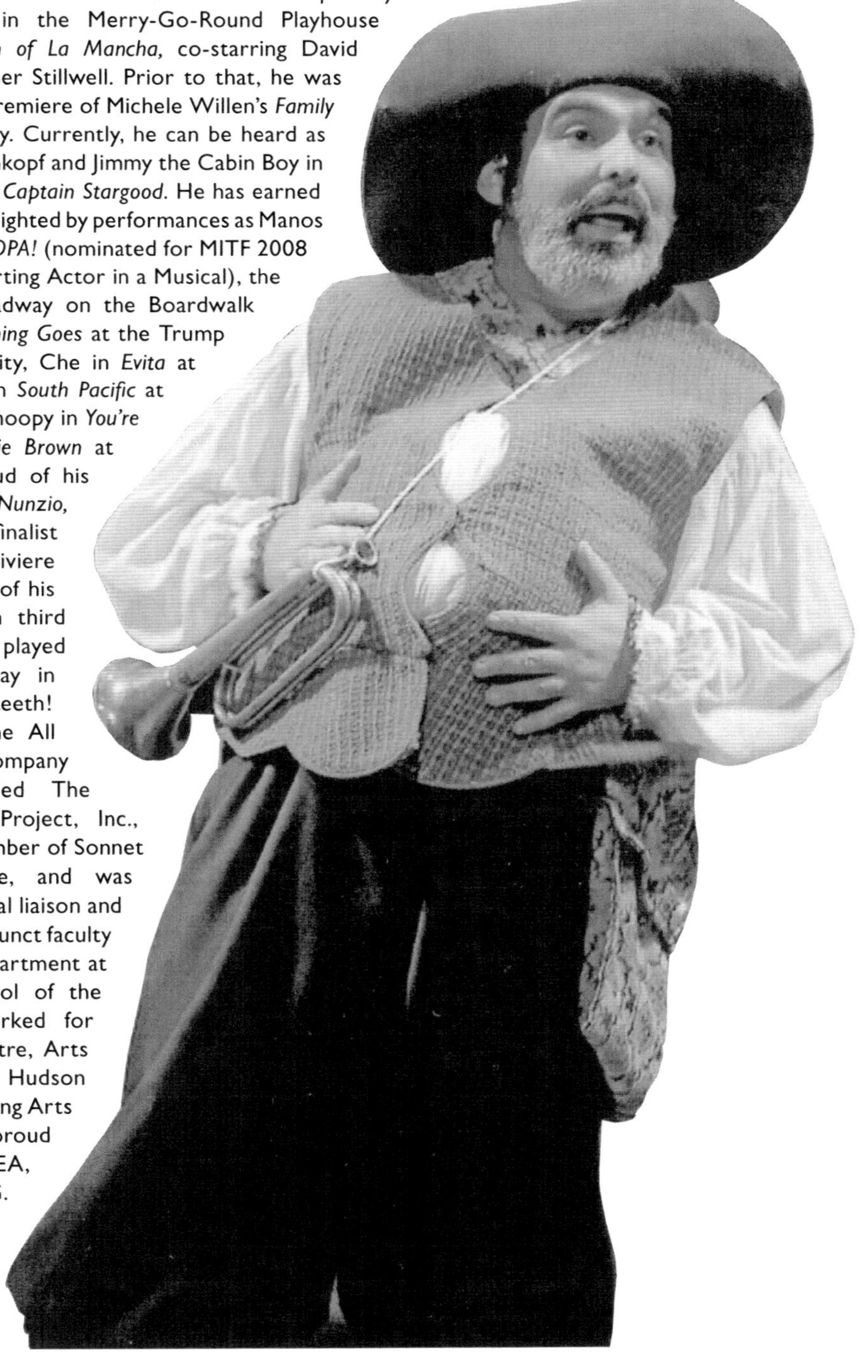

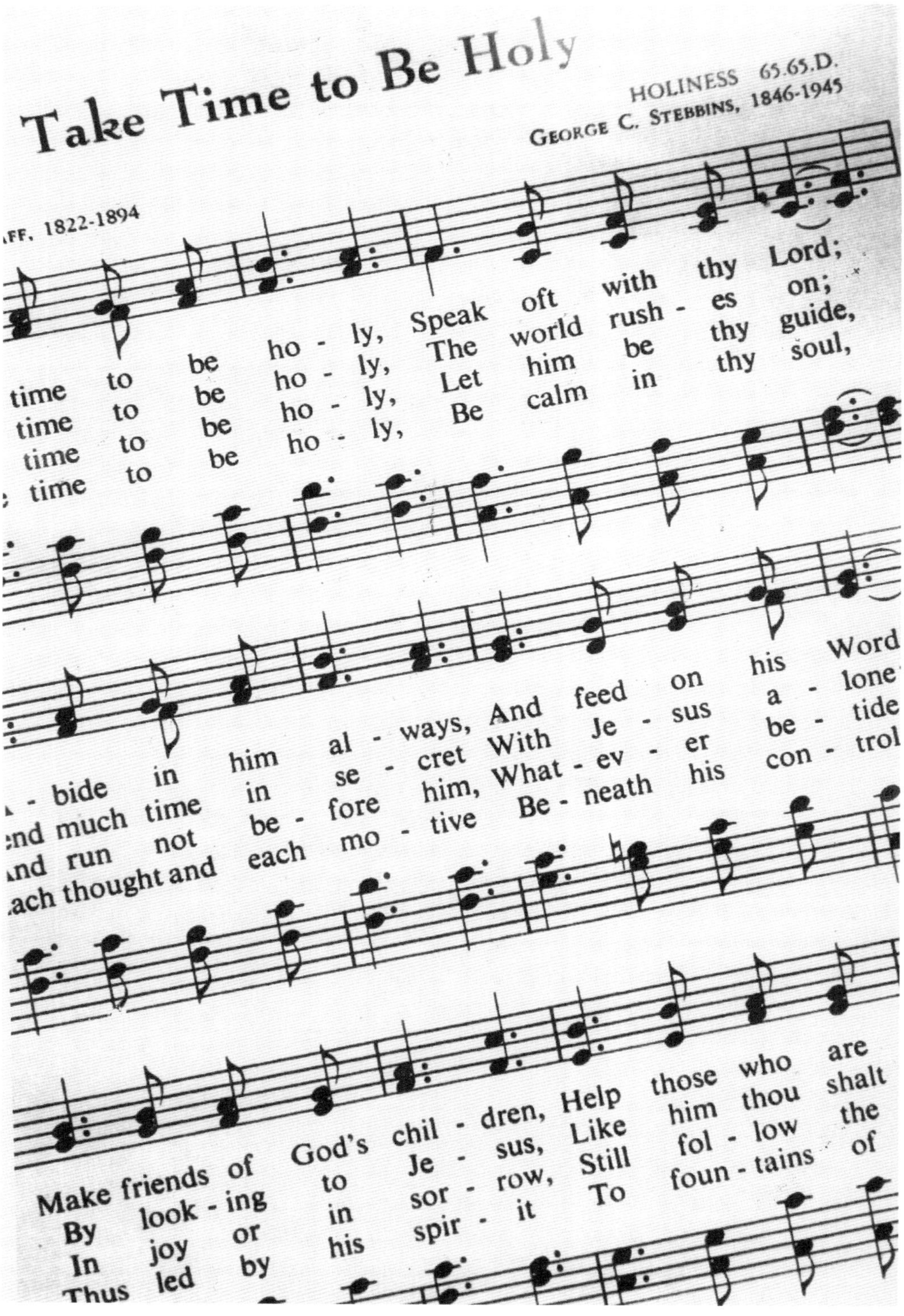
Take Time to Be Holy
HOLINESS 65.65.D.
GEORGE C. STEBBINS, 1846-1945
1822-1894
time to be ho - ly, Speak oft with thy Lord;
time to be ho - ly, The world rush - es on;
time to be ho - ly, Let him be thy guide,
time to be ho - ly, Be calm in thy soul,
- bide in him al - ways, And feed on his Word
much time in se - cret With Je - sus a - lone
run not be - fore him, What - ev - er be - tide
thought and each mo - tive Be - neath his con - trol
Make friends of God's chil - dren, Help those who are
By look - ing to Je - sus, Like him thou shalt
In joy or in sor - row, Still fol - low the
Thus led by his spir - it To foun - tains of

(LEFT)
George Stebbins (1846–1945) was born in East Carlton, where he worked on the family farm until he moved to Chicago at age 23, eventually assuming leadership roles as musical director at various churches. He met and studied under Mr. Dwight Moody and other well-known evangelists in a musical capacity. George served overseas, visiting India, Egypt, Palestine, and Europe. He edited hymnals and composed music for hymns such as "Take Time to Be Holy," "Saved by Grace," and "There Is a Green Hill Far Away." Author Jacob Hall wrote that George "will be remembered best by the music with which his name is associated, for that, if God continues to use it in the future as in the past, will long survive him and the memory of his public ministry." (Courtesy of Orleans County Department of History.)

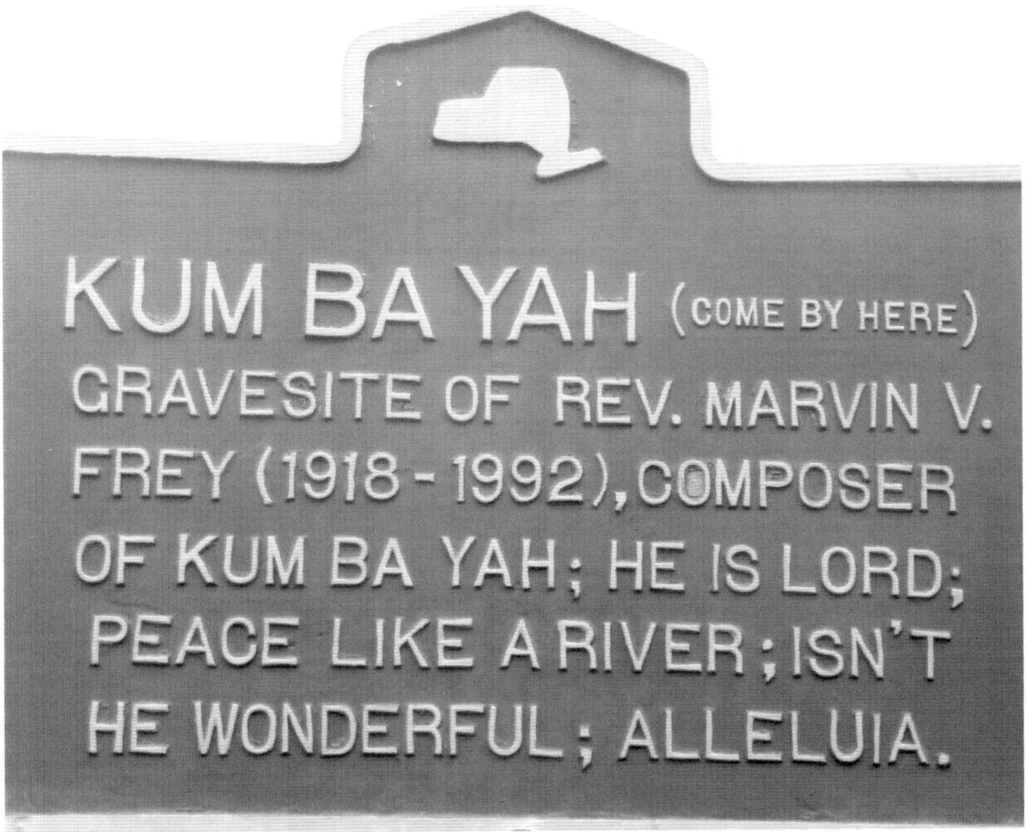

Frey (1918–1992) wrote over 2,000 well-known songs in his lifetime, including "He Is Lord," "I've Got Peace Like a River," and "Do, Lord." A song most of us learned in childhood, "Kum Ba Yah," was copyrighted by Marvin circa 1939 under the title "Come by Here." He claimed the song was inspired by a prayer he heard delivered by a storefront evangelist. His song first appeared as a lyric sheet printed in 1939. The origins of this song are disputed, as a nearly identical Gullah (Creole pidgin) version of this song is believed to have been sung by former slaves living in the southeastern United States. The song has been performed by many artists; one of the most recent recordings was done by Peter, Paul and Mary in 1998. (Courtesy of Andrew Canham.)

(RIGHT)

Porter (1900–1951) was born in Albion on November 14, 1900. Porter was an accomplished artist and musician. He played piano during silent movies at local theaters and area hotels as early as 1925, but he was most known for his artwork. At age 17, Porter was a political cartoonist for the *Knickerbocker Press* in Albany, and later a commercial artist at the Rochester *Democrat and Chronicle*. Porter moved to Buffalo and opened a successful commercial art studio. That success impressed Disney Studios, and he started his new career on June 16, 1936. Porter's first assignment was to assist other artists with Disney's *Snow White and the Seven Dwarfs*. Porter was later transferred to the publicity department, where he made a name for himself as a "ranking artist" drawing *Walt Disney's Comics and Stories*, *Good Housekeeping* magazine installments, and the Sunday comics *Pinocchio* and *Snow White and the Seven Dwarfs*. In 1942, Walt Disney approached Porter to work on requests for military insignia and government war bond advertisements, stating "Mister, you have yourself a job. Just settle down to it. Make as many insignia as you can. If you get overloaded with work, let me know." With a small staff, Porter did just that. He and Roy Williams are believed to have created the now famous "Flying Tigers" nose art, and Porter is singularly credited with designing about 80 percent of his studio's war effort drawings (estimated at 1,200 in total). Legend has it that General Chennault sent Porter a gold clasp with the Flying Tiger insignia as a gift. In 1943, Disney called Porter "a one-man art department." After the war, Porter continued working for both Disney and the commercial sector on a variety of projects. Locally, Porter is credited for creating a masthead for the *Albion Advertiser*. He had three children: Maxine, Gordon, and Diane. Porter passed away on October 17, 1951 in California. His remains are interred at Mount Albion Cemetery near his mother. (Self-portrait by Hank Porter, Courtesy of C.W. Lattin.)

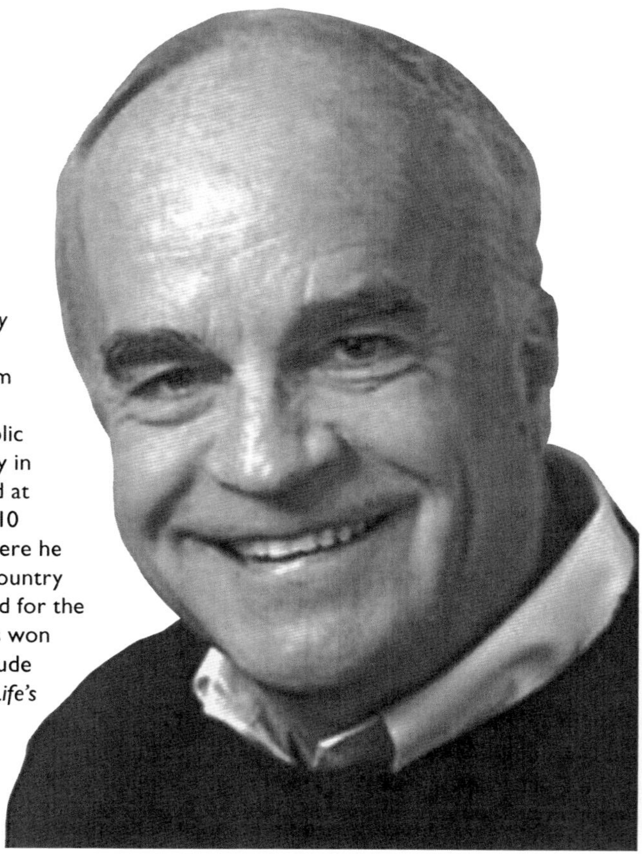

Craig Wilson has worked at *USA Today* since 1984. The son of Roy and June Wilson of Kuckville, he graduated from Lyndonville High School in 1967 and from the S.I. Newhouse School of Public Communication at Syracuse University in 1971. Following graduation, he worked at the *Saratogian* in Saratoga Springs for 10 years before moving to *USA Today*, where he is also a feature writer, traveling the country on assignment. He has been nominated for the Pulitzer Prize numerous times and has won several writing awards. His books include *It's the Little Things: An Appreciation of Life's Simple Pleasures,* which was published by Random House, and *Mothers and Children,* which was published by the National Geographic Society. (Courtesy of Craig Wilson.)

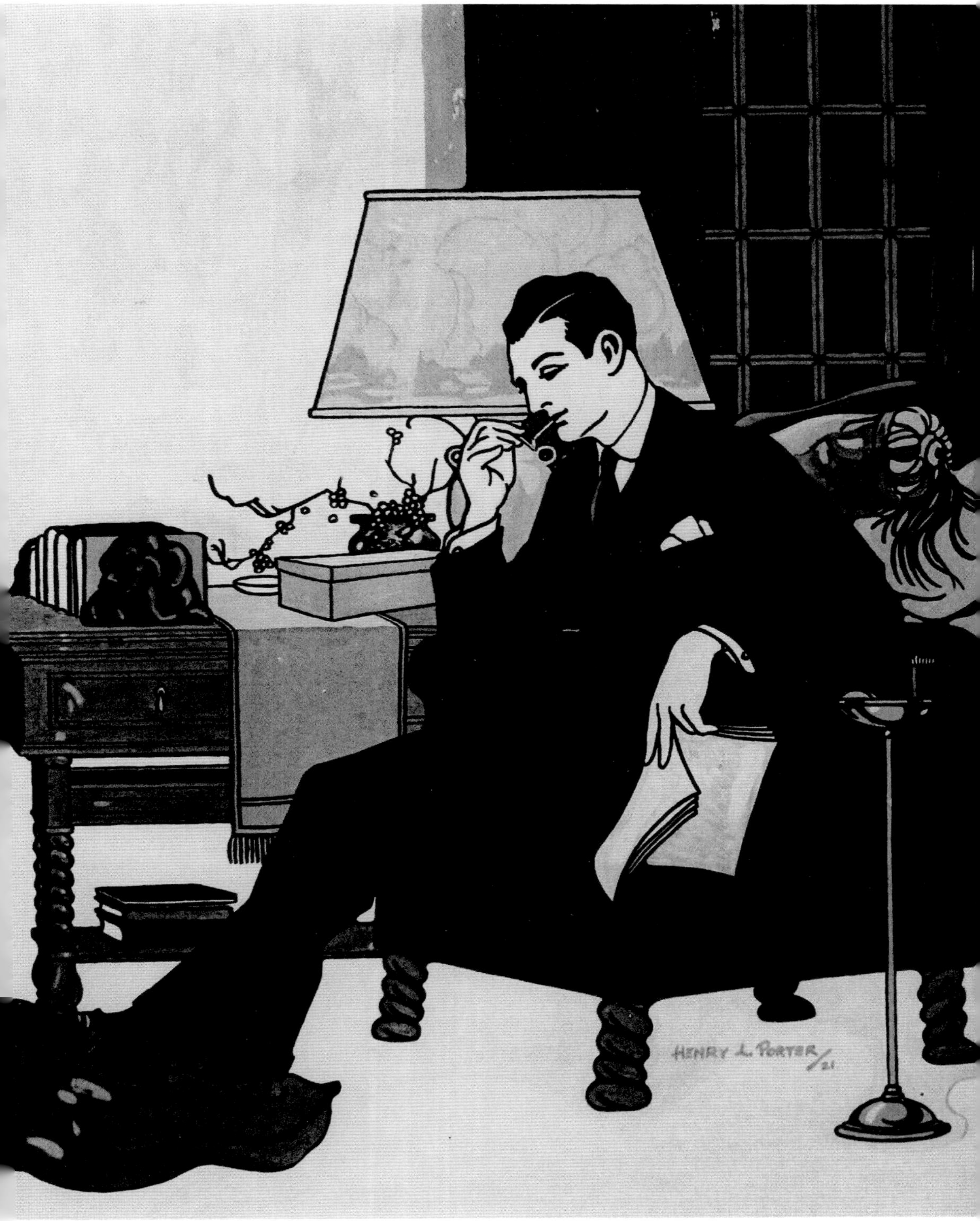
HENRY L. PORTER /21

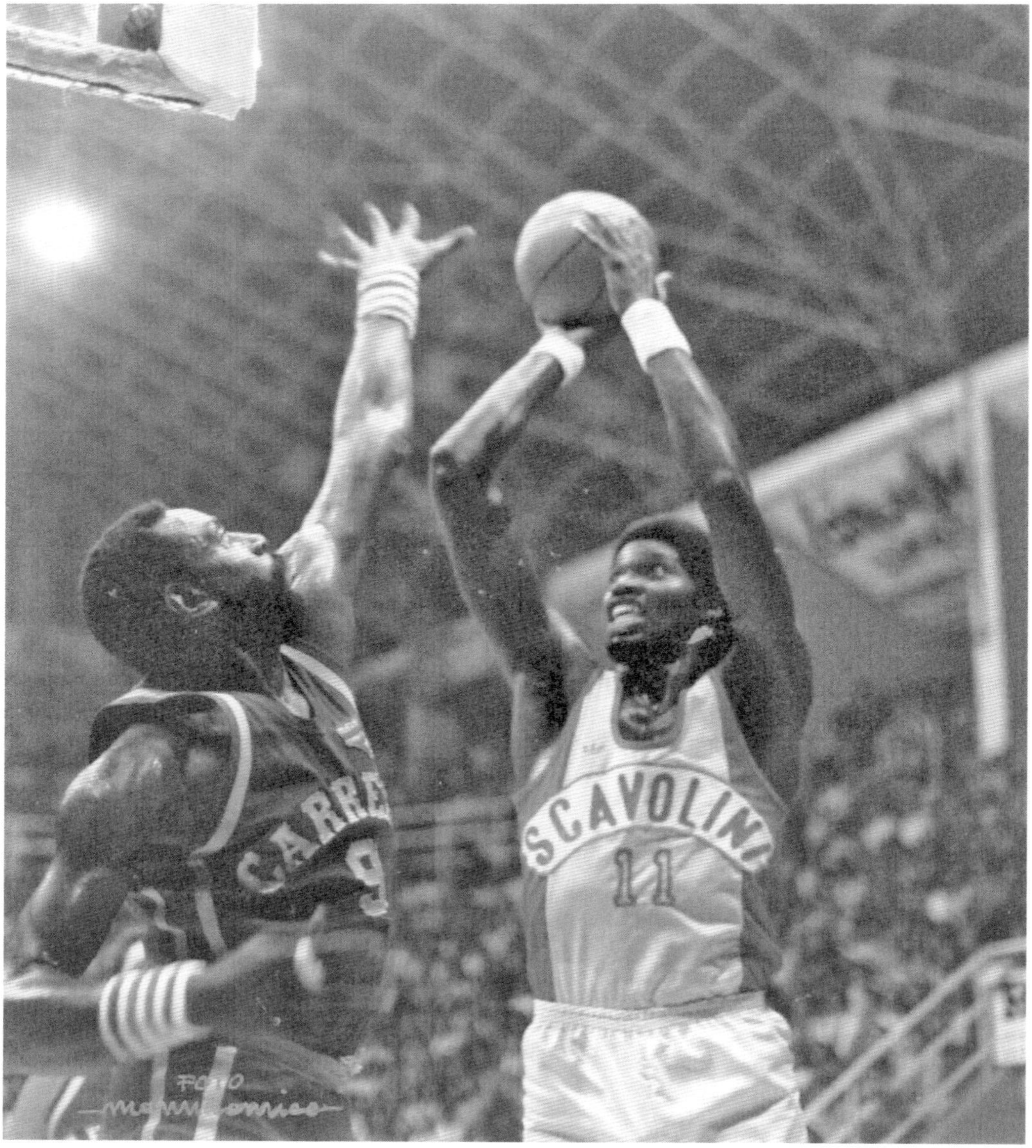

Bouie played basketball for Syracuse University (1976–1980) and graduated with a BA in speech communication. His collegiate honors include: NCAA Freshman All-American; NCAA All-American Team (1980); SU's All-Century Team (2000); and the Vic Hanson Outstanding Citizenship Award (1994). For 20 years he held the blocked shots record at Syracuse. After college, he was drafted by the NBA's Dallas Mavericks. Bouie was a member of the US pre-Olympic team with numerous future NBA stars, including Magic Johnson; this team never played because of the 1980 Olympic boycott. He played professionally for 14 years (1980–1993) in the Italian League. Upon his retirement, Bouie had the longest consecutive tenure of any American player. While playing overseas, Bouie was a seven-time All-Star nominee, and won the European championship ("Coppa Korac") during the 1991–1992 season. (Courtesy of Roosevelt Bouie.)

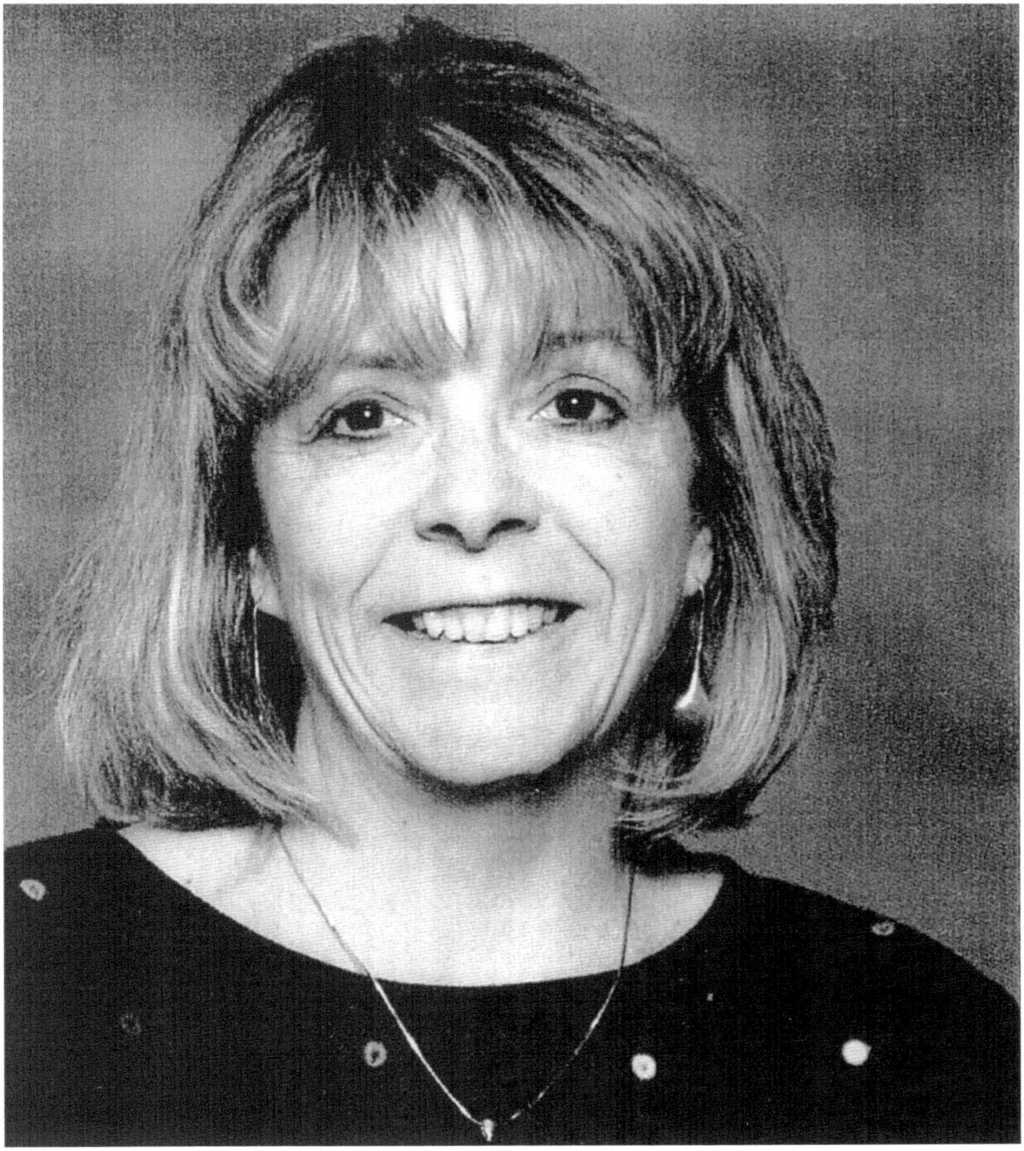

Alman, a former Albionite, earned her PhD in 1985 with a concentration in public personnel management and labor relations and interpersonal communication from the University of Pittsburgh. She pioneered the first online degree program offered there. Currently, she is the director of online education at the Pitt's School of Information Sciences. She teaches in the graduate program, administers the online program, and is involved in several research studies. She has also taught at San Jose State University and the University of the Virgin Islands. Her areas of specialization include asynchronous learning, marketing and PR, interpersonal communication, management and strategic planning, and social media. She has published books and journal articles, conducted multimillion-dollar research projects, and presented at national and international conferences. (Courtesy of Sue Alman.)

Kathy Dibley Samborski founded Klowns for the King, and Neil established Master's Hands Puppeteers in 1996, both as vehicles to "preach the Gospel to every creature." In developing their programs, they have attended a Fellowship of Christian Magic Convention and other creative and performing arts seminars. Their puppetry has reached hundreds of people in a unique way that is long remembered after the performance. (Courtesy of the Samborskis.)

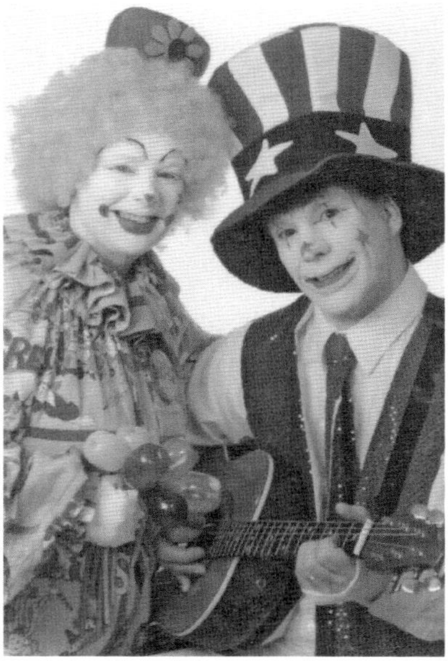

Hailing from Kendall and graduating from SUNY Oswego, Massey interned for the American Film Institute, which launched his extremely successful career. He has produced many primetime network shows including *Expedition Impossible*, *Survivor*, *WWE Tough Enough*, and the *History Channel's Top Shot*. Other TV projects include *Dancing with the Stars*, *Dude What Would Happen?*, and *Undercover Boss*. *Massey* has become a YouTube content partner and produces comedy videos under the name Podunk Pictures. (Courtesy of Aaron Massey.)

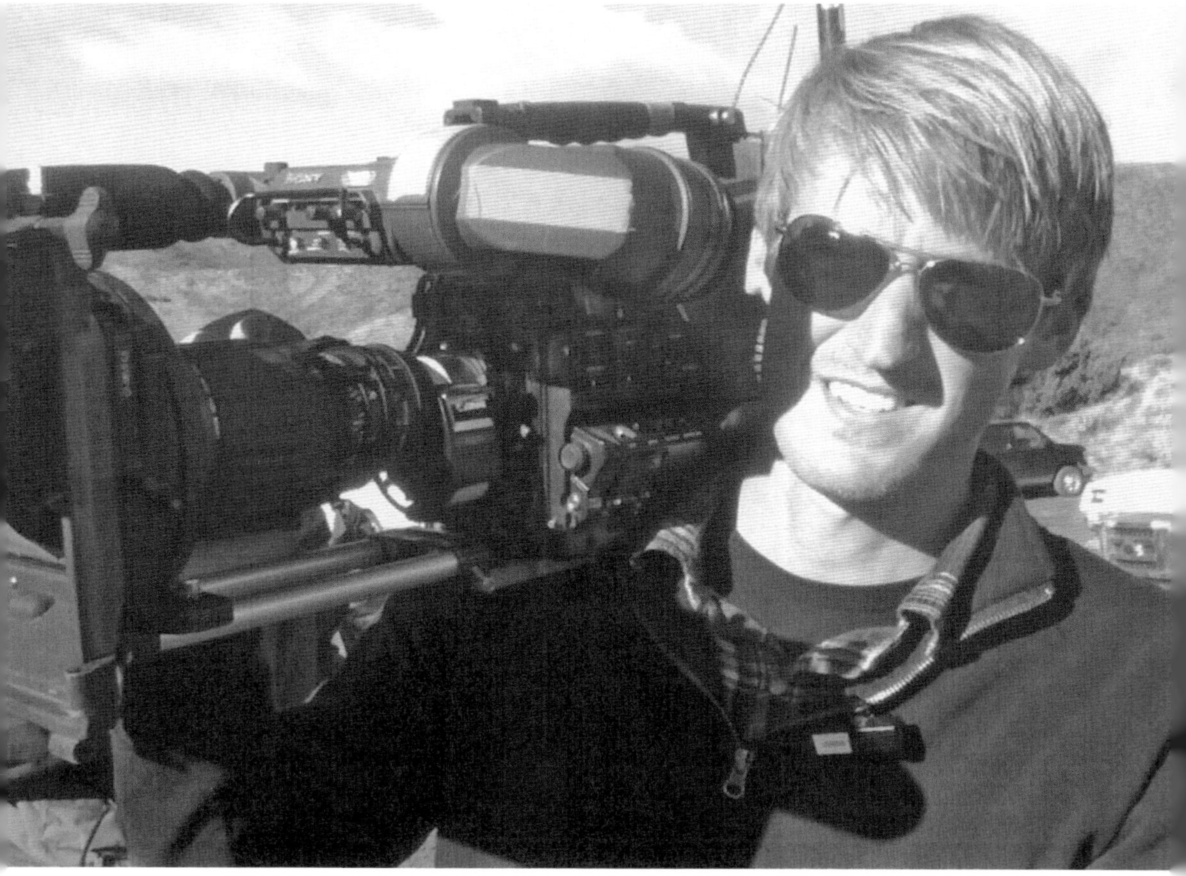

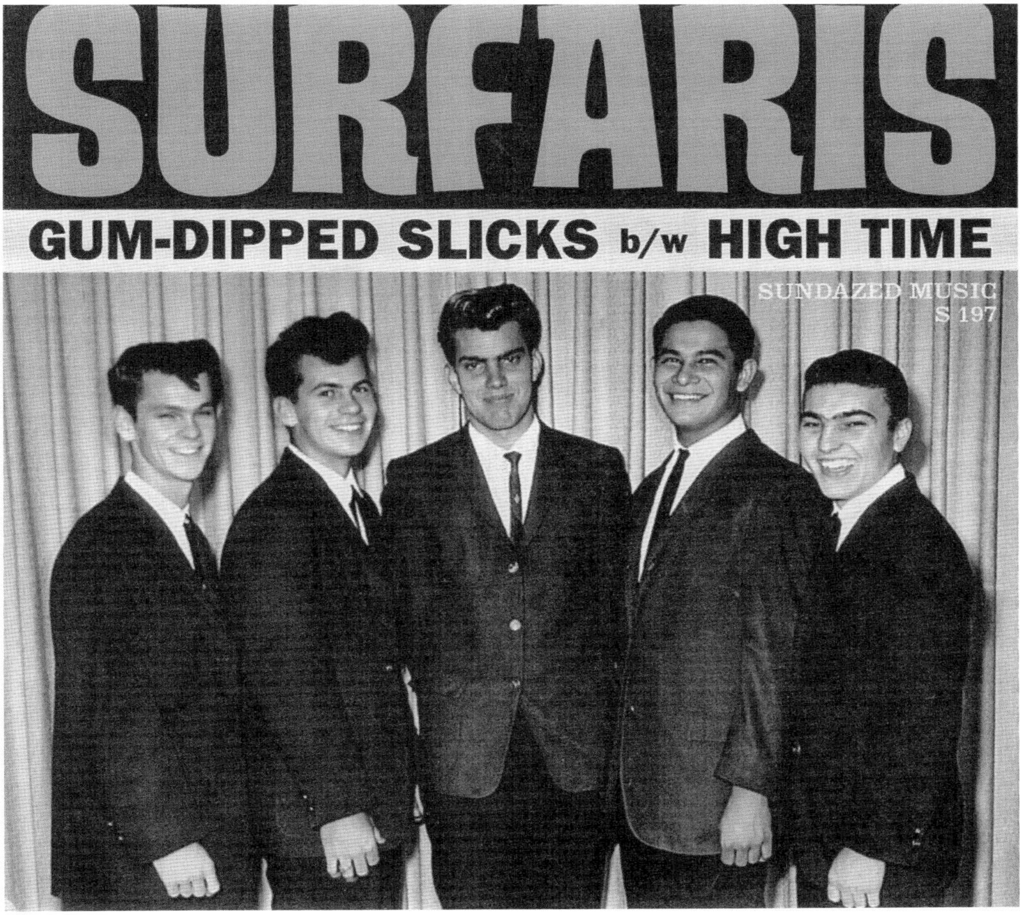

Around 1960, the Original Surfaris were formed. Larry Weed (second from left) of Kendall is one of the band's members. Originally called the Surfaris, they changed their name to the Original Surfaris after another band also called the Surfaris became widely famous for the song "Wipe Out." Larry Weed believes he wrote the song, and Orleans County legend supports him; unfortunately, he lost his court dispute to the other group. Weed's Original Surfaris are best known for their hits "Surfari" and "Bombora." (Courtesy of Larry Weed.)

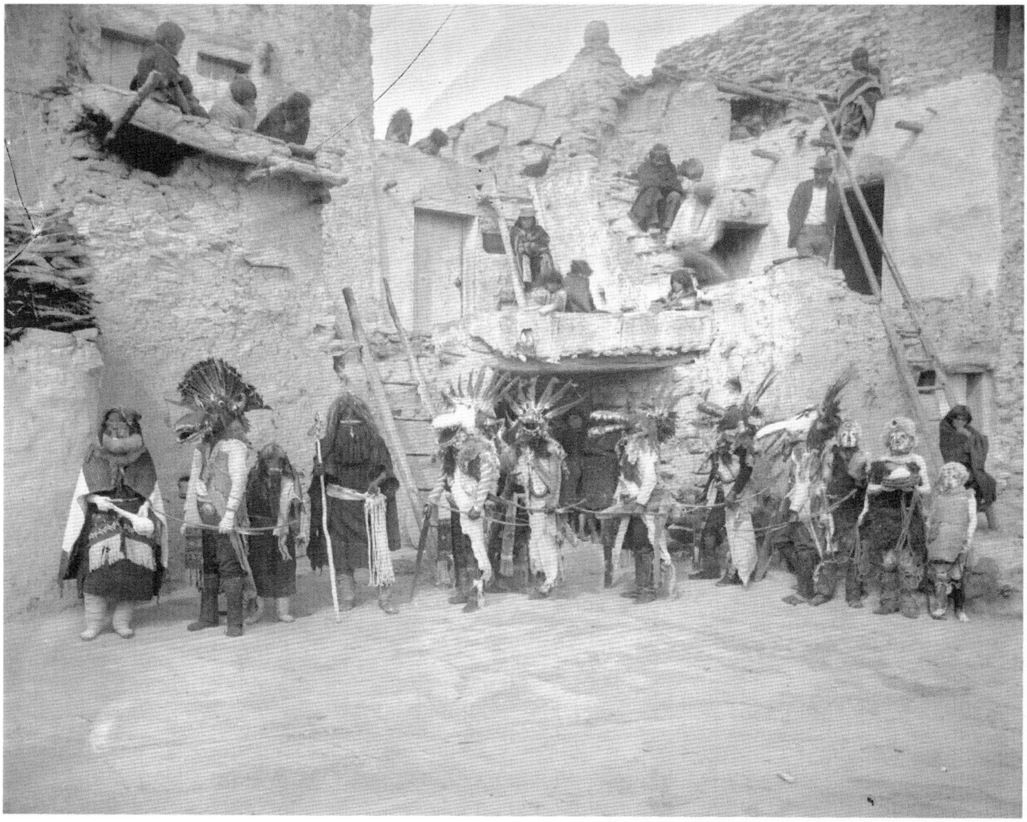

Weighing only one and a half pounds at birth and being kept on a pillow for the first year of his life did not seem to cause Frank Cushing any lasting problems. "When I was a boy, less than ten years of age, my father's man, while plowing one day, picked up and threw to me across the furrows, a little blue flint arrow point, saying, 'the Indians made that; it is one of their arrowheads.' I took it up fearfully, wonderingly, in my hands. It was small, cold, shining, and sharp-perfect in shape. Nothing had ever aroused my interest so much. That little arrow point decided the purpose and calling of my whole life. When nearly fourteen years of age, I discovered, in the woods south of Medina, an ancient Indian Fort. I built a hut and used to go there for days on a time, digging for relics when the sun shone, and, at night, in the light of the camp fire, studying by experiment how the more curious of the relics had been made and used." Cushing accidently made the acquaintance of L.W. Ledyard, a man interested in geology and archaeology. Mr. Ledyard introduced Frank to Spencer F. Baird, assistant secretary of the Smithsonian. Baird invited Cushing to write a paper on the old Medina fort. After a short course at Cornell, Cushing joined the Smithsonian staff as ethnologist and by 1876 was curator of the Smithsonian's archaeological collections at the Centennial Exposition in Philadelphia. In 1877, he was appointed curator of the Ethnological Department of the National Museum in Washington, DC. By 1879, Cushing was selected for an expedition to live with the Zuni and the Pueblos of the ancient province of Tusayan. From 1879 to 1884, he became anthropology's first participant observer. After some initial difficulties (the Zuni seriously considered killing him as he was obviously after their secrets), he was accepted by the community, adopted by the governor of the Pueblo, and participated in Zuni activities. In 1881, he was initiated into the warrior society, the Priesthood of the Bow. (Courtesy of National Anthropological Archives, Smithsonian Institution, [06662400].)

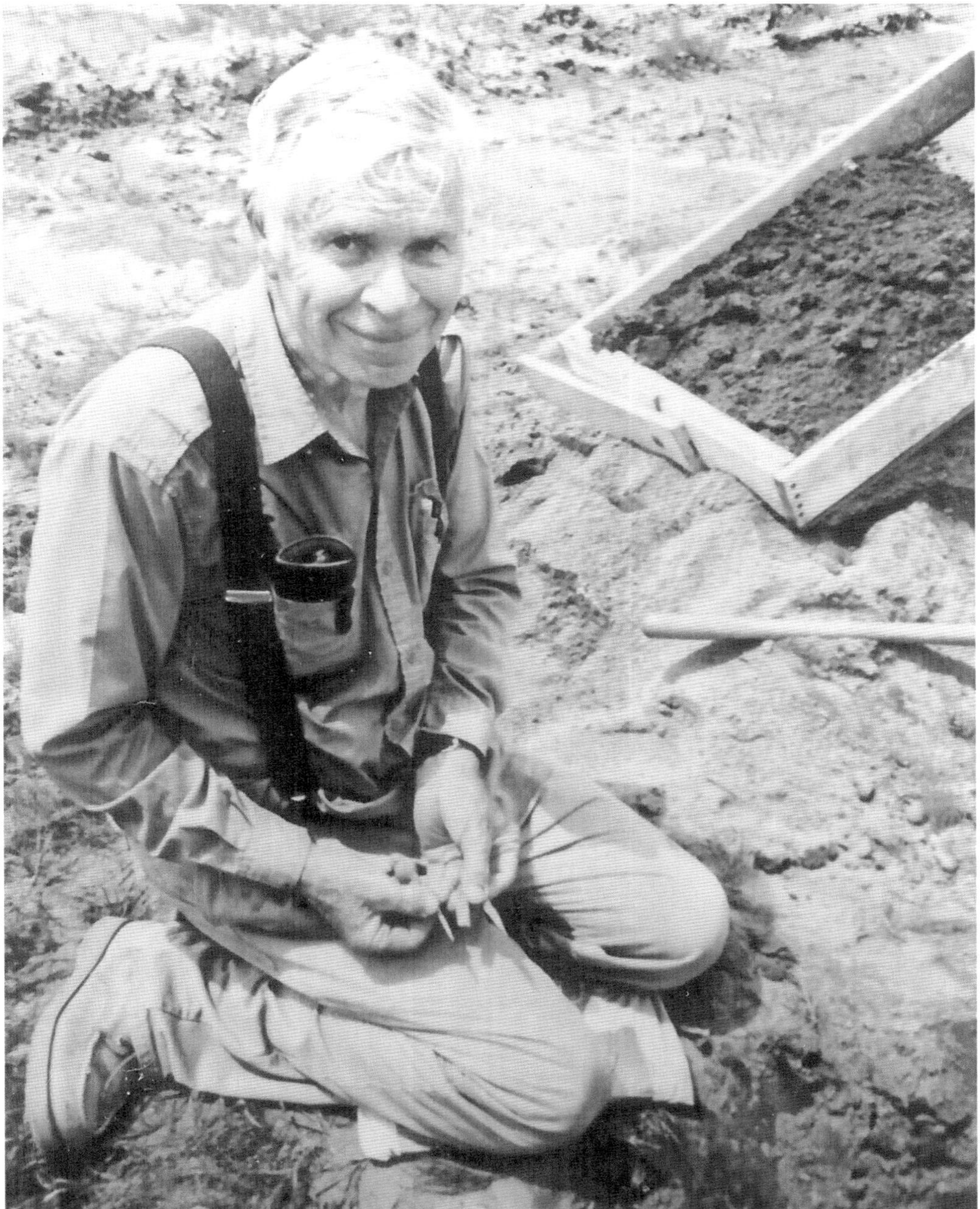

Vanderlaan's quest for history began in 1956 when he discovered two perfect arrow points while hunting. He has discovered many important artifacts, catalogued them, and published his findings. Vanderlaan has made significant discoveries and has been recognized as a fellow by the New York State Archaeological Association and the Rochester Museum and Science Center for his "distinguished contributions to archaeology." (Courtesy of Stanley Vanderlaan.)

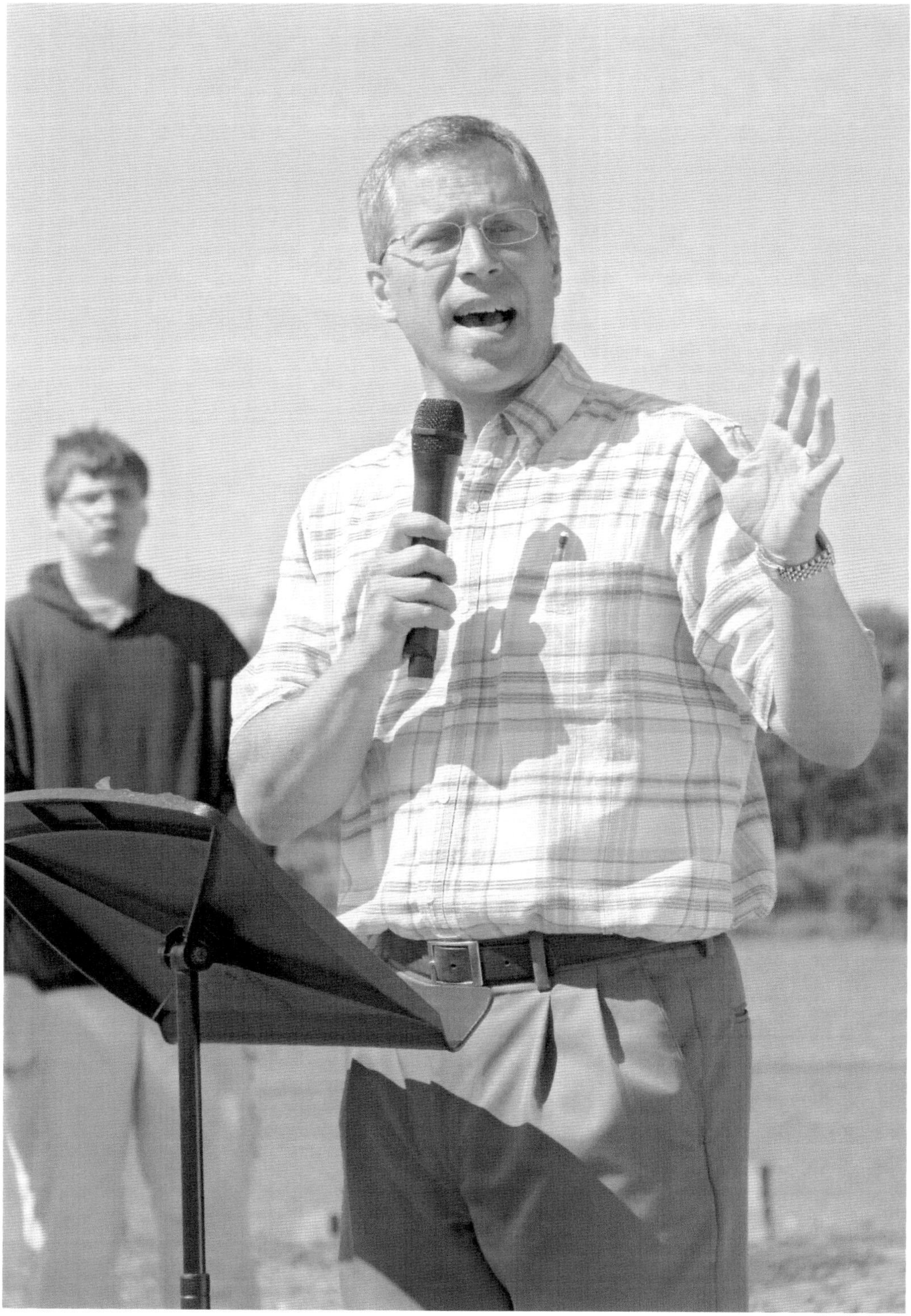

(LEFT)
Archer is the seventh grade service learning teacher at the Albion Middle School. His classes study local history and current events and perform numerous community service projects throughout the school year. Somehow, Archer manages to guide his students into extraordinary performance. Inspired by a classroom presentation by Bill Lattin, students were curious about the abandoned cemetery located behind the site of the former Alms Poor House on County House Road. On a service field trip, students visited an overgrown burial ground, and discovered 10 small stone grave markers etched with only a number. While delighted with the discovery, the sadness of the situation spurred these students into action—their mission was to discover who was buried there and clean up the cemetery. Archer divided students into groups to accomplish a variety of tasks essential to accomplishing their mission: researching death and institutional records, appealing to the County Legislature for restoration and maintenance, and physical cleanup of the junglelike area. His students worked hard for an entire year, and it paid off. They uncovered 66 stones, now reset in rows. They learned the names of 160 residents likely buried in that cemetery, and restored the history of life at the Alms House that served destitute residents for 130 years. People of every nationality, some paupers, and some displaced professionals lived there. The sandstone building, and later a medical building, stood on a working 155-acre farm. Able-bodied residents worked the farm, which produced all kinds of grains, fruits, and vegetables that were sold to help support it. In addition, the Alms House sold over 125,000 pounds of milk annually. To assist in the project, the Albion School District used a Learn and Serve America grant to recognize the cemetery by erecting a historical marker by the road and building a post and chain fence that now lines the site. Local businesspeople donated an etched memorial and built a stoned quarter-mile laneway to the burial ground. The work of Archer's students drew a community together and they are recognized for their excellent citizenship. (Courtesy of C.W. Lattin.)

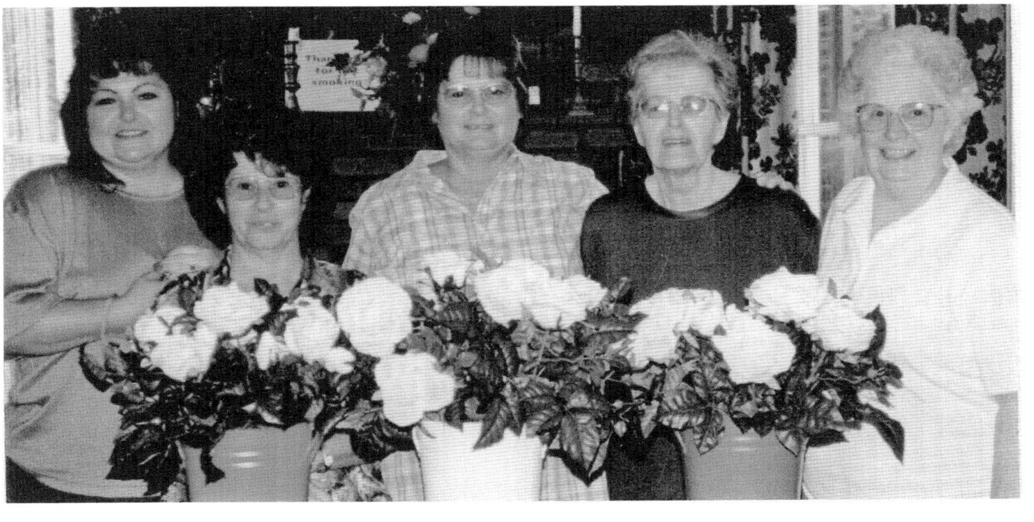

For Sharon Kerridge, Orleans County GenWeb County Coordinator, it began with headstone readings in the Town of Gaines and Carlton Cemeteries. She connected with Marge Schultz, Mary Stack, Bob Hales, Doug Murphy, and Stu Van Orden, and the rest is history. To date, the group has placed information from over 80 cemeteries online. Jason Zicari, superintendent of Mt. Albion Cemetery, serves to keep the group updated—a tremendous help. Tom Taber is the site's "Civil War Guy." Richard Nellist, Ridgeway historian, compiled Ridgeway Cemetery information. The site went online in June 1997 and in September 1997 won "Best New York State Website." This site is of invaluable assistance to researchers, saving them time and money. Pictured above, from left to right, are Nicole Wieme, Sandy Freeman, Sharon Kerridge, Marge Schultz, and Mary Stack. (Courtesy of Holly Canham.)

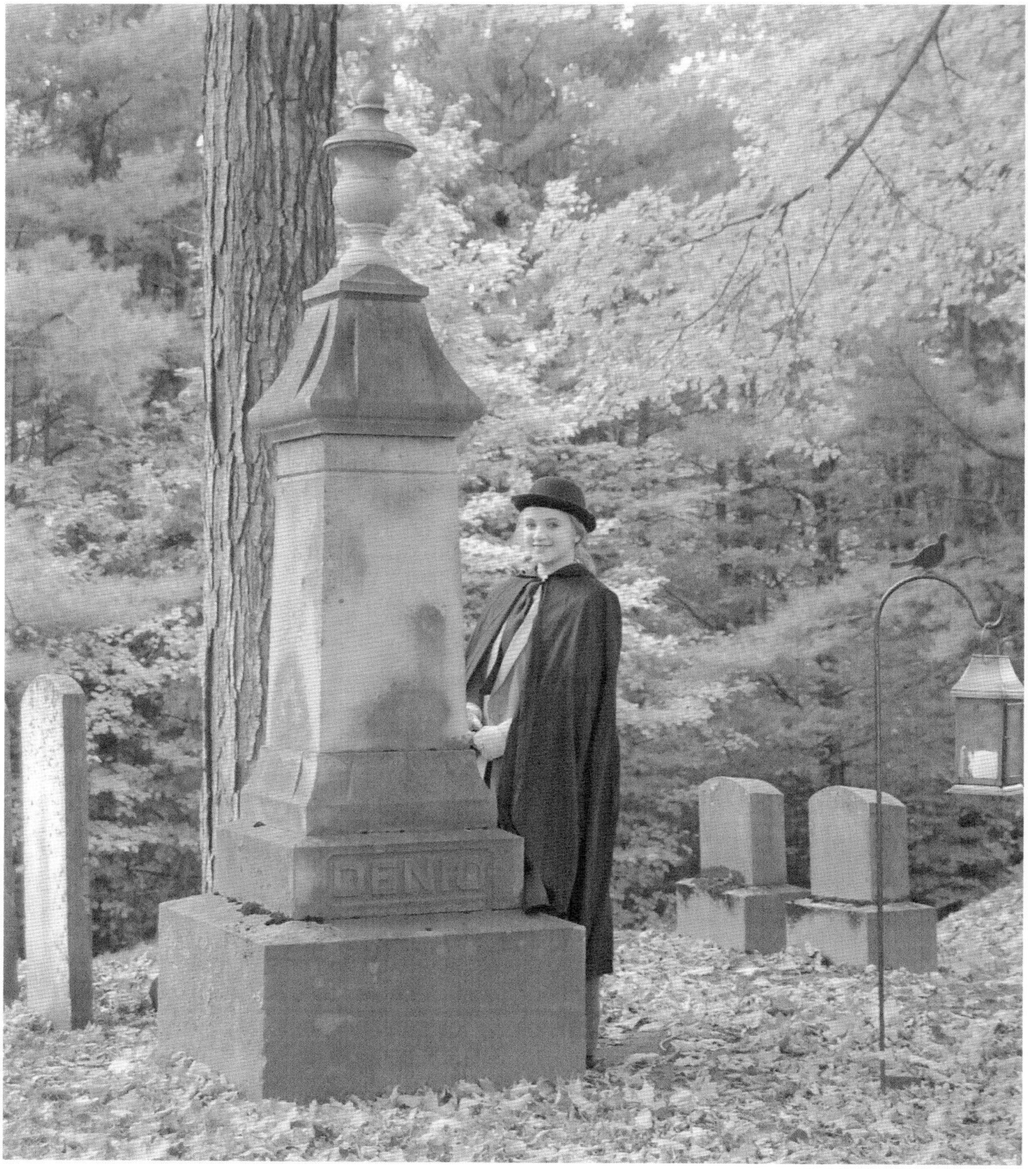

Inspired by the desire to foster an excitement within students about history and community service, Gary Simboli, Mike Thaine, and Sue Starkweather got together and planned what has become an annual event. The first year saw about 50 student participants, who performed various roles such as actor, tour guide, and technical crew-member; there was also instrumental music that students pre-recorded and played throughout the tour. Last year, more than 90 students participated; live music was added to improve upon the already successful student production. Faculty and staff supporters report that students love to dress up in period-correct costumes, perform their roles, learn about local history, and, importantly, share their knowledge and community appreciation. (Pictured above: Joyce LaLonde as "Denio"; page 71: Mark Graham (top) as "Bullock," and Michaela Miller (bottom) as "Phipps.")

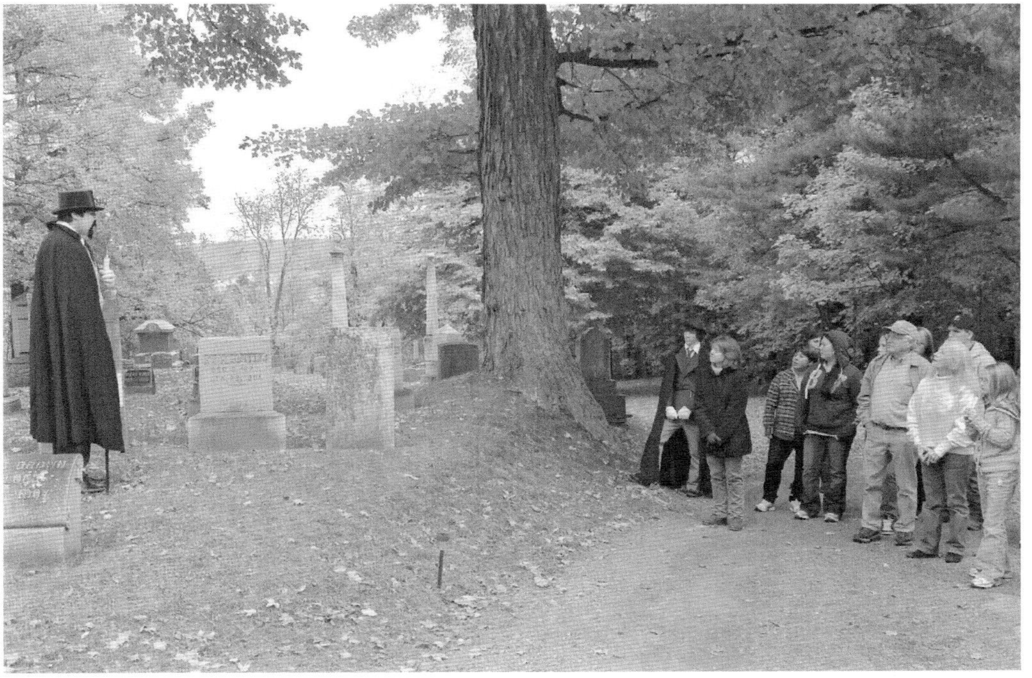

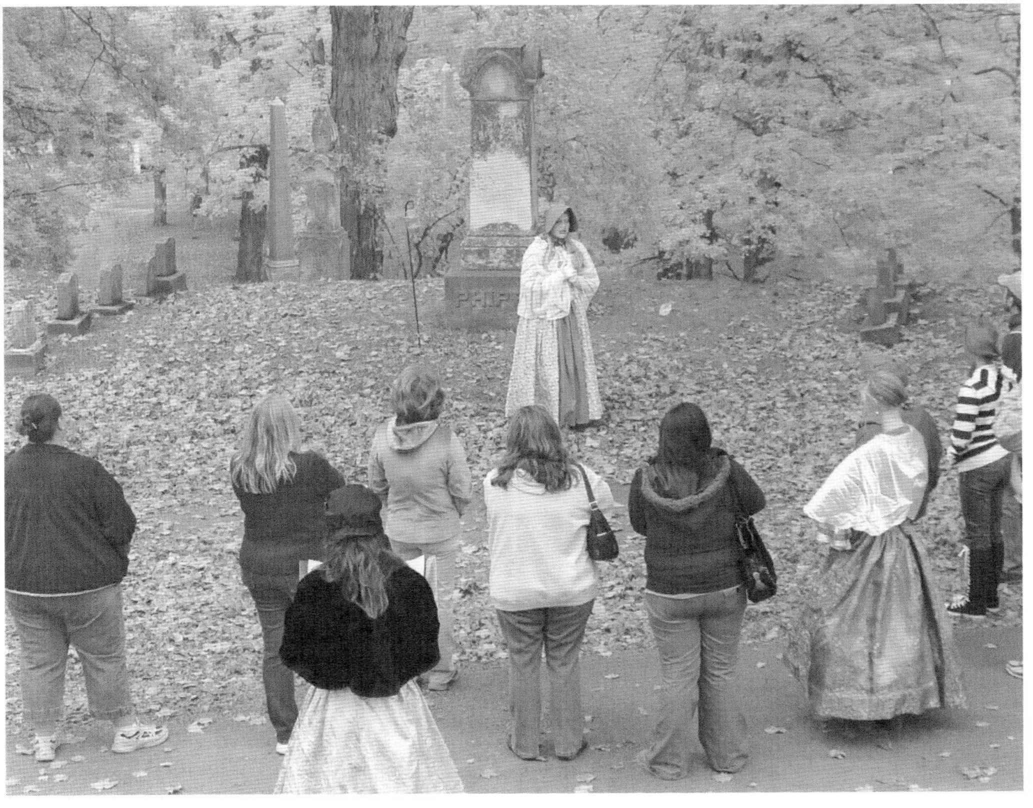

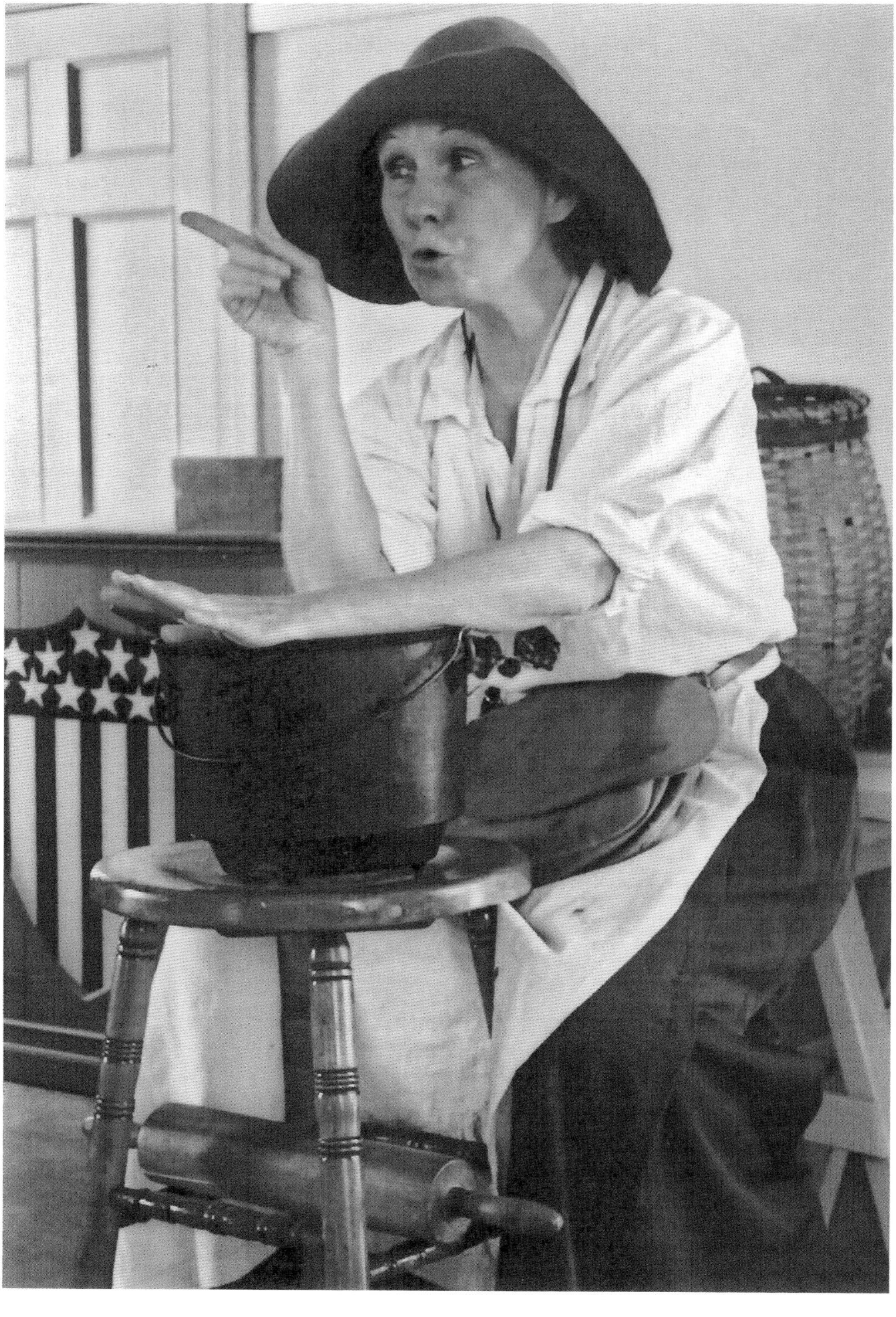

(LEFT)

Actress, storyteller, playwright, author, and illustrator, Sepik presents *Erie Canal Sal*, a theatrical characterization of Sal McMurray, an Irish cook working on a packet boat traveling the Erie Canal in 1840. The program combines Irish folk tales and facts about the canal, so folks can learn about one of the engineering wonders of the world either watching Sepik's performance or by reading her book, *Erie Canal Sal*. Ms. Sepik majored in modern dance at Point Park College, where she also studied acting and writing. She has performed with the Paddy Toon Modern Ensemble in Pittsburgh, with the Rochester Philharmonic's "Phil Revue" with mime troupe, and Flash in the Pan. Sepik has also studied with the Bottom of the Bucket and Garth Fagan Dance. Her dance career ended suddenly in the 1980s. Sepik cofounded the Flight of Fancy Experimental Theatre (F.O.F.) and is an artist working with Young Audiences of Rochester and Young Audiences of Western New York. She presents 200 to 300 programs a year. In 2004, she was honored by Young Audiences of Western New York for her work with students and her commitment to learning through the arts. "My storytelling started when a teacher's aide asked me to do storytelling. I was too shy to tell stories as myself, so I developed characters to tell the stories for me. Storytelling helped me overcome my shyness." Sepik portrays Mary Jemison, a white woman who, as a young girl, was captured by the Indians and when offered her freedom chose to remain with her Indian family. Her other characters include 19th-century womens' rights leader Susan B. Anthony, who not only speaks of life in the 1800s, but also comments on current issues, and Beatrix Potter, who narrates "The Tale of Peter Rabbit" and "The Tale of Mrs. Tittlemouse." "When performing in schools my goal is to awaken children to the joy of learning, the joy of life and the joy of who they are. As one child so aptly put it, someone finally got me to like history." (Courtesy of Pat Mead.)

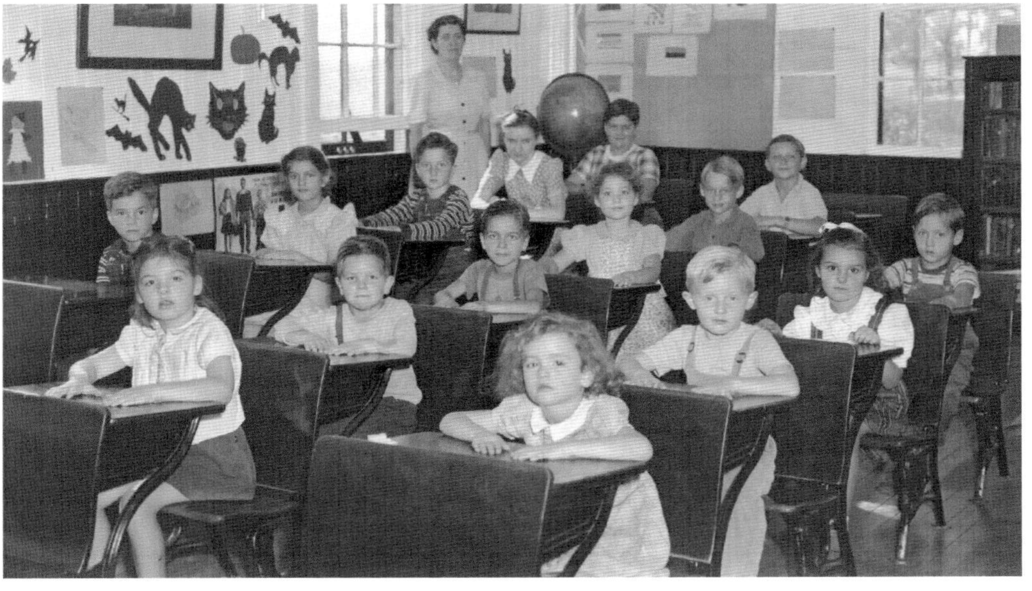

The citizens of Orleans County have been generous with school funding since its inception. Early pioneers made sure children attended their lessons in log cabin homes until schoolhouses could be built and scholars brought in to serve as teachers. Early Orleans County boasted a high number of country schools similar to the one in this photo. Miss Spaulding lived a long life (1906–2004), and is fondly remembered by many. Students pictured are (row by the wall) Peter Allen, Mary Lou Hughes, Billy Allen, Lucile Rowley, and David Vipham; (middle row) Lotti Rhodey, Allen Horsch, Henry Horsch, Betty Huber, Wilbur Mull, and Warren Snyder; (front row) Sandra Myers, Barry Mix, Marcia Carr, and Teddy Brace. (Courtesy of Wilbur C. Mull.)

Tierney began pole vaulting for Medina High School in 2002. In 2003, he began training with Rick Suhr. In March 2004, Tierney entered the New Balance National Championship in New York City as an unknown. He won with a high of 15 feet, 11 1/2 inches. That spring, Tierney set the Medina High School, Niagara-Orleans League, and Section VI record of 16 feet, 1 inch. He competed in the state meet in North Syracuse and won—reaching a height of 16 feet, 1 inch. Tierney entered Ashland University with an athletic scholarship. In 2009, he won the NCAA Division II Nationals in Houston with a height of 17 feet, 9 inches, and set Ashland's indoor record. Tierney was recognized as one of Ashland's top scholar-athletes in 2009, and was an All-American seven times. (Courtesy of Wendi Pencille—Horsefeathers Studio.)

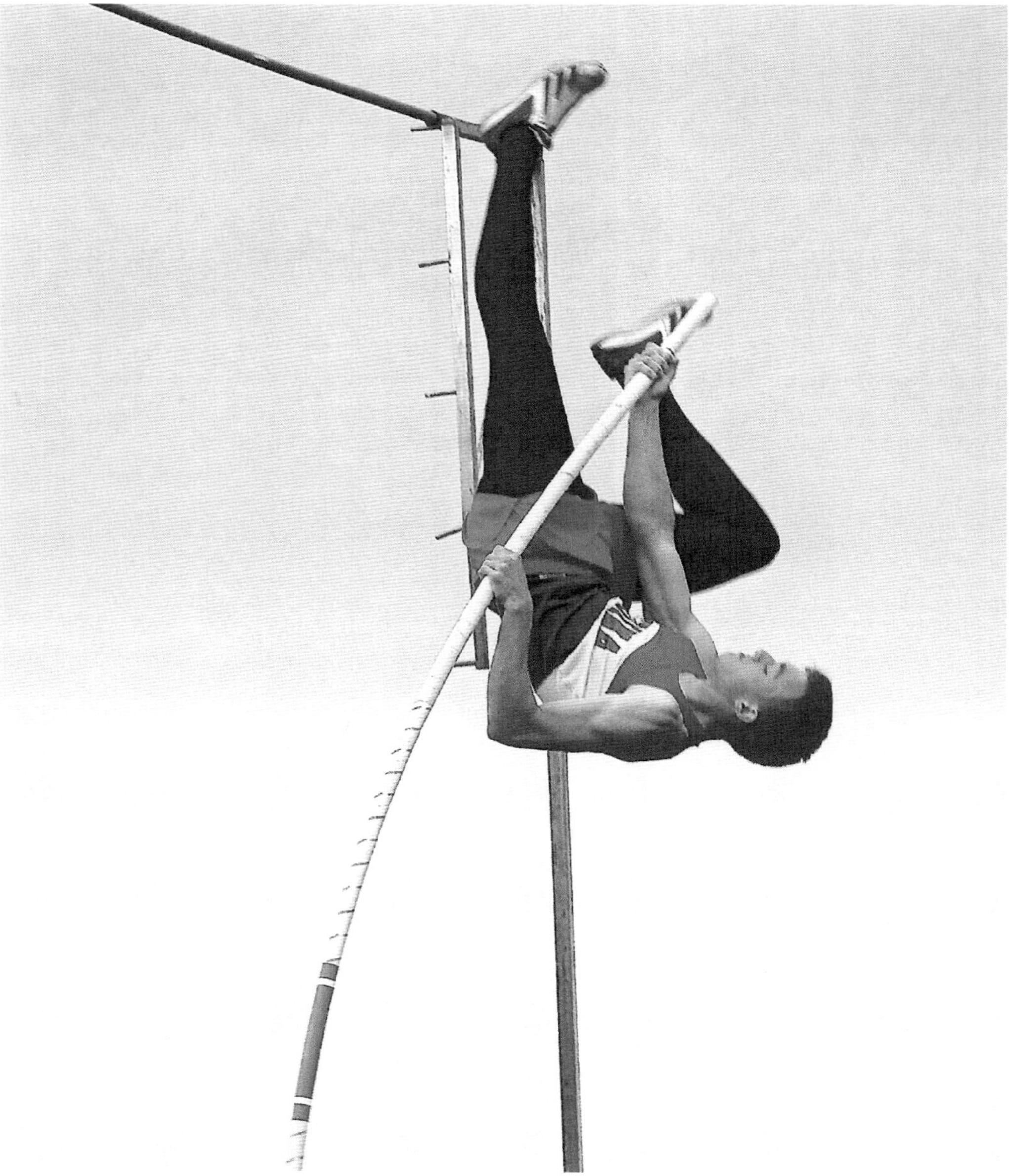

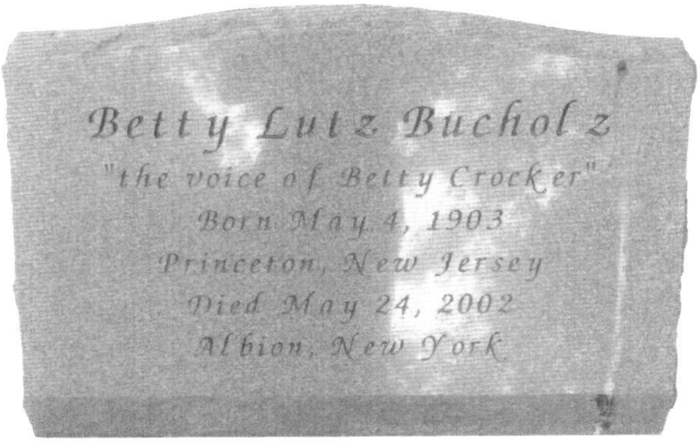

(ABOVE)
Bucholz (1903–2002), according to this unusual memorial record, was "the voice of Betty Crocker." She had a lengthy radio career from 1934 to 1951, broadcasting three times a week from Chicago's Merchandise Mart via NBC's radio network. Current television personality Hugh Downs worked with her. She retired to Albion and is buried in Mt. Albion Cemetery. (Courtesy of Bud Canham.)

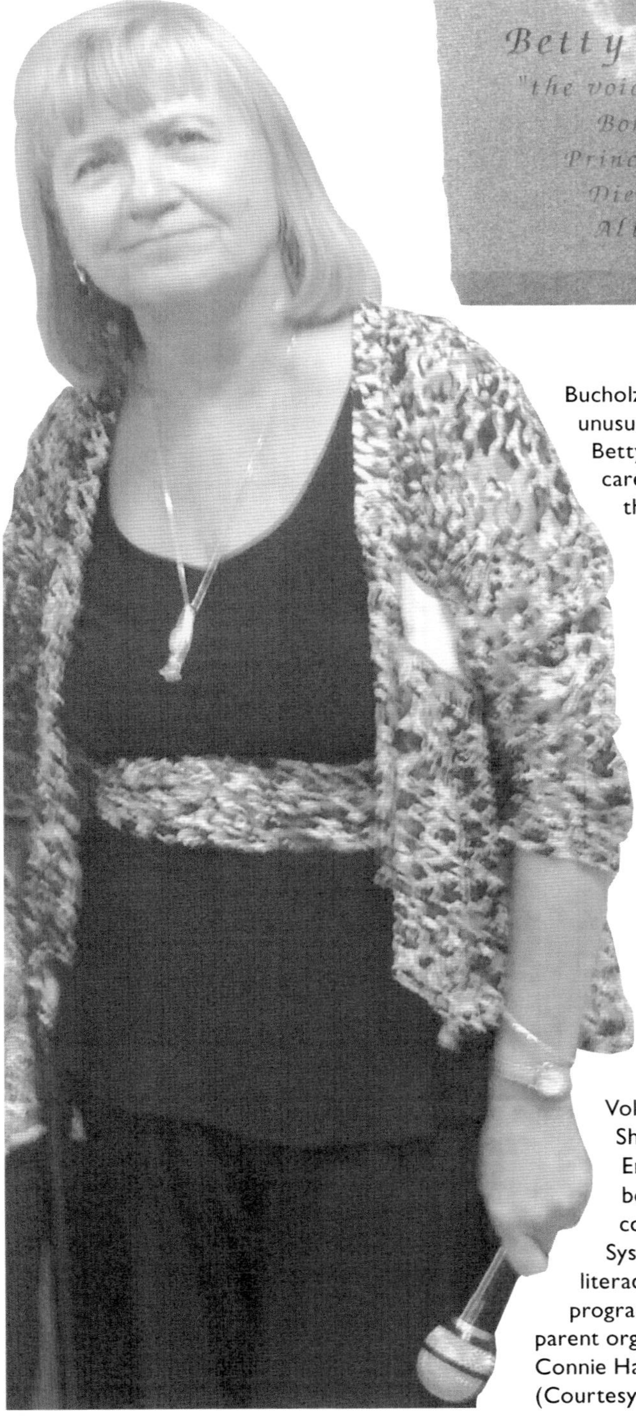

Ruck assumed leadership of Literacy Volunteers of Orleans County in 1989. She expanded services to include English as a Second Language, and both GED and disability assistance. In collaboration with the Albion School System, she established the first family literacy program in western New York. Her program received the Literacy Volunteers parent organization's highest honor in 1996—the Connie Haendle Program Excellence Award. (Courtesy of Rose Ruck.)

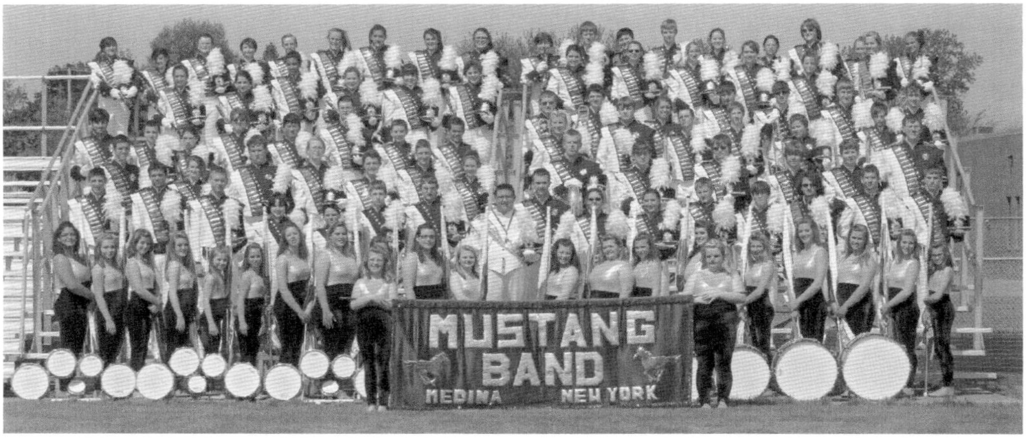

Formed in the 1970s under the direction of Joseph McKain, the band performs and competes all over the United States and Canada. They have earned many awards while competing in categories such as parade, drum line, twirling, and jazz, including 10 Governor's Cup awards and the prestigious Grand Champion award. (Courtesy of Kathy Dreyfus.)

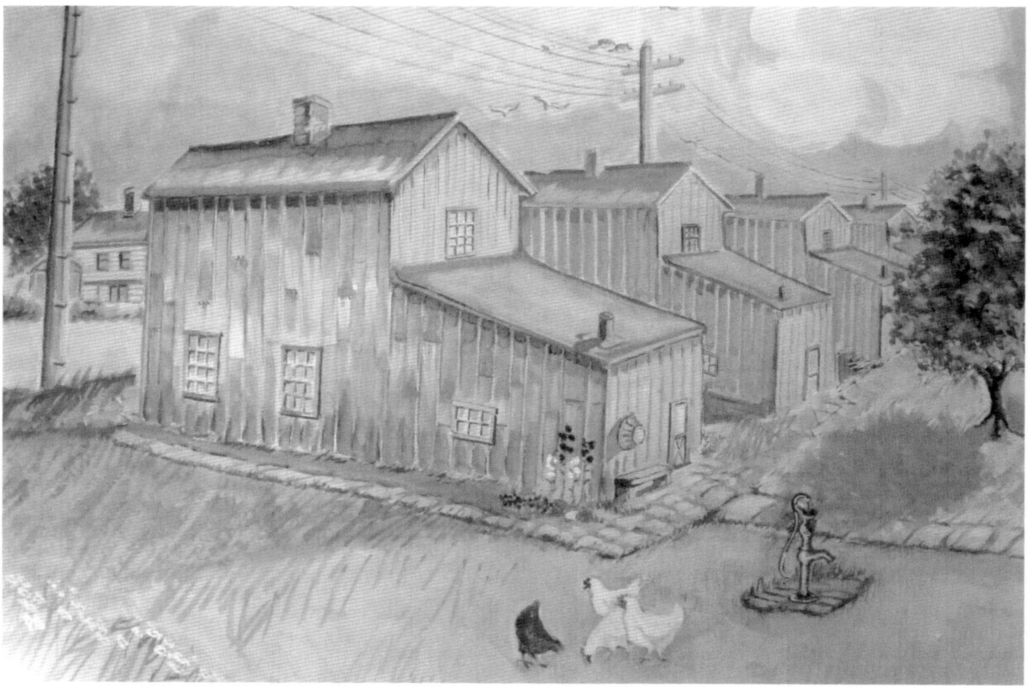

Ciarico (1909–1993) created the logo for Rolling Rock beer, which is still in use by the company today. He also created the image above called "7 Shacks"; it depicts temporary housing built by quarry owners for their immigrant workers. Often their first lodging upon arrival, the shacks provided minimal protection from the elements. (Courtesy of Joseph Ciarico.)

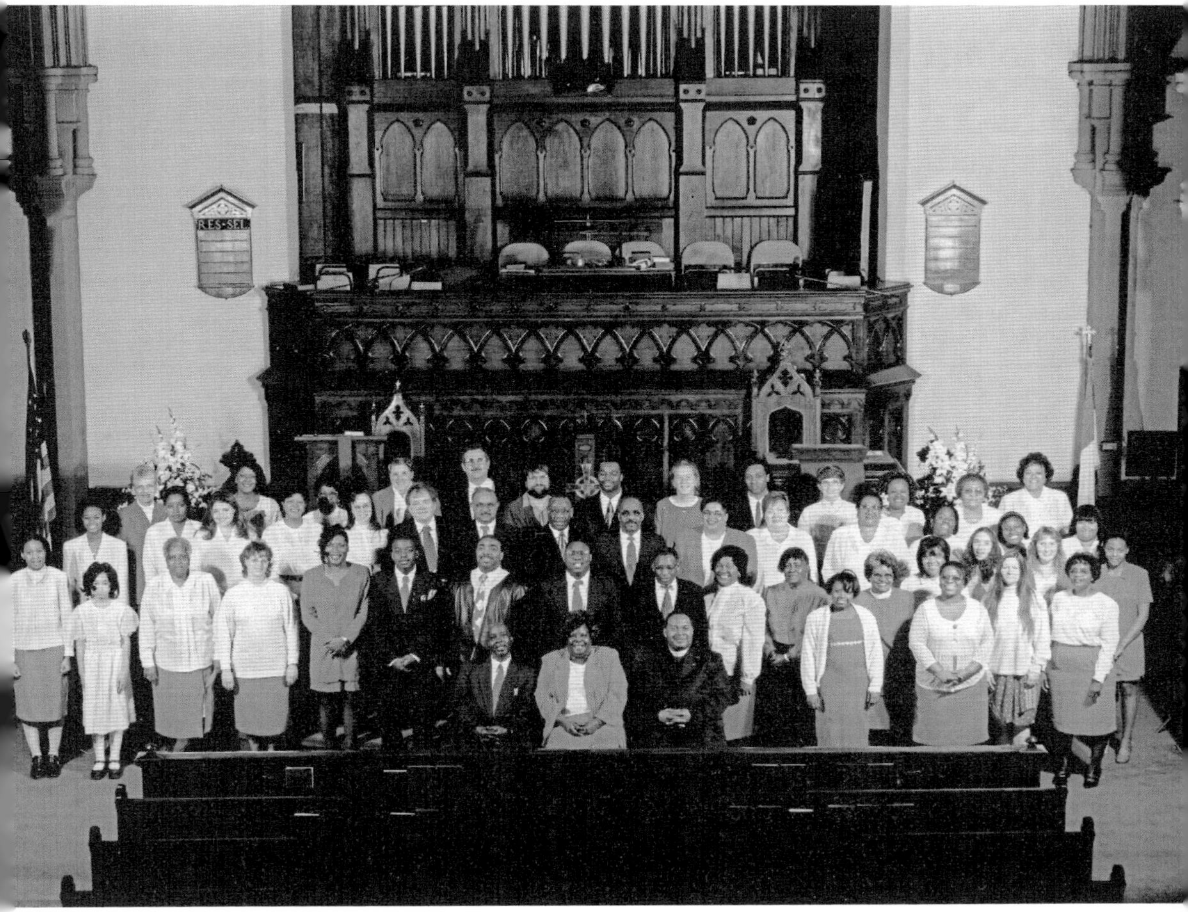

Racial tensions began to escalate locally in 1998. Linda Sisson decided to attempt to ease that tension. She brought area churches together by forming a community choir. This became a family affair with up to three generations participating from about 20 different churches. Age, race, or religious affiliation was not a barrier. In fact, diversity was encouraged. The mission of the choir was and is: "to provide spiritual enrichment through gospel singing with Orleans and surrounding counties; to promote *Unity, Equality, and Christian Love* to all people, regardless of race, creed or color; and to provide positive outreach to the Youth of Orleans County by encouraging their enrollment as a member of the choir." Current musical directors are Rev. William Washington, Gloria and Doug Powell, and Dolores Patterson. (Courtesy of Grace Denniston.)

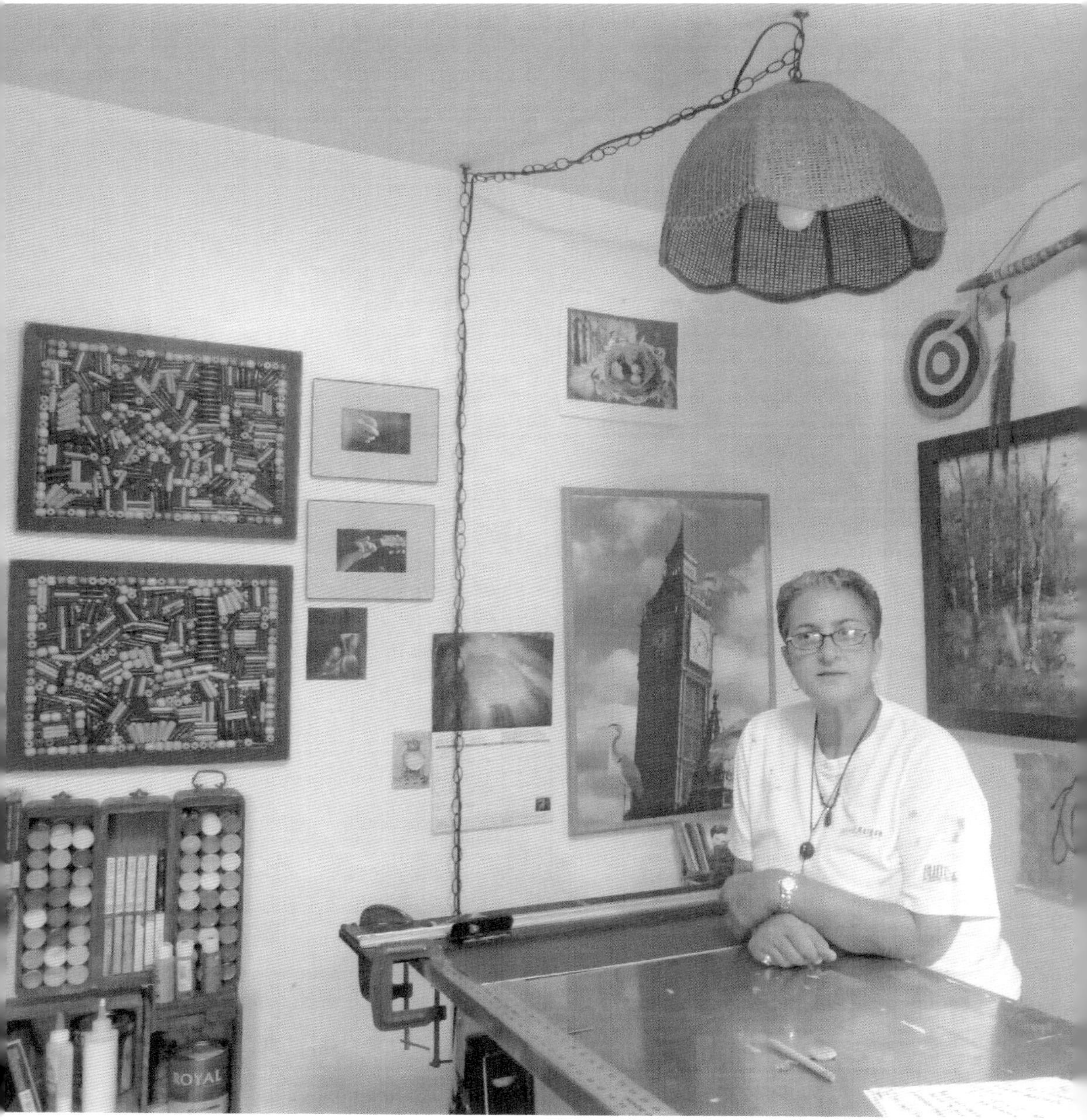

Martilotta works in several mediums, classifying her work under surrealistic assemblage art: sculptures, collages, and shadow boxes. She has studied painting, and is ready to begin a painting career. Martilotta graduated with a degree in studio art from SUNY Brockport in 1993. She and husband Neal Muscarella operate a European-style art gallery, Marti's On Main, featuring the work of local artists, "Artists of the Oak." Kim says, "[The term "Artists of the Oak"] comes from the many rivers and streams fed by the Oak Orchard watersheds known collectively as 'The Oak.' Our group now has about 20 artists, consisting of a very diverse group." (Courtesy of Holly Canham.)

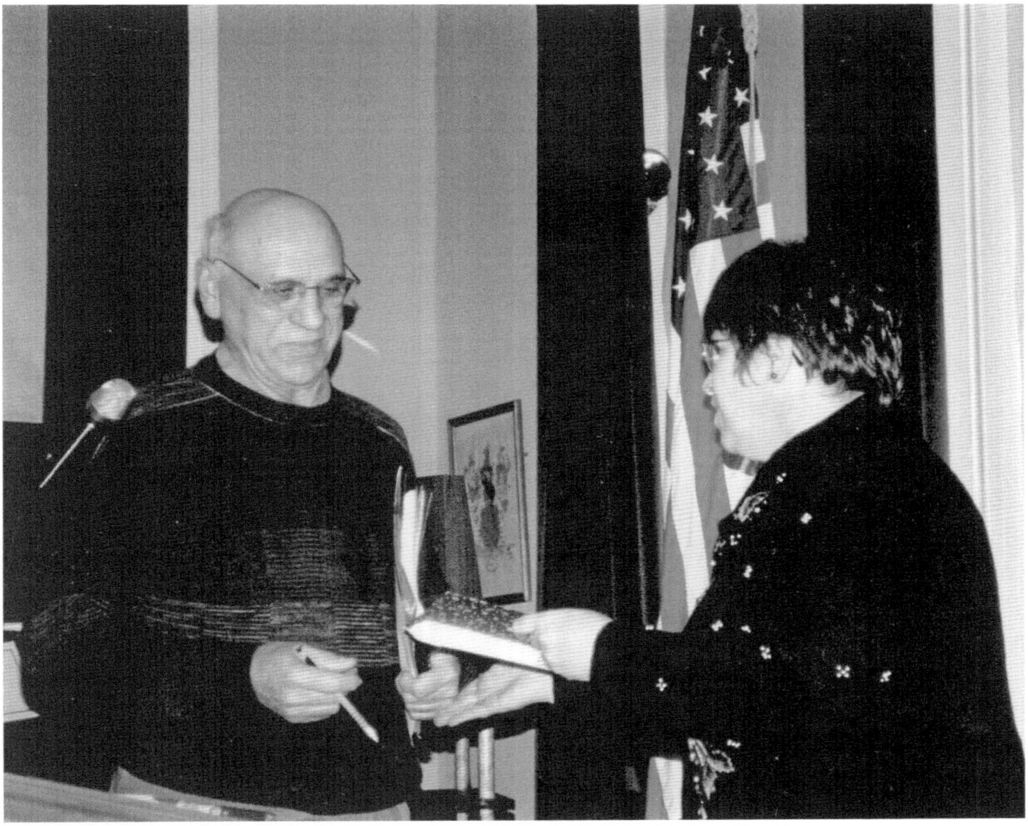

Roses and Garlic: A Nostalgic and Personal Look at Life on State Street, Holley, New York from 1900–1941 is now out of print, but continues to be a vital resource documenting the daily lives of Italian-American families in this community. Charles (1921–2007) used the personalities of residents from 43 homes on State Street to describe their cultural influences. In a time when neighbors looked after each other's kids as their own, Charles explained, "Most of our gang wars were stopped by whatever mother had decided it had gone far enough. My mother used to charge into a brawl with her deadly broom, taking care to keep only her own boys in the line of fire. Whack! Ma, you're hurting me with that broom! 'Of course, you imbecile,' she'd reply, 'you think I came out here to sweep?' Whack!" A superstition that colored Italian people's lives was the "Malocchio" or "Evil Eye." Charles said, "Once Old Franco was proclaimed by Zia Angellucia as being the spell-caster himself when his cow gave tainted milk. She advised he caused this bad milk because he was carrying a knife in his pocket while milking the cow. He was incensed by the accusation and stormed out of her house after calling her names. She responded with a curse and that night the cow died. East Holley buzzed with excitement as rumors flew about poisonings, curses and intrigue. In all probability the cow ate an oleander plant, which would have killed her. The kids forever believed this woman not only could make a cow die, but thought she could turn small boys into dogs! 'Malocchio!'" Charles also wrote about Italian craftsmanship. Wonderful red sandstone architecture is evident today in Orleans County as a result of the Italian immigrants' work. Their contribution came at huge expense—the work was hard, dirty and extremely dangerous. Accidents were common and if you got hurt, you got fired—no insurance, no compensation. Charles reported, "I remember being in the quarry when there was a great crash. The crane toppled, killing Joe. The quarrymen paid for his funeral." (Courtesy of Evan Cady.)

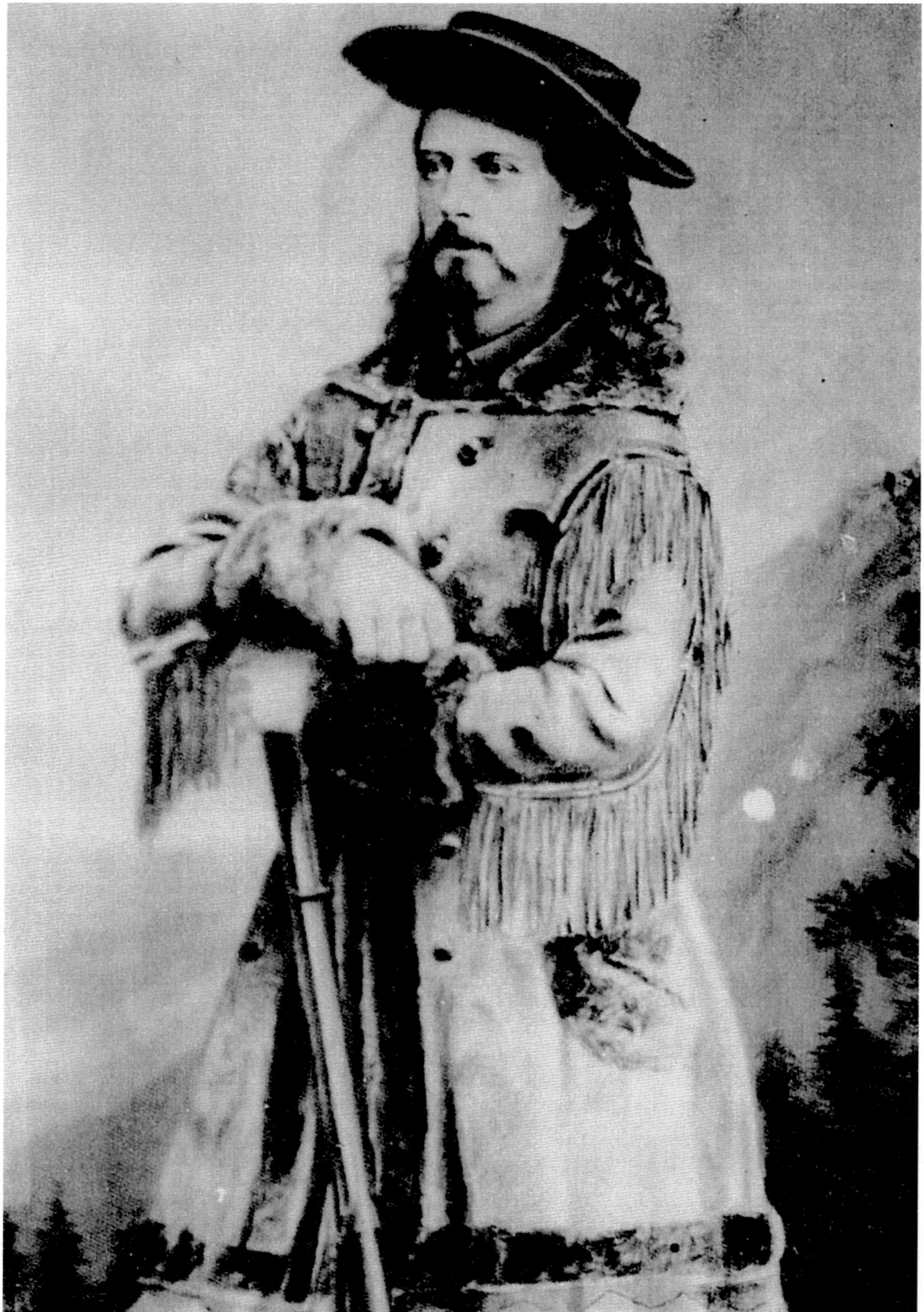

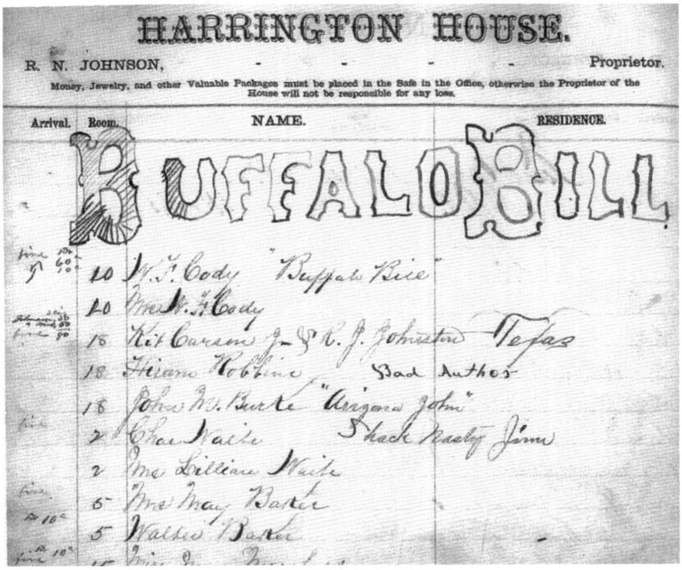

HARRINGTON HOUSE.

R. N. JOHNSON, - - - - - Proprietor.

Money, Jewelry, and other Valuable Packages must be placed in the Safe in the Office, otherwise the Proprietor of the House will not be responsible for any loss.

Arrival.	Room.	NAME.	RESIDENCE.
		BUFFALO BILL	
	10	W. F. Cody "Buffalo Bill"	
	10	Mrs W. F. Cody	
	18	Kit Carson Jr & R. J. Johnston	Texas
	18	Hiram Robbins Bad Author	
	18	John M. Burke "Arizona John"	
	2	Chas Waite Shack Nasty Jim	
	2	Mrs Lillian Waite	
	5	Mrs May Baker	
	5	Walter Baker	

Sometimes, the legends visited Orleans County. Buffalo Bill (1846–1917) and his troupe performed in Albion in February of 1881, and in 1875—when it is believed Buffalo Bill himself signed the register above. Buffalo Bill Cody was the most recognizable celebrity on earth in his era. He educated the world about America's western and American Indian cultures. (Harrington's Orleans Hotel and Ledger photograph courtesy of Orleans County Department of History; Buffalo Bill Cody image courtesy of Buffalo Bill Museum and Grave, Golden, Colorado.)

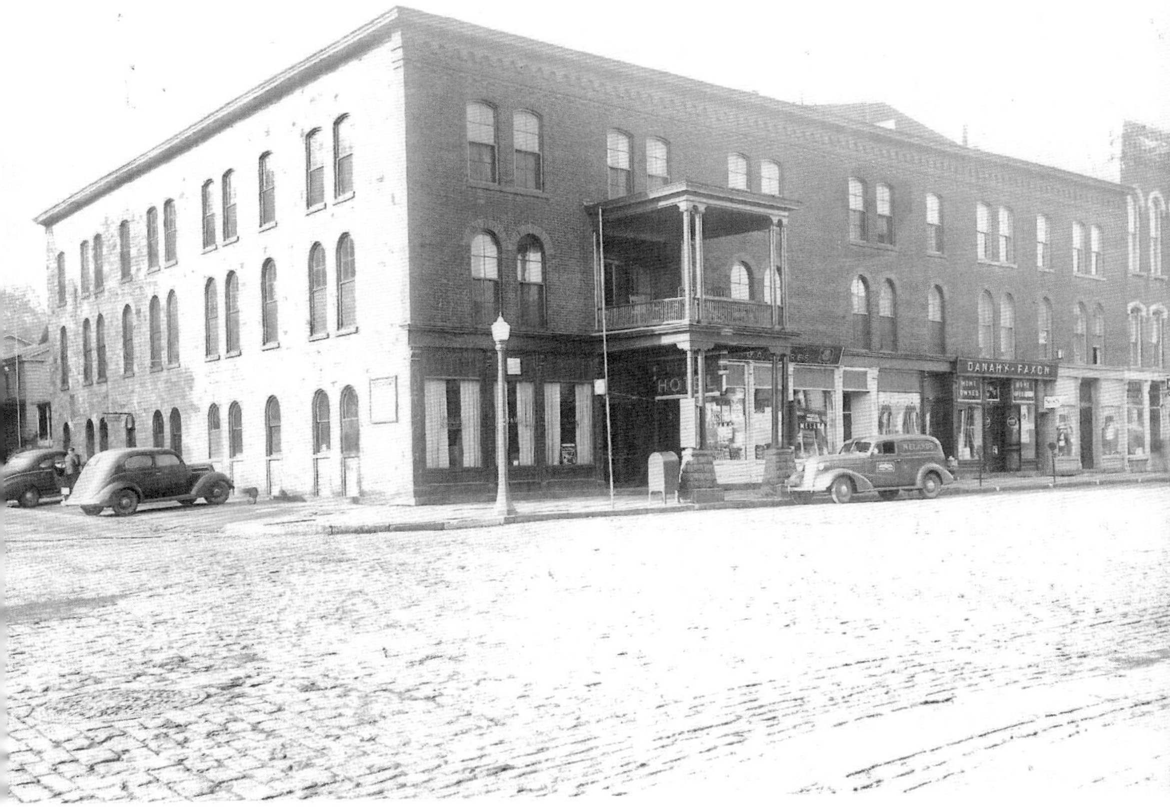

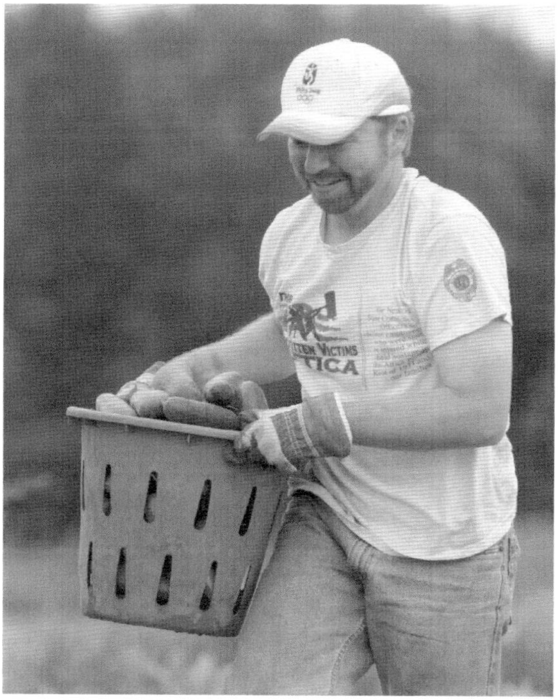

In *Farm Hands: Hard Work and Hard Lessons from Western New York Fields*, Rivers, a reporter for the *Daily News* in Batavia, introduces readers to the rigors of farm labor and some of the people who do the grueling work, including cabbage cutter "King Kong" and apple-picking pro "Stretch." Rivers self-published the 153-page book in 2010. *Farm Hands* is based on a newspaper series in 2008, for which Rivers worked at 13 farms in western New York. That series won national honors from the North American Agricultural Journalists and Columbia Journalism School. The Associated Press also recognized the series for "in-depth reporting" and the New York Agricultural Society presented Rivers with a "golden pitchfork" for the project. The book is in its fifth printing and has sold more than 5,000 copies. (Courtesy of Tom Rivers.)

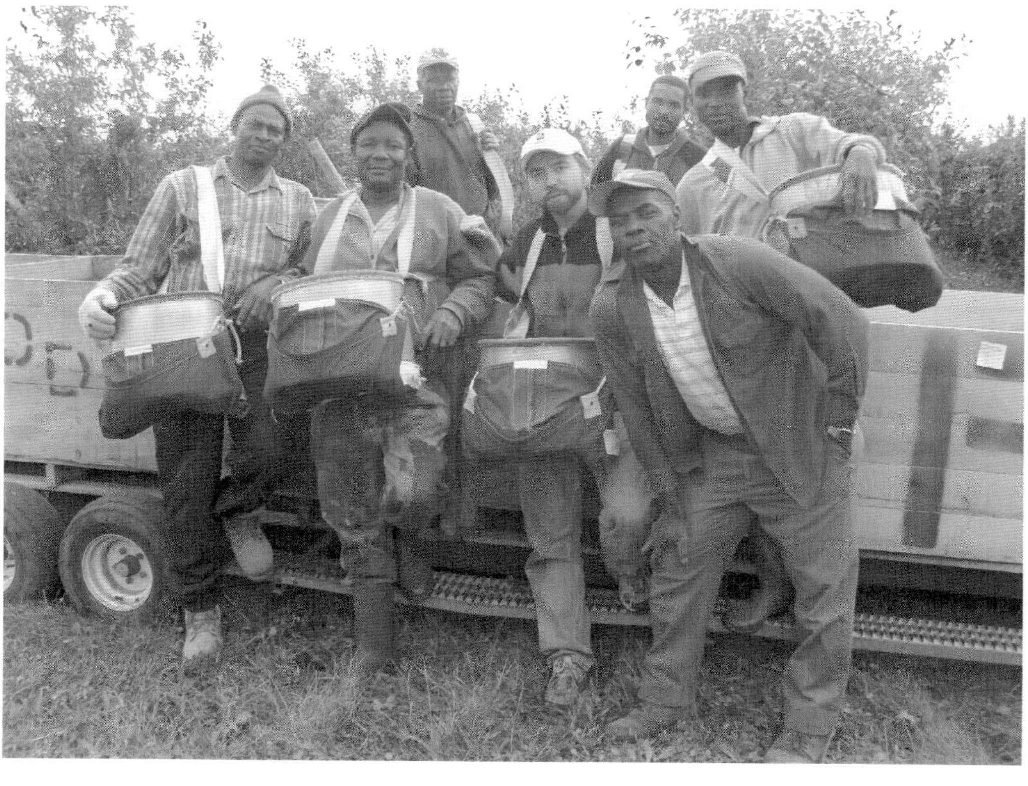

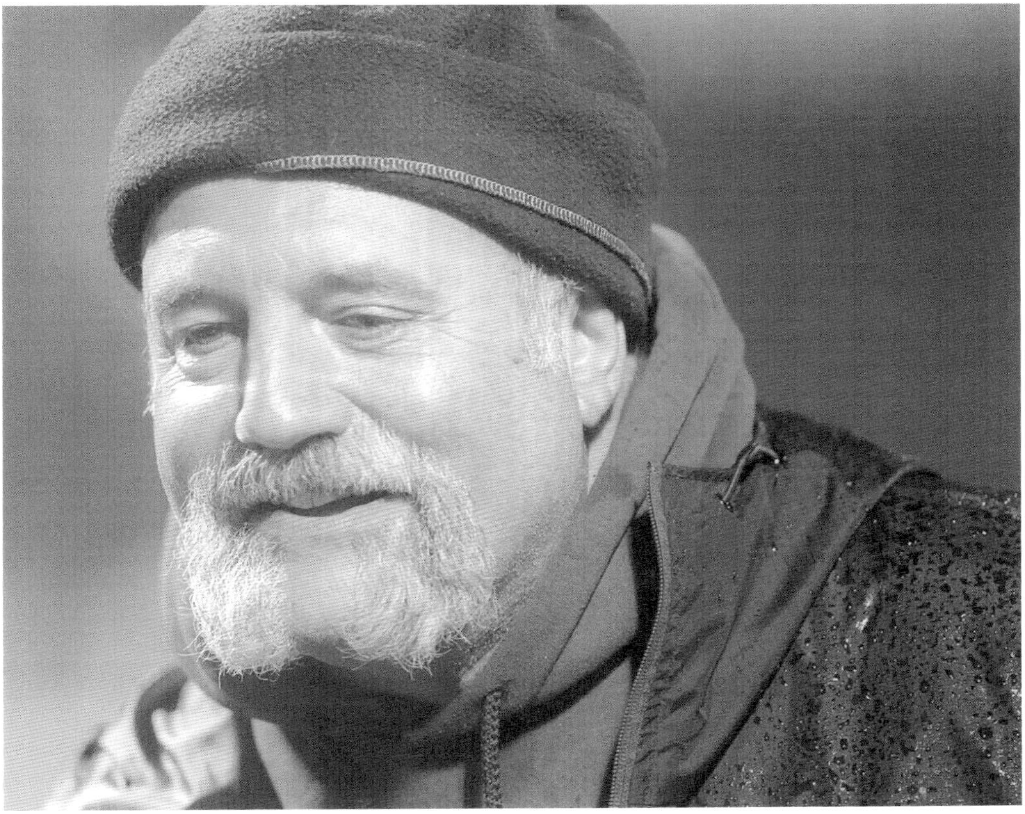

Monacelli grew up in Albion, playing several sports, including football and baseball for Albion High. He graduated in 1967 and went on to teach and coach for his entire career at nearby Caledonia-Mumford High School. Monacelli retired from coaching football at the end of the 2010 season, amassing an impressive 186-50 record as head coach over 23 seasons, following two as assistant varsity and 14 as head JV coach. Having only one losing season, his first, Coach Monacelli went on to lead the powerhouse small school team to 10 Section V titles and four state titles in six appearances, plus a No. 1 state ranking before official state championships were instituted. Winning streaks of 35 and 17 games plus 21 straight sectional wins added to the legacy of Cal-Mum's ranking among the best winning percentages in the nation. During the last years of his tenure, Monacelli also served as athletic director and was instrumental in the building of a state-of-the-art sports complex in 2006, at which C-M hosted their first prestigious state sports event in 2011 for the NYSPHYSSA Track & Field Championships. Known for his die-hard traditions, Monacelli is not one for changing "what isn't broken," whether it's running the football or his old faithful truck! However, after learning about testing and management of head injuries at an athletic directors' conference in 2006, he established baseline testing for all students in his middle and high schools; other area schools followed suit. In May 2010, Monacelli was invited to testify at a US House Education and Labor Committee hearing on the incidence rate, management, and effect of concussions on academic performance. Coach believes that the well-being of his athletes has always been much more important than winning or losing. Monacelli's character and record have earned him several "coach of the year" honors and the respect of all, including his coaching fraternity. He is treasured for his willingness to instill values and teach life lessons to his "football kids," including his own three sons who played for him. (Courtesy of Michael Johnson/*Livingston County News*.)

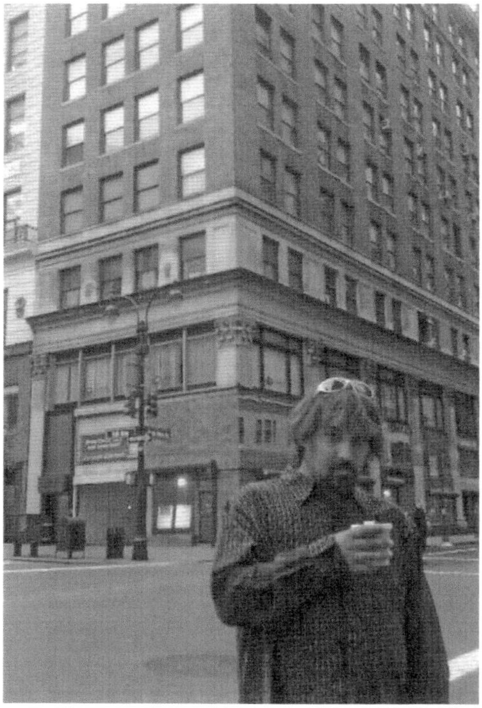

Russo began working in theater while attending Albion High School and has come to enjoy various aspects of the performing arts. Over the last 10 years, he has tried his hand at directing, designing, and acting. He recently enjoyed portraying Gov. DeWitt Clinton for Musicalfare's *Erie Canal Comes to Life* show. (Courtesy of Nick Russo.)

Bellavia is an assistant professor in the School of Education and Psychology, Graduate Division, at Touro College in New York City. He is celebrating the 10th anniversary of his book, *We Are All the Same Inside*. He is the recipient of the Skowhegan School of Painting and Sculpture's Fellowship Grant, Principal for a Day, and Young Adult Institute Teacher Recognition Award. (Courtesy of Holly Canham.)

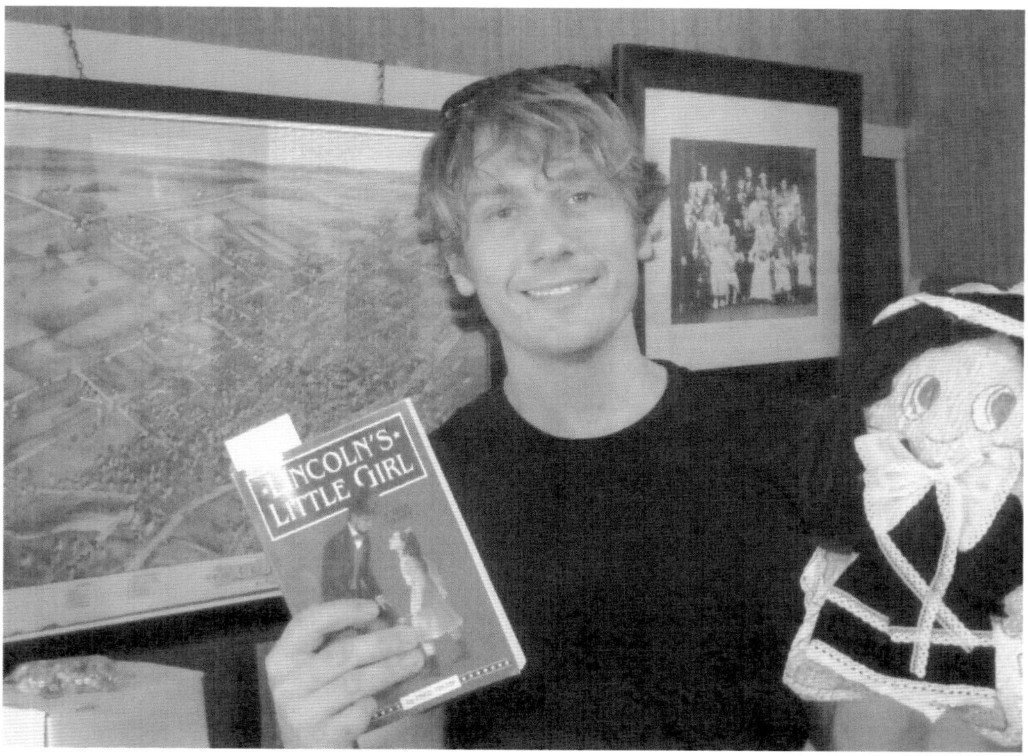

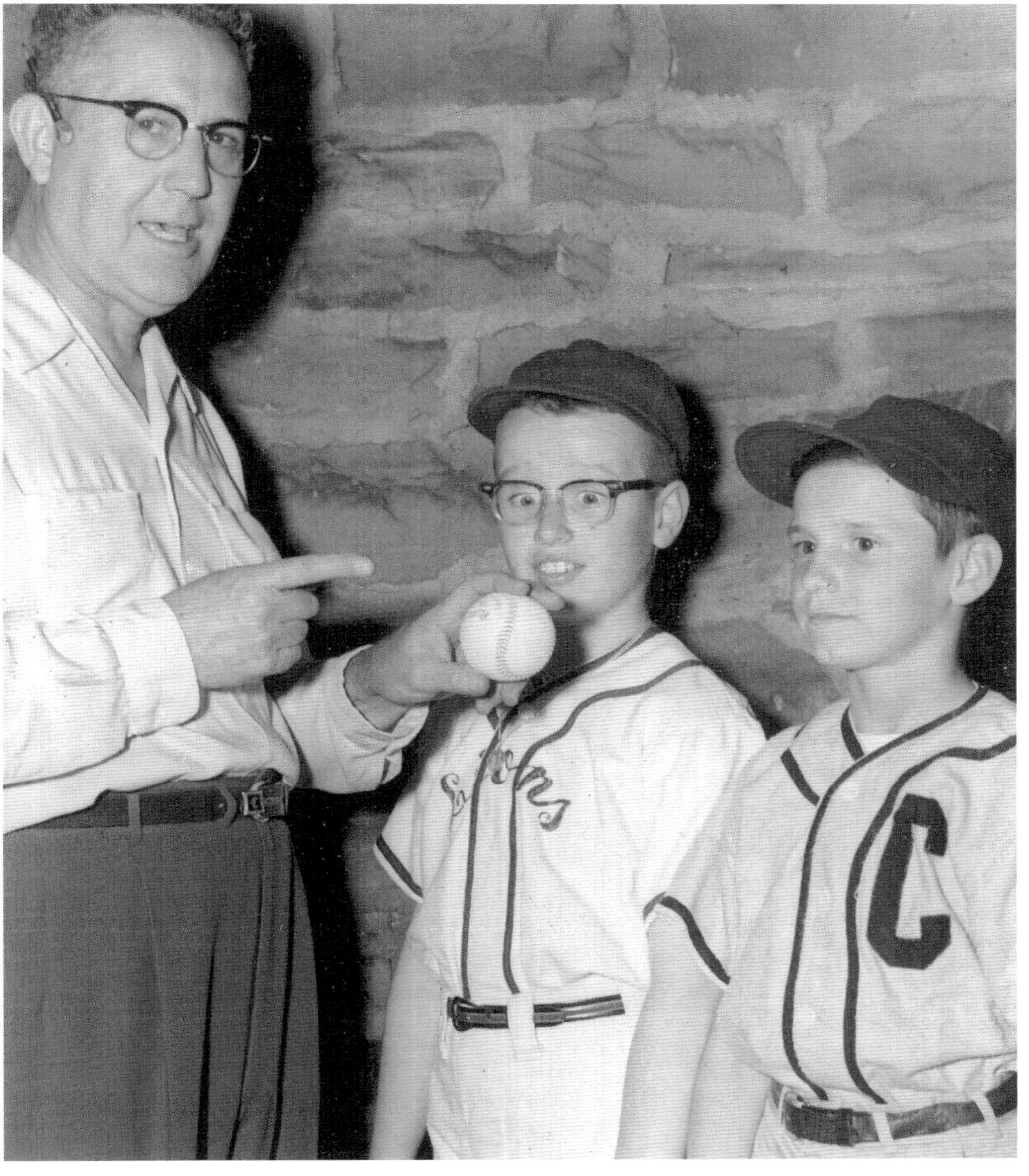

Carl Fischer, of Medina, was born in 1905. At age 24, he began his major league pitching career, eventually playing for four teams—the Washington Senators, Chicago White Sox, Cleveland Indians, and St. Louis Browns. On May 30, 1931, the New York Yankees visited Griffith Stadium to play Fischer's Washington Senators in a doubleheader. In game one, Fischer pitched the ninth inning, striking out pinch hitter Sammy Byrd and the legendary Babe Ruth. He earned a save and secured a 3-2 win when Lou Gehrig hit a pop fly to end the game. Fischer played for seven years and earned the nickname "the Medina Mauler." Locally, he established Fischer's News Stand in Albion, and founded the Carl Fischer Little League of Albion. Pictured with Carl are a young Mr. Vick (center) and Ronnie Carlston (right). He died in Medina on December 10, 1963. (Courtesy of Orleans County Department of History.)

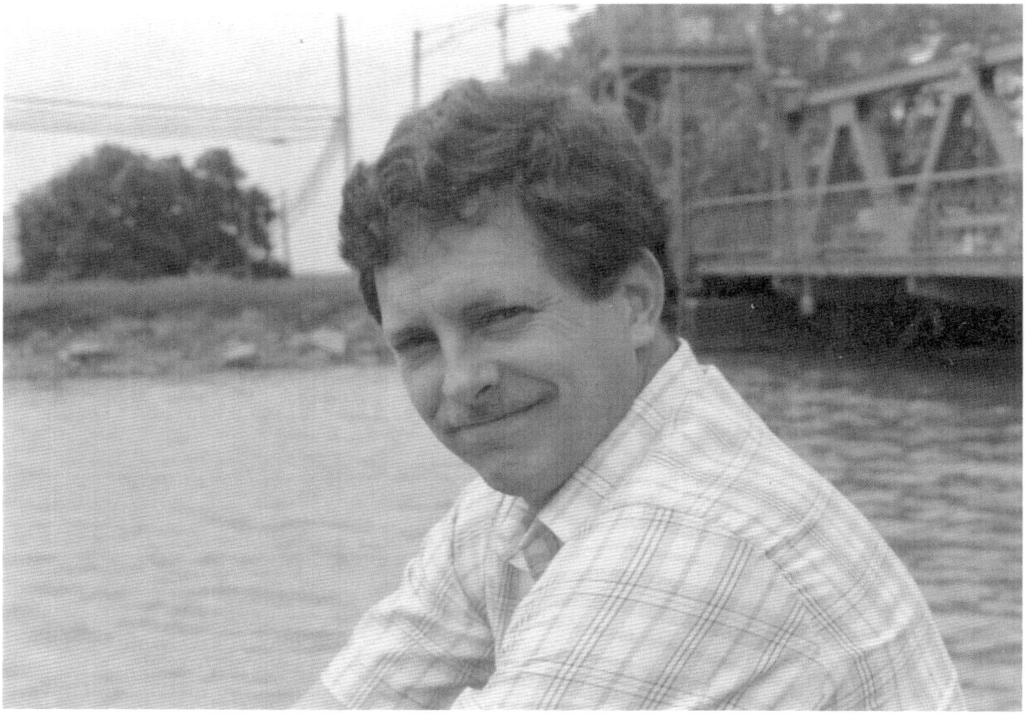

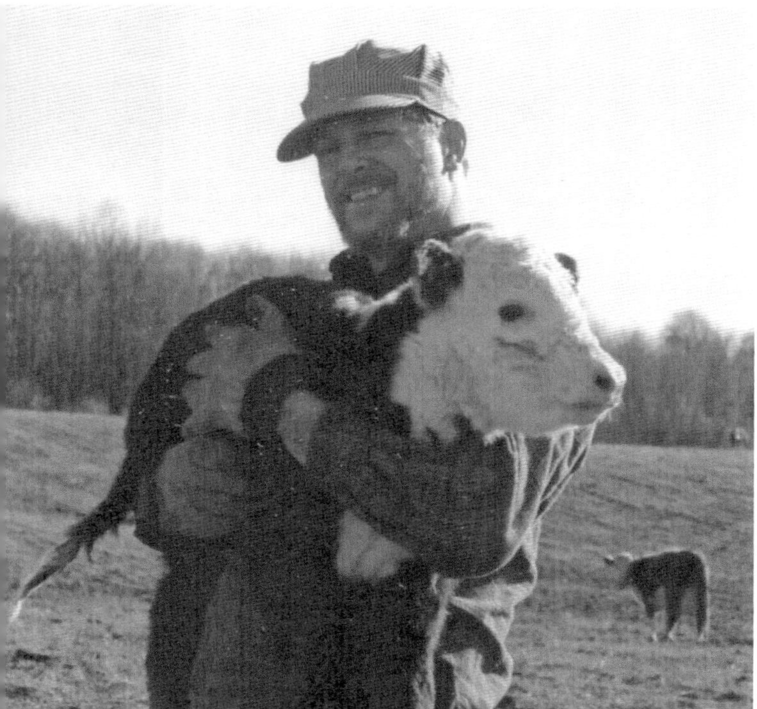

A high school English teacher for 35 years, Sillick penned insightful pieces about living on the farm that brought him simple joy. His weekly column, "The Alps Road Journal," was carried for 10 years in the *Medina Journal-Register*, the *Buffalo News*, and *Country Folks* newspapers. He seemed astonished when he considered, "a million people might read my column, if they didn't turn the newspaper page too quickly." An artist when it came to cabinetry and an excellent musician, his published writings included articles on fine woodworking, cattle-raising, organic gardening, fishing, and education. A farm tractor accident took his life, a reminder to all of us the dangers farmers encounter while feeding our community. (Courtesy of Kathleen Sillick.)

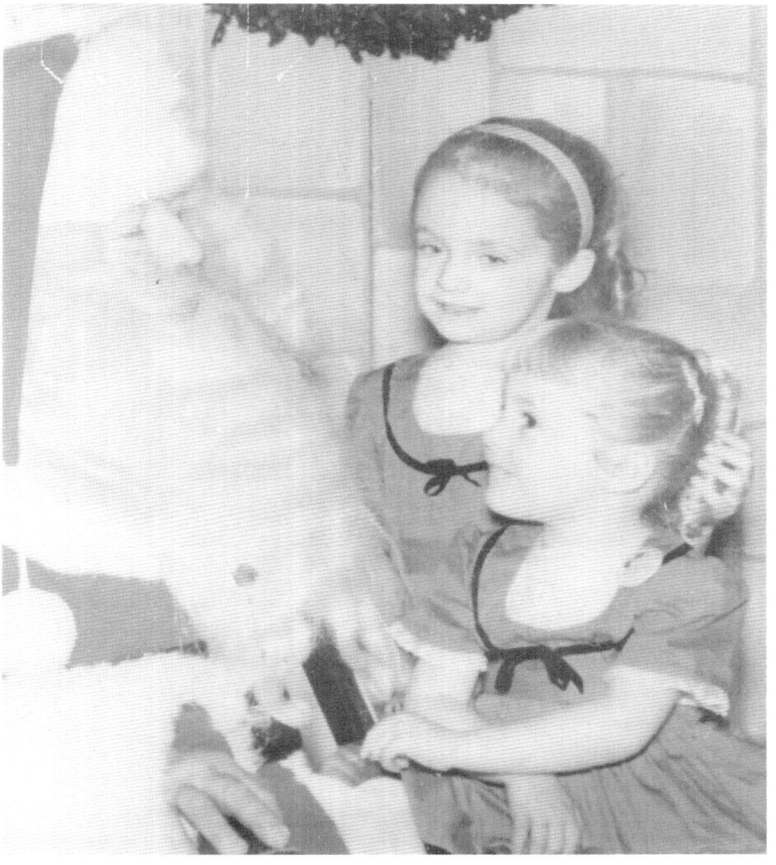

In 1937, Howard (1896–1966) established a Santa Claus School in Albion, the first of its kind. Then, in 1953, he opened a theme village called Christmas Park. Over 100,000 people visited Christmas Park in 1959 alone. At age seven he began making toys using a coping saw he received as a gift from an aunt. He eventually opened a toymaking business that operated until after World War I. He simultaneously operated the family's 400-acre farm until he suffered a broken neck when he fell from a silo ladder. The inability to farm gave him the opportunity to focus on his passion—the Santa Claus School. Santas in training learned child psychology, had formal dance instruction, took acting classes, received toy orientation, and even studied Santa Claus etiquette. There were even refresher classes! Howard said, "Santa was a character of dignity, a man of years and wisdom, a rugged outdoors man who dealt daily with reindeer, multitudinous gifts, and physical labors." Thus, Howard's Santas' clothing came to be made of expensive wools, silks, and thick rabbit fur. Wigs and beards were made from yak fur imported from Asia. Howard's school became world famous, and he traveled widely to train men to be Santa. Among his students were Edward G. Robinson and James Cagney. He was the Macy's Thanksgiving Day Parade Santa from 1949 until 1965, and Howard was the technical advisor for the original motion picture *Miracle on 34th Street*. He also made appearances on television shows such as *What's My Line* and *To Tell the Truth*. Christmas Park was unequaled anywhere in the world and investors finally were able to convince Charlie to incorporate, which was the beginning of the end. On May 25, 1968, items from the park were sold at auction. Howard's motto was "they err who think Santa Claus enters through the chimney. He enters through the heart." As someone said, "Charlie Howard didn't die with a million dollars. He died with a million friends." (Courtesy of Cindy and Sandy Weaver.)

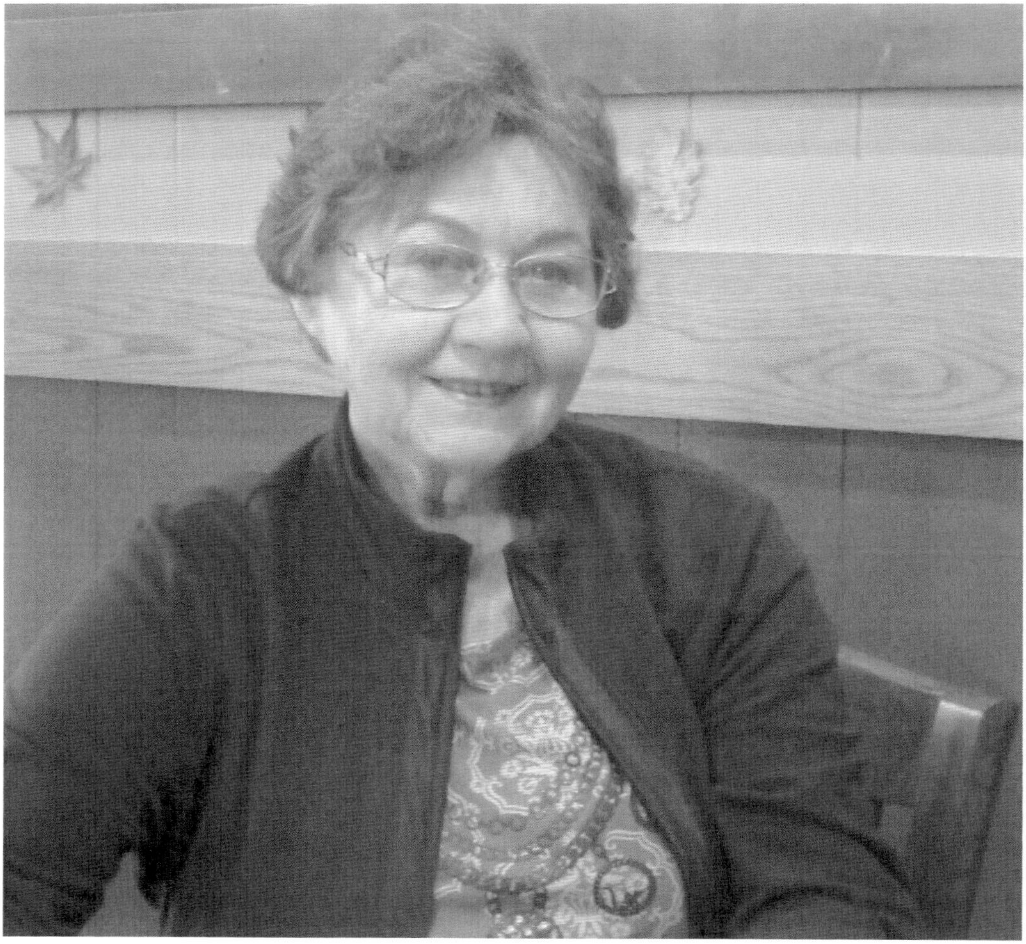

"Delivering *Buffalo Courier Express* newspapers led to my career in writing," Kropf remarked. "I always liked writing and got my first experience as editor of the Medina High School newspaper." Being hired by the *Daily News* in Batavia has afforded Kropf many privileges, including riding in several B-17 bombers. She also flew with the Red Barons in their Stearman stunt planes and the nine-plane Canadian Snowbirds team. At the age of 53, she learned to fly an airplane and solo piloted a Piper Arrow. "One of my jobs at the paper was to write obituaries; at first I didn't realize the importance of a person's obituary—and doing a good job of it, as it's likely the last thing ever written about the person. My duties grew and now I cover any story that needs to be told. I also personally interviewed Donny Osmond." Kropf's proudest achievement is meeting Gen. Charles Sweeney, the man who dropped the atomic bomb on Nagasaki, thereby ending World War II. "It is he, and men like Col. Robert Morgan, pilot of the B-17 *Memphis Belle* (the first B-17 to fly 25 missions and return), who have given me an appreciation of veterans, and I am honored to write about them. When my paper started covering Orleans County, I was thrilled to be able to write about my community and the people I know there. For my dedication, the Orleans County Chamber of Commerce gave me their second Lifetime Achievement Award, which reads, 'For her commitment and passion to Orleans County, including spending time with local seniors, reporting on local history and promoting the people, places and history of Orleans County.'" (Courtesy of Andrew Canham.)

Outstanding Citizens and Notable Personalities

Sometimes life just isn't fair. Some people can sing; that's okay. Some can dance; that's okay, too. But, someone who can sing *and* dance—well, that's downright bordering on being a showoff. But, there is also a level of performance that is simply stellar, and we mere mortals have to wonder, "How is she able to do that?" And sometimes we just have to say "Wow!" outside the world of music too. Such is the case with Donna Rodden; there have only been three people honored with the International Peace Award: Mother Teresa, Jacqueline Kennedy Onassis, and Orleans County's Donna Rodden. And, what about Wilbur Mull? There's a man who can sing money for charity out of people's pockets, to the tune of $2 million. And then there's Richard Gordineer, who had a really tough start in life; he was born into slavery. His list of accomplishments will put a song in your heart. The size of this book limits the acknowledgment of all the great folks in the county, but remember and be thankful for the efforts and contributions many folks have made and are making. This chapter honors Orleans County citizens who make, or have made, a difference.

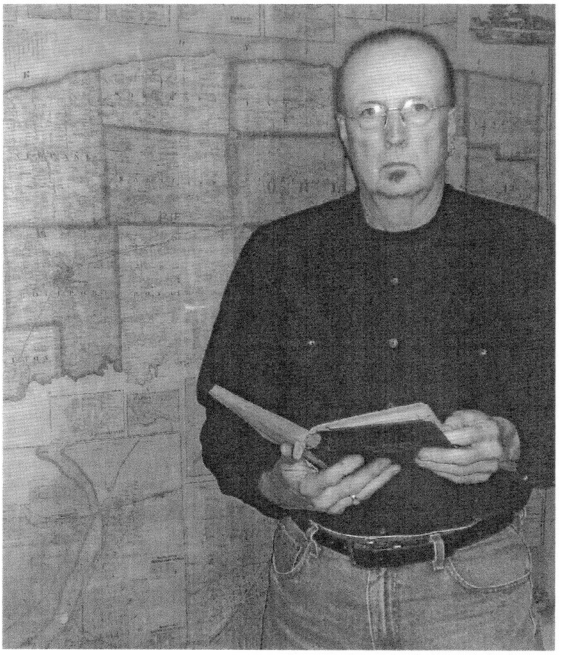

Born in Orleans County and dedicated to the preservation of local history, Bill Lattin has served Orleans County in ways too varied and numerous to include in this work. Highlights include cemetery tours, positions on boards of various civic groups, and several published books. He recently retired as curator of the Cobblestone Museum. One of Lattin's favorite quotes, written by Norman poet Master Wace, is provided below:

All things to nothingness descend,
Grow old and die and meet their end;
Man dies, iron rusts, wood goes decayed,
Towers fall, walls crumble, roses fade . . .
Nor long shall any name resound
Beyond the grave, unless be found
In some clerk's book; it is the pen
Gives immortality to men.

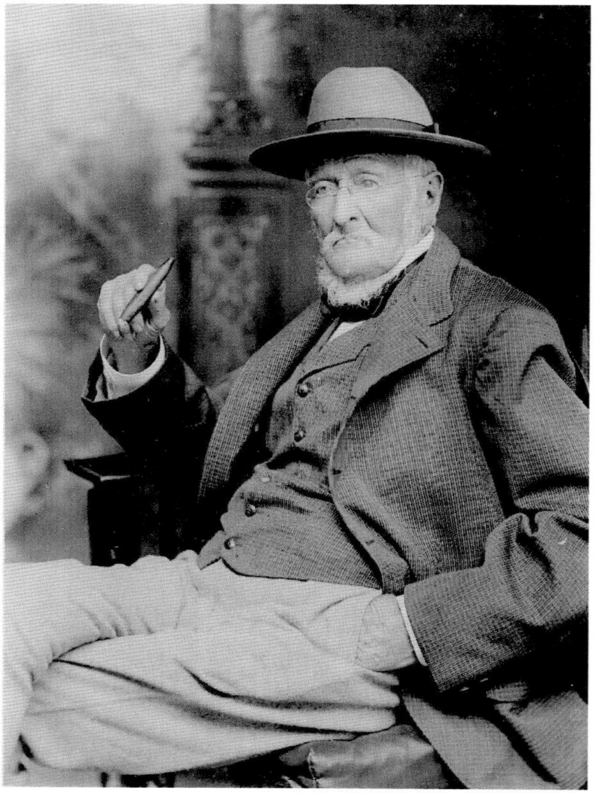

Glidden (1813–1906) lived in Clarendon before moving to Illinois. He invented barbed wire by using a coffee mill to create the barbs; he placed the barbs along a wire, and then twisted with another wire around them to keep the barbs in place. He created the Barb Fence Company in Illinois. Upon his death in 1906, he was one of the richest men in America. (Courtesy of the Joseph F. Glidden Homestead and Historical Center, DeKalb, Illinois.)

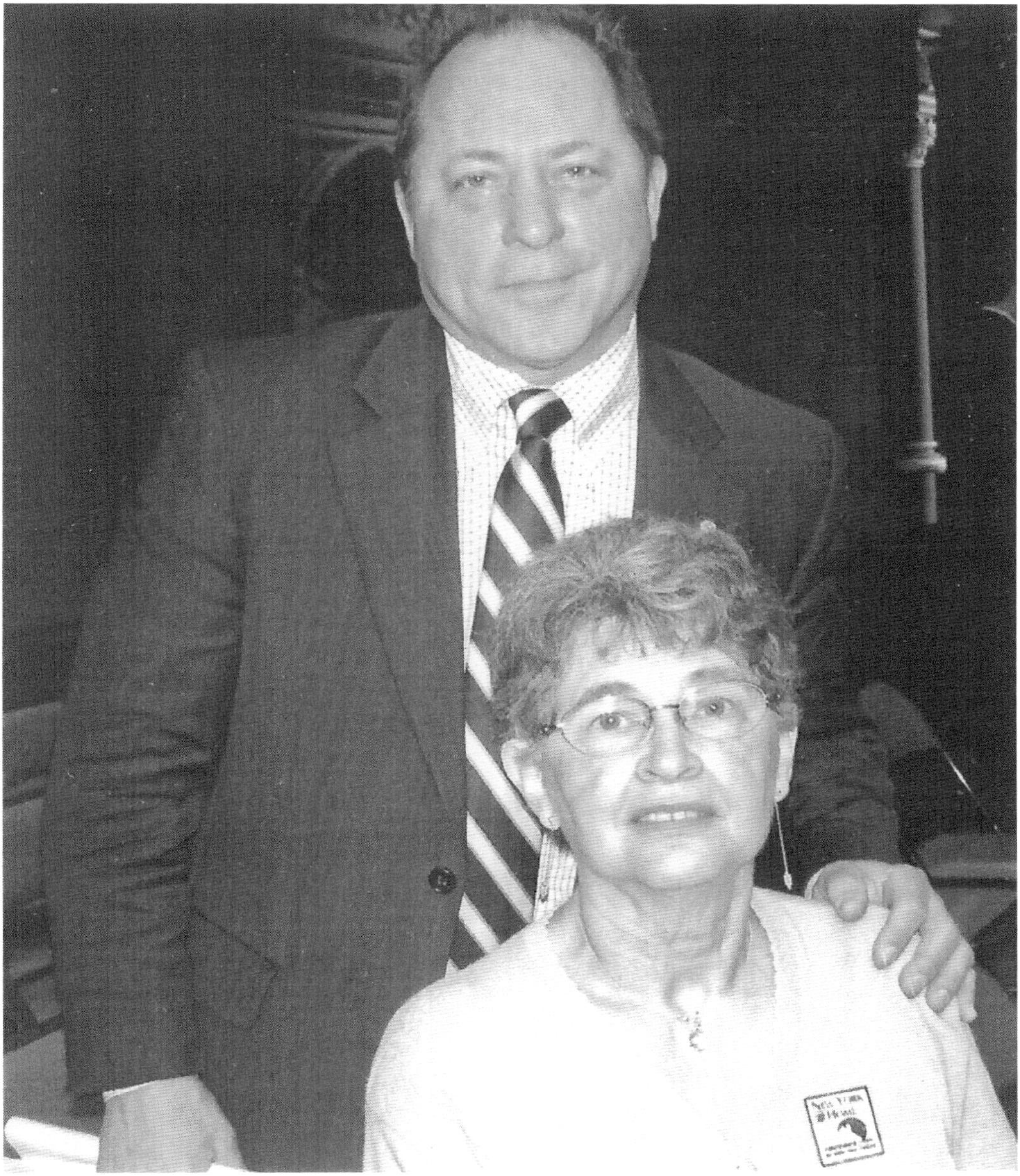

Denniston put her degree in social work to great service for the residents of Orleans County. She retired in 2004 as director of the Orleans County Office for the Aging. She served on the board of directors of Community Action. As a retiree, she has been trained with Hospice of Orleans County to serve as a companion to terminally ill citizens. She was able to provide training to other volunteers on topics such as health care proxies, Do Not Resuscitate (DNR) orders, and Alzheimer's disease. Denniston has held many positions in the Rotary Club and her church group over the years and remains a vital member of the community. The importance of her service was recognized in 2010 as she was awarded the New York State 2010 Outstanding Contribution by a Senior Citizen Award. Denniston is pictured with Assemblyman Steve Hawley. (Courtesy of Monica London.)

Pullman (1831–1897) spent the early years of his life in Albion and is believed to be the most internationally recognized figure from Orleans County. Though primarily a cabinetmaker and contractor during his time in Albion, in 1853 he accepted a contract working on the Erie Canal. Pullman moved buildings so that the canal could be widened. He later moved to Chicago, where at age 28 he raised several-story city buildings so efficiently that business could continue during the process! There, among other things, he invented the luxury Pullman Sleeping Car for comfortable railroad travel. When President Lincoln's body was returned to Illinois via a Pullman car, word spread about the railcar's popularity and the cars were put into use in Europe as well. Pullman built a new plant and, in an effort to solve the issue of labor unrest and poverty, he also built a town adjacent to his factory with its own housing, shopping areas, churches, theaters, parks, hotel, and library for his employees. There were 1,300 original structures. The centerpiece of the complex was the Administration Building and its man-made lake. The Hotel Florence, named for Pullman's daughter, was built nearby. Pullman allegedly ruled the town like a feudal baron. When business fell off in 1894, Pullman cut jobs and wages, leading his workers to launch "the Pullman Strike," a violent upheaval that was eventually broken up by federal troops sent in by Pres. Grover Cleveland. Pullman later joined forces with Andrew Carnegie, who controlled key patents, to secure the transcontinental sleeping car business. As early as 1893, his company was worth $62 million. Two of George's brothers, (Royal) Henry Pullman (1826–1900) and James Minton Pullman (1836–1903), became prominent Universalist ministers, the family's chosen religion. George Pullman built the Universalist church—the Pullman Memorial—in the hometown of his youth, Albion, New York; the church was dedicated in 1895. The church remains a place of worship and a popular meeting place today. (Courtesy of Cobblestone Museum.)

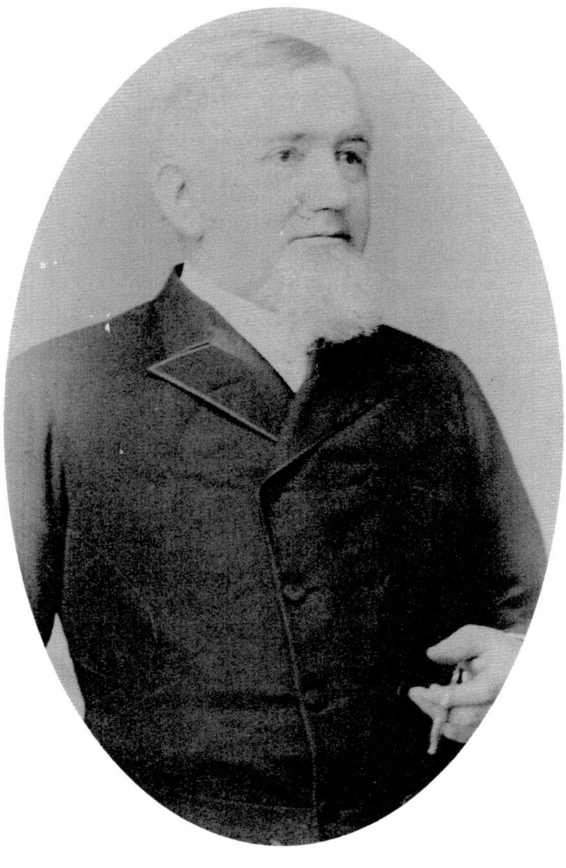

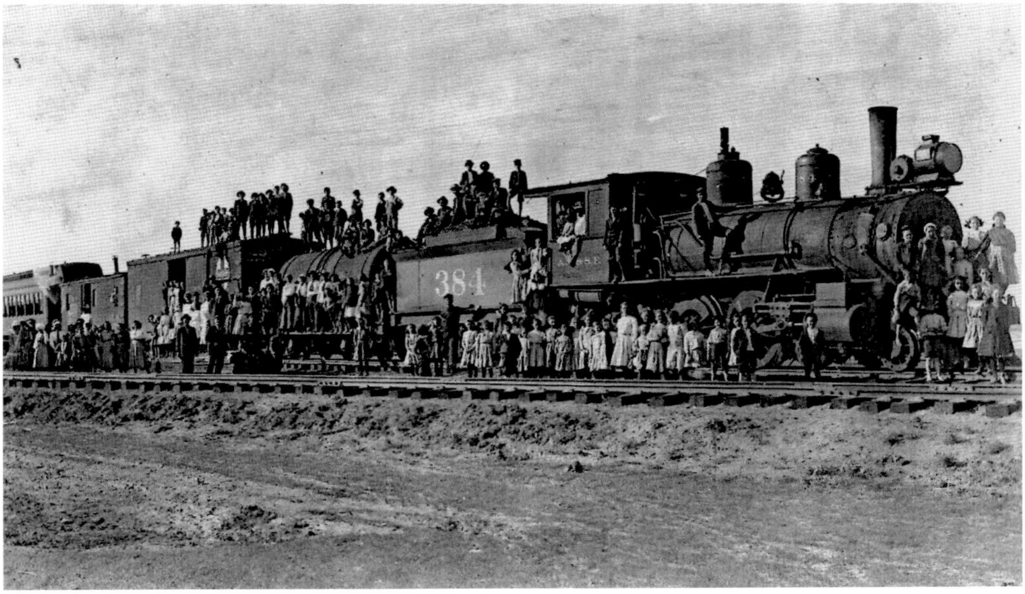

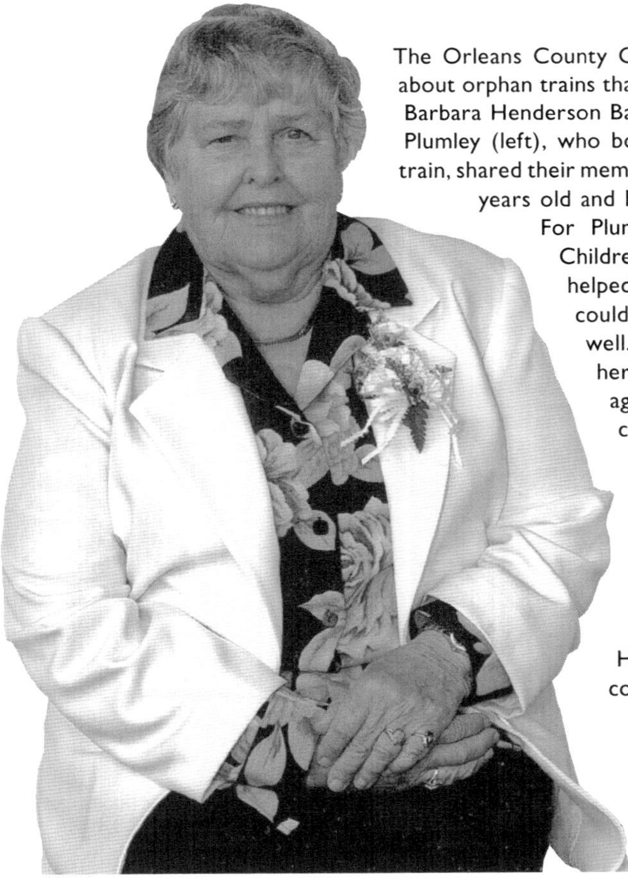

The Orleans County Genealogical Society hosted an event about orphan trains that restored a lost part of local history. Barbara Henderson Bacon (not pictured) and Beth Cooper Plumley (left), who both came into Medina via an orphan train, shared their memories and experiences. Bacon was nine years old and Plumley only 18 months upon arrival. For Plumley, remembering annual visits by Children's Aid Society agent Clara Comstock helped her trace her lineage. Bacon, however, could remember her circumstance very well. She spent about 30 years researching her past and eventually met her middle-aged biological siblings. Over 200,000 children of unhappy circumstances were relocated by rail throughout America from 1853 to 1929. The program, founded by Charles Loring Brace, was deemed 87 percent successful and led to modern-day social services programs. (Image above courtesy of the Kansas State Historical Society; bottom image courtesy of Holly Canham.)

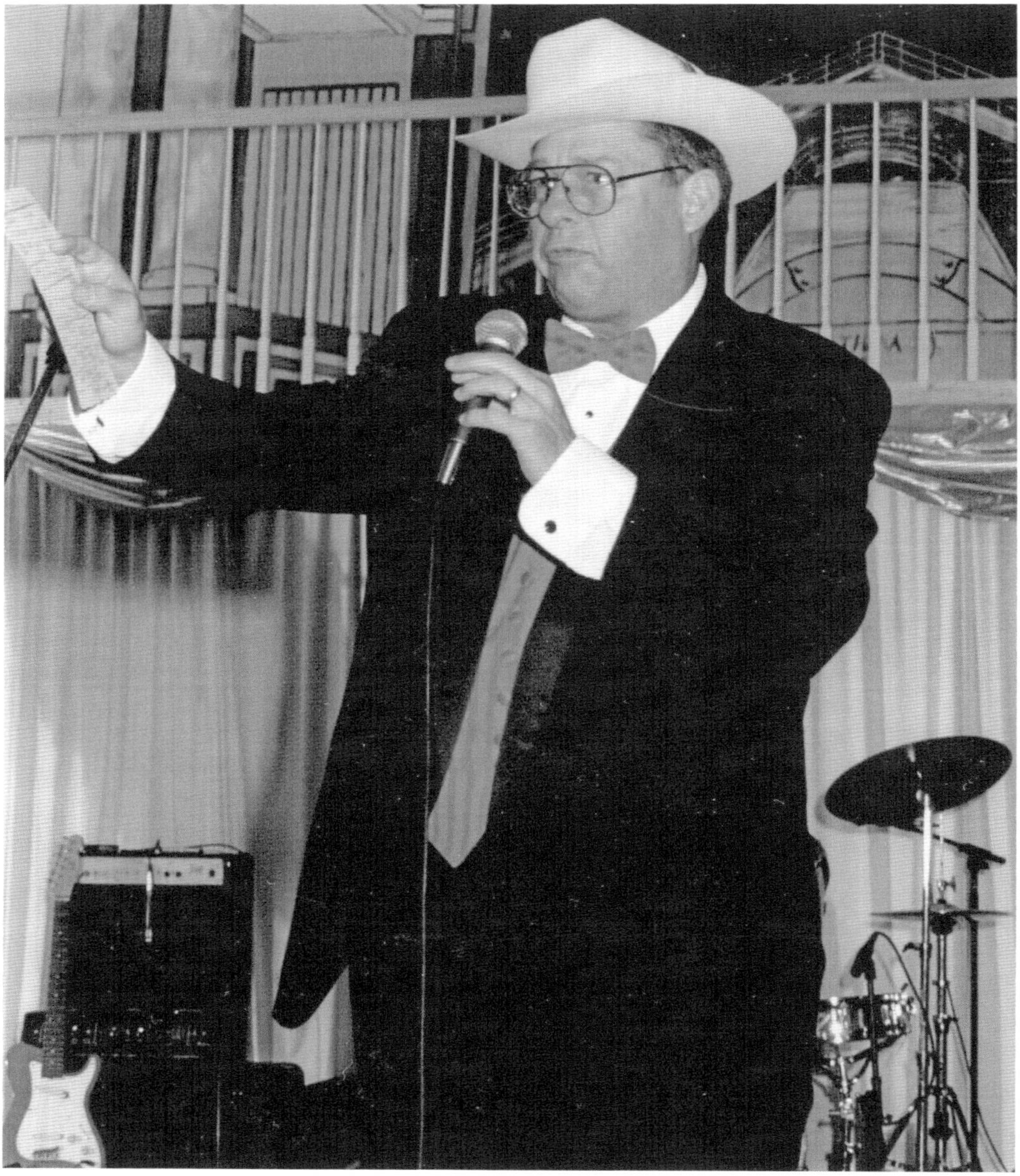

Mull is proud to have come from a pioneer farming family from Barre, so proud that he donated land and substantial funds (in part for a softball field and a large picnic shelter) to become Mull-Barre Park as a memorial to them. From his one-room schoolhouse early education, he went on to earn an MS from the University of Georgia. Recently inducted in the State of Georgia Auctioneers Hall of Fame, he is credited with raising over $2 million auctioneering for charities. Mull credits his early start in auctioneering at age 12 for his success. Mull founded Classic Groundcovers, which today is a multimillion-dollar international nursery supplier. The recipient of numerous prestigious honors, he affirms "the most important lessons learned in life are patience, consistency, honesty, and the golden rule." (Courtesy of Wilbur C. Mull.)

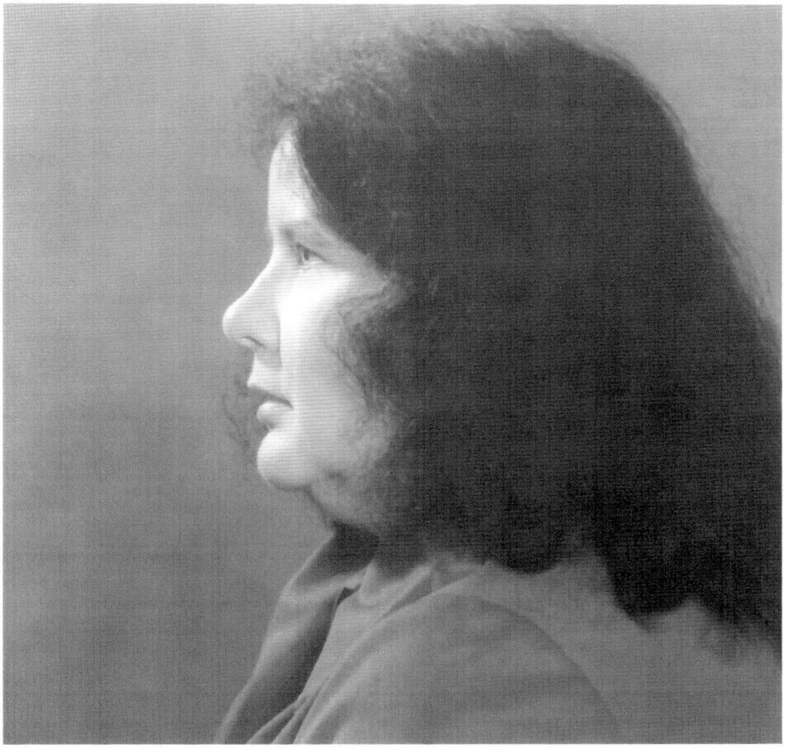

Rodden (1926–1985) encountered much resistance in the field of journalism. Her daughter said, "She would submit articles for publication, and when they learned she was a woman, they refused her. She eventually wrote under the pseudonym of Robert Quigley." A freelance writer, she wrote two books and for several years was editor of the *Herald Tribune* and *Lyndonville Enterprise* in Orleans County. As a radio and television director of Cayton TV Advertising and the company's vice president, she became the first woman to direct a television program—a documentary called *Great Fights of the Century.* She later directed segments of *Captain Kangaroo* and other documentaries. Donna also taught and served as a librarian in Albion. She served on numerous county board positions, including the Task Force on Alcoholism, Historical Monument Corp., and Mental Hygiene Services. Her efforts got Mt. Albion on the National Register of Historic Places. Donna served as Albion's mayor for 13 years. Her political influence included appointments to the New York State Friendship Force, the "Thalwil Conference" (a Swiss event fostering international peace), and a US State Department Foreign Policy Conference. Rodden has been a White House dinner guest on more than one occasion. She was recognized worldwide for her service. Rodden earned the International Peace Award from Brazil—one of only three people to ever win the award (Mother Teresa and Jackie Kennedy Onassis are the others). She received the Presidential Commendation Citation from President Nixon for exceptional service to others, the Peacemakers' Award from the United Service Club, and the International Amity Award and Distinguished Service Award from Girl Scouts of America. Rodden has also been honored by Queen Elizabeth (Royal Award), the League of Women Voters (Women in Government Award), the US Coast Guard (Certificate of Achievement), and she received a Kennedy Foundation Medal (first Special Olympics in Orleans County). She was a teacher, lawyer, and close to completing ministerial studies when she died. In her eulogy, Orleans County historian Bill Lattin summed up Rodden's life, saying, "Donna was an individualist, a brilliant thinker, creative writer, renowned speaker, diligent public servant and humanitarian. She has left her mark on this community." (Courtesy of Photos by Bruce.)

Paul (1892–1976) led a hobo-like lifestyle on the streets of Medina for the greater part of his life. He was an affectionately received town character. In fact, he was trusted to make bank deposits, deliver telegrams, and performed as a general handyman to Main Street proprietors. His days were spent sitting in the old Murphy's store on Main Street in a chair at the back of the store. If area businesspeople needed him for an errand, they knew where to find him. Dan came to Medina as a young boy to work on railroad maintenance gangs. He originally stayed with the Paul family and adopted their surname as his own. Returning to Medina after his military service during World War I, he displayed signs of trauma causing some to refer to him as "the crazy eye-talian." He dressed in a long hand-me-down overcoat, felt hat, and usually had a corsage on his lapel. One newspaper account described his appearance as "Charlie Chaplin-like." He could be seen darting around town with his long coat sweeping the streets while he chattered away to himself. His semi-reclusive lifestyle found him sleeping in private rooms, barns, garages, the stairwell on the south side of the JCPenney building, and in bad weather on the city hall porch. During the summer months, he would thumb rides or walk north to Lake Ontario to bathe in its waters. Late in his life, when he was hospitalized, considerable amounts of money were found in secret folds within his legendary overcoat. While being cared for at the local VA Hospital, it was also discovered that he had many uncashed pension checks. His only known possessions were a trunk of lacy items, like doilies, which some believed were made by his mother. He would occasionally give one away as a gift. A newspaper article summed it up well, "He took with him an unwritten history of Medina that few could record, for he mingled with all; he was everybody's friend—and who was not a friend of Dan's?" (Painting by Gene Massey, courtesy of Debbie Russo.)

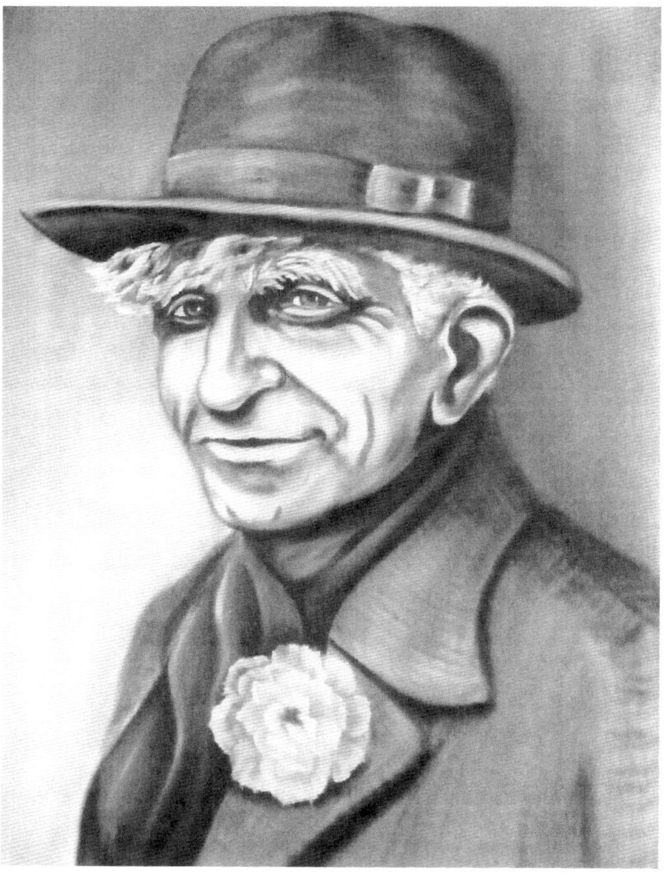

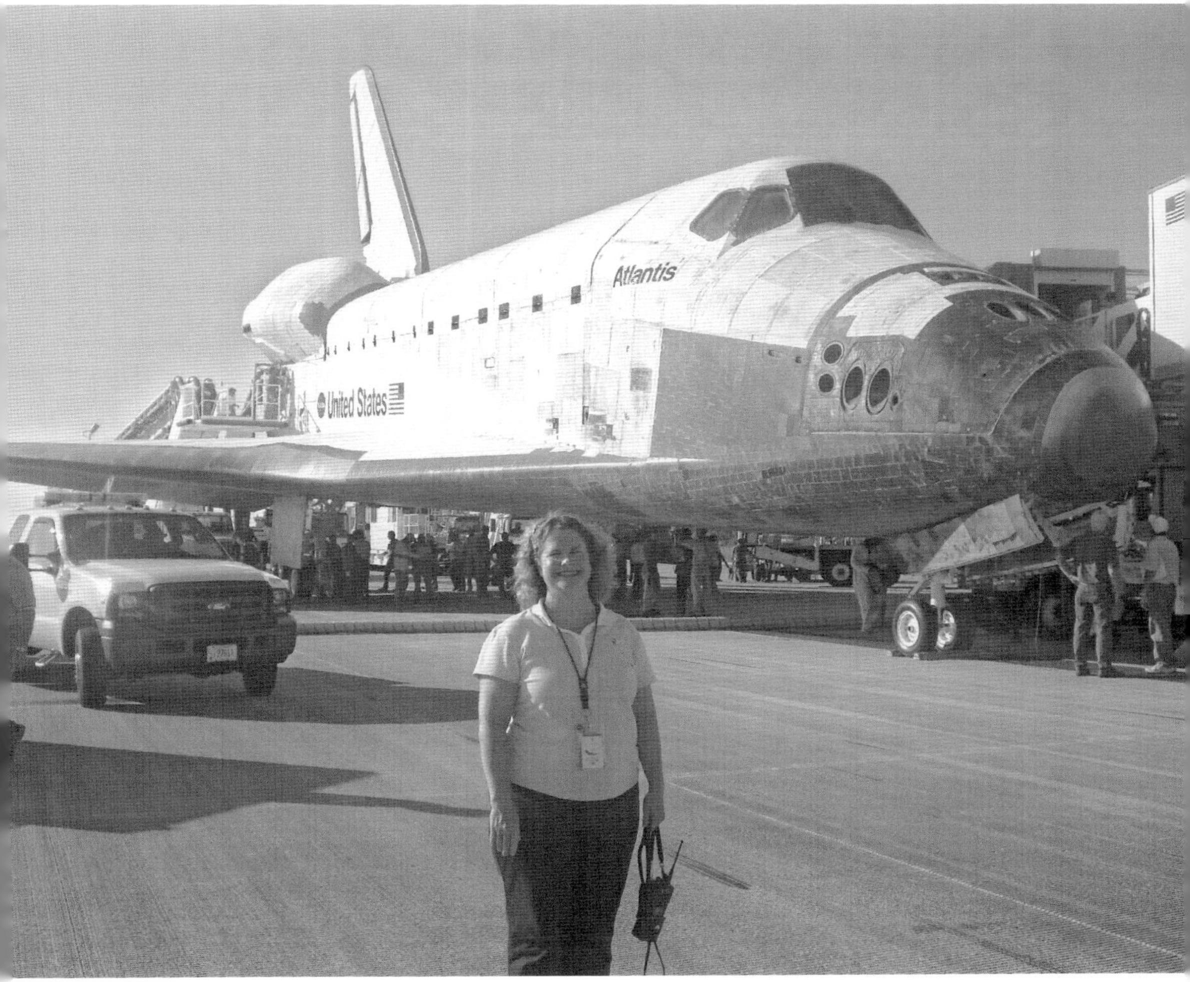

From the time she was in high school, Huff knew she wanted to be an aeronautical engineer. After graduating from Medina High School in 1983, Huff enrolled at Penn State, where she earned a bachelor of science in aerospace engineering. When NASA visited the college to recruit new employees, Huff was interviewed and hired. She has been at the Kennedy Space Center since 1987, working in the thermal protection system program. Part of Huff's job requires her to inspect the external service of the shuttle upon landing. She and her team were in position on the runway to inspect the space shuttle Columbia on February 1, 2003, when they heard over their radios that there would be no routine landing—the shuttle had broken up in the skies over Texas. Huff has worked on all four NASA shuttles and has witnessed most of NASA's 113 launches. Her duties require her to be in the engineers' support area of the launch control center, and often she is in the firing room (where the launch is triggered) visually scanning the shuttle for problems. She and her team would not have been able to see with the naked eye the infamous piece of foam insulation that was later photographed hitting the wing of the shuttle Columbia at liftoff, she said. Although losing a shuttle is quite a shock, Huff said they know the danger is always there. She continues to love her job and has complete confidence in the space program. Now that the shuttle program has ended, Huff's duties will change, but she has not disclosed exactly what she will be doing in the future. One thing is sure—it will be at NASA. (Courtesy of Joy Huff.)

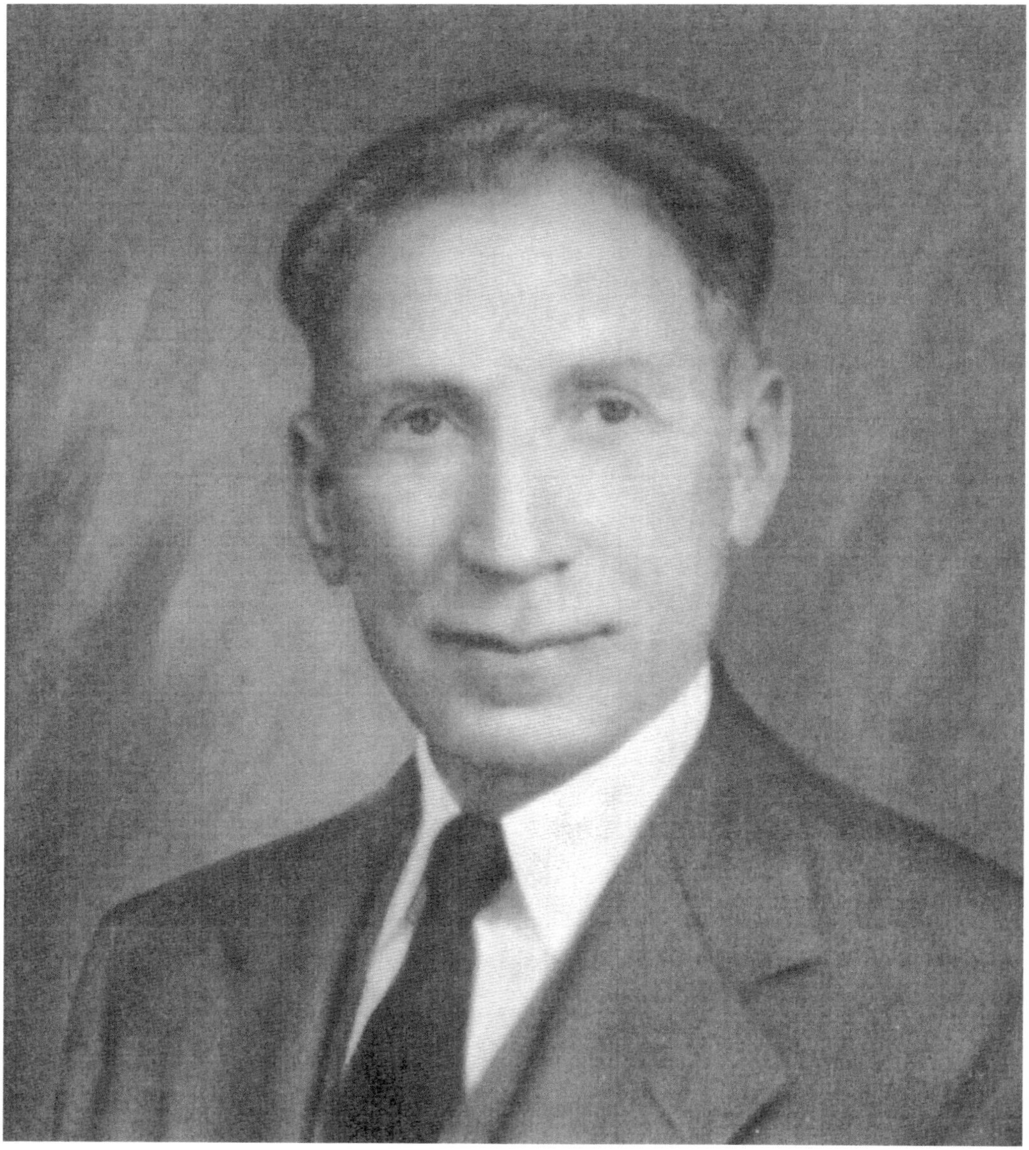

In 1925, William Smith, already an established commercial applesauce canner, moved to Lyndonville where he and his brother-in-law Wilson McCagg assumed half-ownership of the Lyndonville Canning Company, Inc. Of critical importance to the company's success was Smith's applesauce patent (related to steaming apples and sugar)—which dramatically improved the canning process nationwide. Smith served as company president for 41 years and eventually he and his partner acquired full company ownership. He had several hobbies, including his Robin Hill Arboretum located in Yates. The preserve contains over 450 varieties of shrubs and trees, which he acquired nationwide. An award-winning photographer, he gained acclaim for his collection of fungi prints—featured in *National Geographic* magazine and Eastman Kodak displays. His family donated land and funds for the Yates Community Library. (Courtesy of Yates Community Library.)

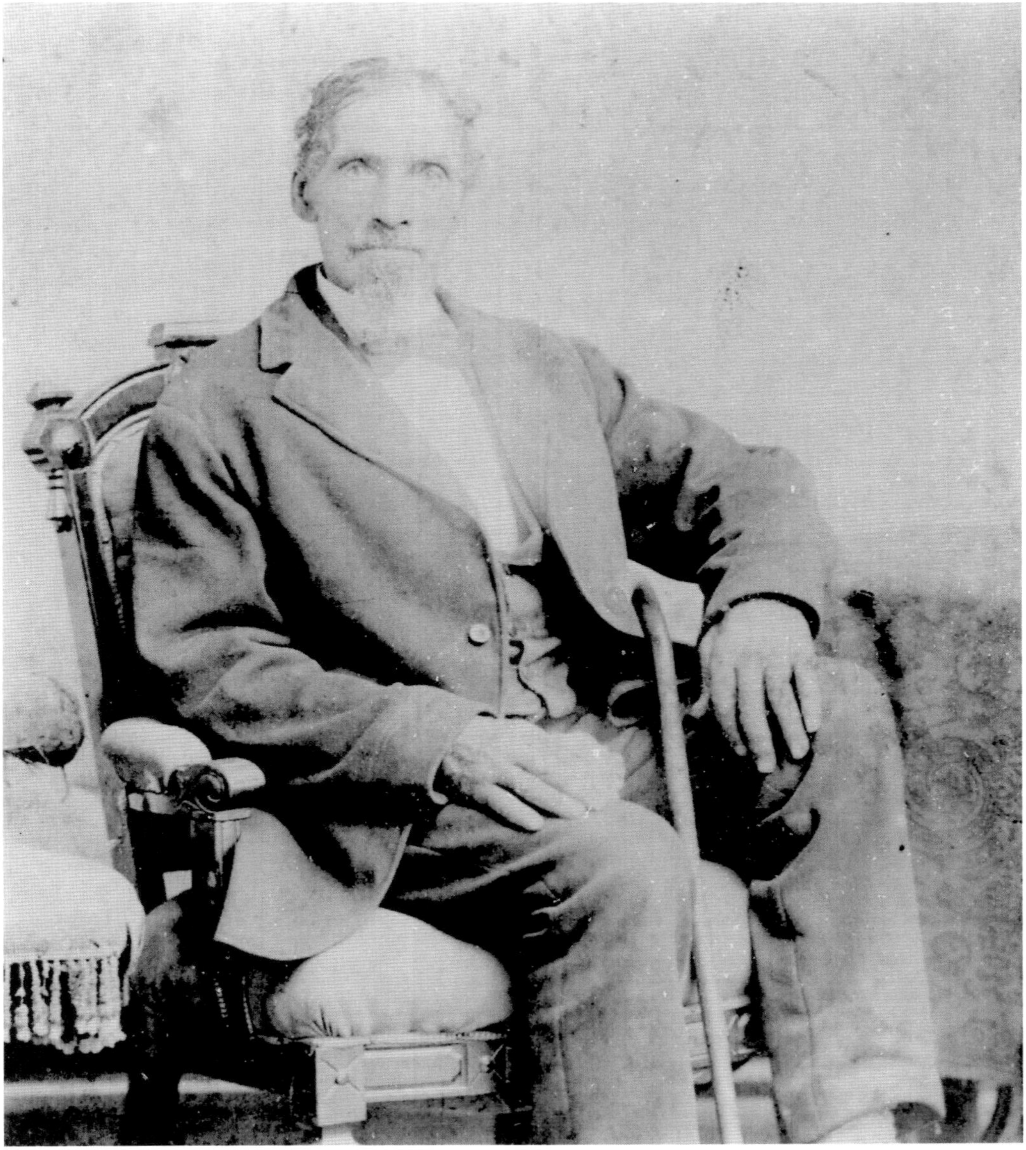

Gordineer was said to have been, at the time of his death, the oldest resident of Orleans County. Born in Schohaire County, New York, his father was Jacob Gardineer and his mother was a slave belonging to Jacob. When he was two months old, he and his mother were sold to Joseph Grant. They came to Medina in 1823 and lived with the family of Walton Grant. Gordineer served as the cook. In 1825, they were liberated by the New York State Emancipation Act. Gordineer then worked on the Erie Canal until 1839. It is believed that Gordineer cooked on the first boat ran in the canal and catered parties. He was the only successful drayman here for many years and a whitewasher. He accumulated considerable property at one point. He was said to have been a steward of several fire companies, "the oldest fireman in town." (Courtesy of Orleans County Department of History.)

Two decades of service on Medina Memorial Hospital's board, including a term as president, gave Waters the knowledge to improve and reform health care for seniors. She was influential in the construction of Orchard Manor Nursing Home and the Willows adult home for ambulatory residents. Waters has served on the Genesee Region Planning Council and Orleans Medical Scholarship Board. (Courtesy of the Waters Family.)

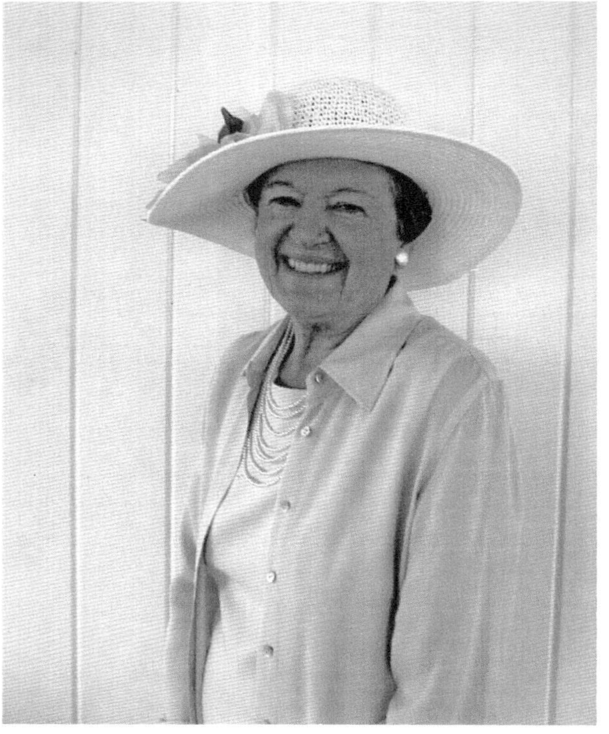

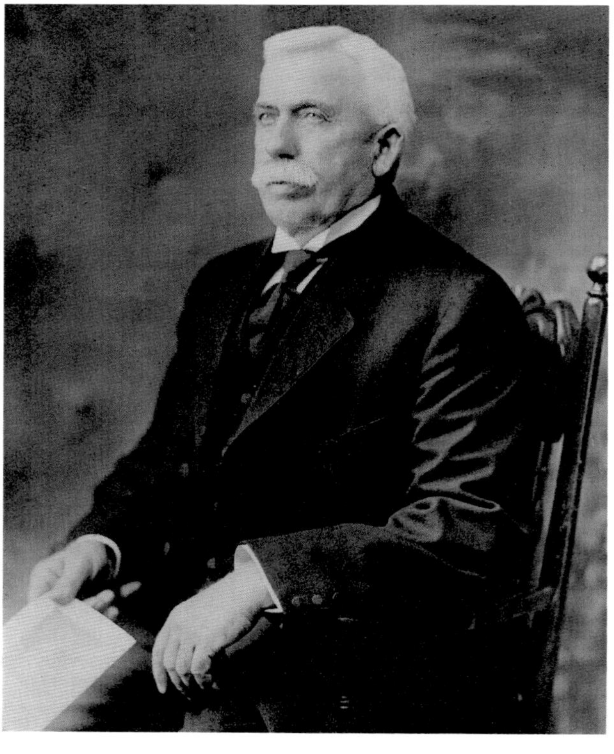

Bogue (1851–1922) was a very successful nurseryman whose fortune, combined with that of his wife's, amounted to over a million dollars. Having no children, they donated their fortune to help those in need. The Bogue Home was established in Albion. Although no buildings remain, their bequest still provides assistance today. (Courtesy of Orleans County Department of History.)

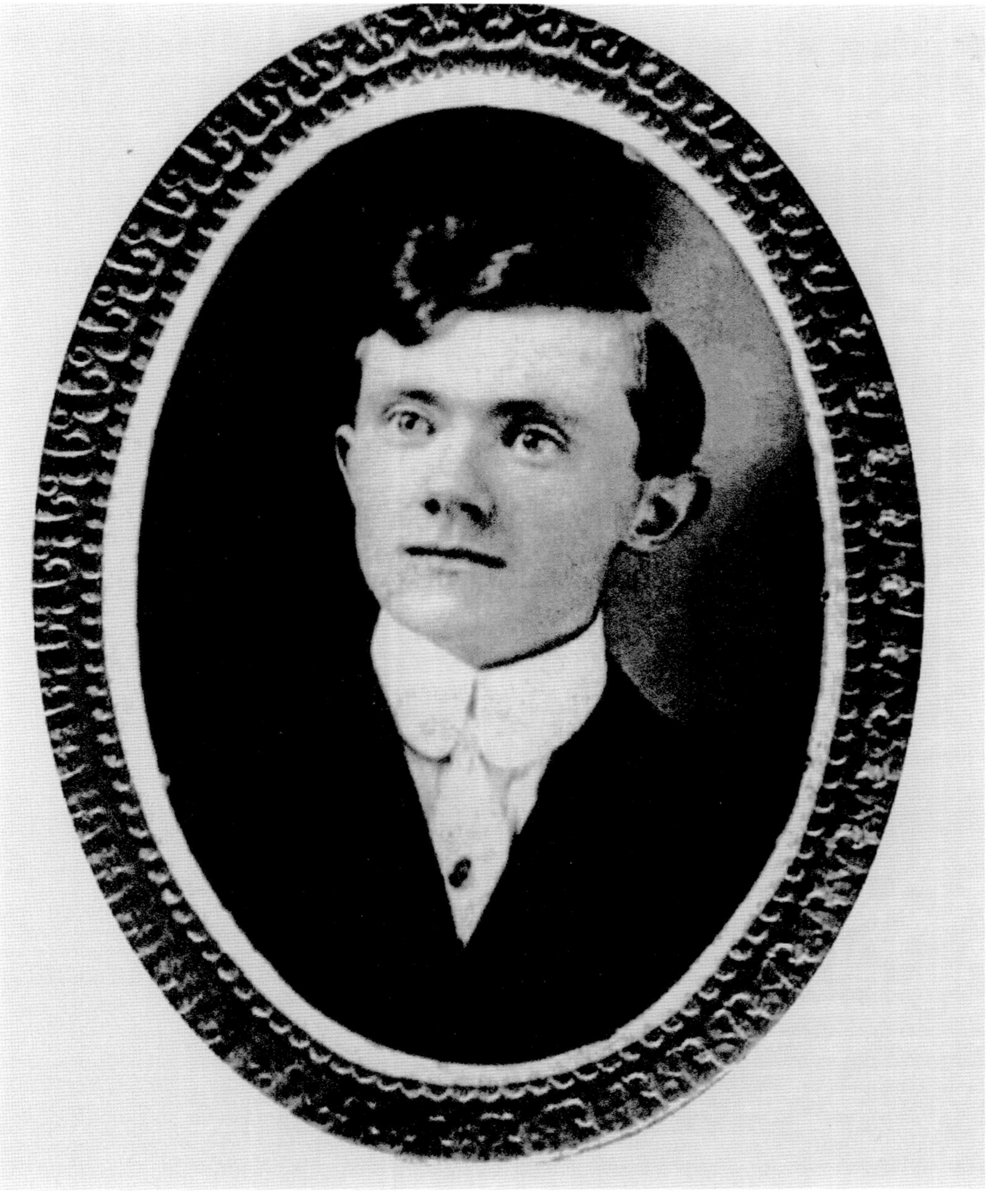

Pratt (1889–1988) spent his life in Gaines, where his ancestors settled in the early 1800s. His early days were spent teaching in one-room schoolhouses and dairy farming. Pratt developed an avid interest in Abraham Lincoln—dressing in like garb and visiting schools. He was once questioned by the Secret Service when outside the White House in his costume. His many and varied interests kept him active into his 99th year. Known by many for his interest in antiques and his years as Town of Gaines historian, he also authored three books on the area's history. He was active in the Cobblestone Society (charter member) and the Universalist Church. (Courtesy of Orleans County Department of History.)

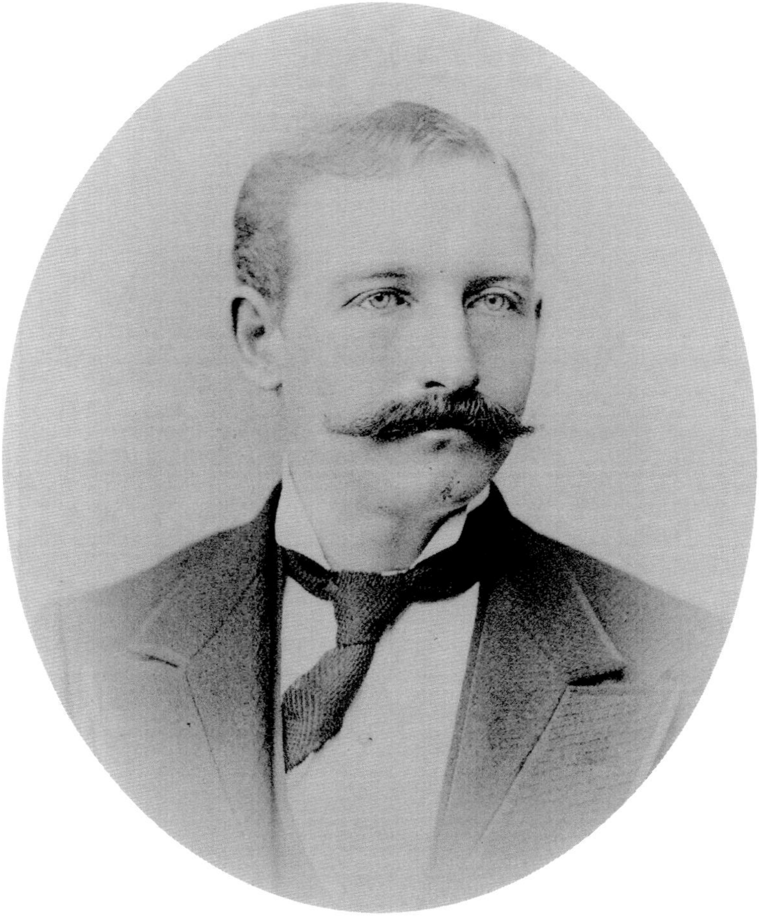

Burroughs (1846–1895) was born in Medina to prominent parents, both of whom died young leaving Silas Jr. and his siblings to be raised by an aunt and uncle. Industrious by nature, he became a traveling pharmaceutical salesman and graduated from the Philadelphia College of Pharmacy in 1877. In 1878, Burroughs traveled to England on business for others and ended up establishing his own Burroughs & Company, importing American drugs. He invited a friend into partnership, and together they formed Burroughs, Welcome and Company. His political persuasion was toward active Christian socialism. He believed in shared profits and eight-hour workdays. He was almost fanatical in his support of free trade, sincerely believing it would prevent war. Hugely successful in business, Burroughs established the Livingstone Cottage Hospital in England, still in existence. The Rolling Stones' Mick Jagger and Keith Richards were both born there. Burroughs kept a demanding schedule of world travel. He kept up a regular, loving postcard correspondence with his family that he secured in albums, providing many details about his lifestyle. By the end of December 1894, Burroughs was exhausted and had the flu. He visited his sister in the south of France, where he enjoyed combining work and cycling along the beautiful coast resorts. Unfortunately, the normally warm climate suddenly changed to snow, and Burroughs landed in bed at the Windsor Hotel in Monte Carlo on February 4th. His wife left London the next day, arriving at Marseilles Station to learn of his death. In his will, he left half his wealth to charitable causes. Boxwood Cemetery in Medina was given a large bequest by Burroughs, and a chapel was built at the entrance, which includes a memorial window dedicated to him. (Courtesy of Julia Sheppard.)

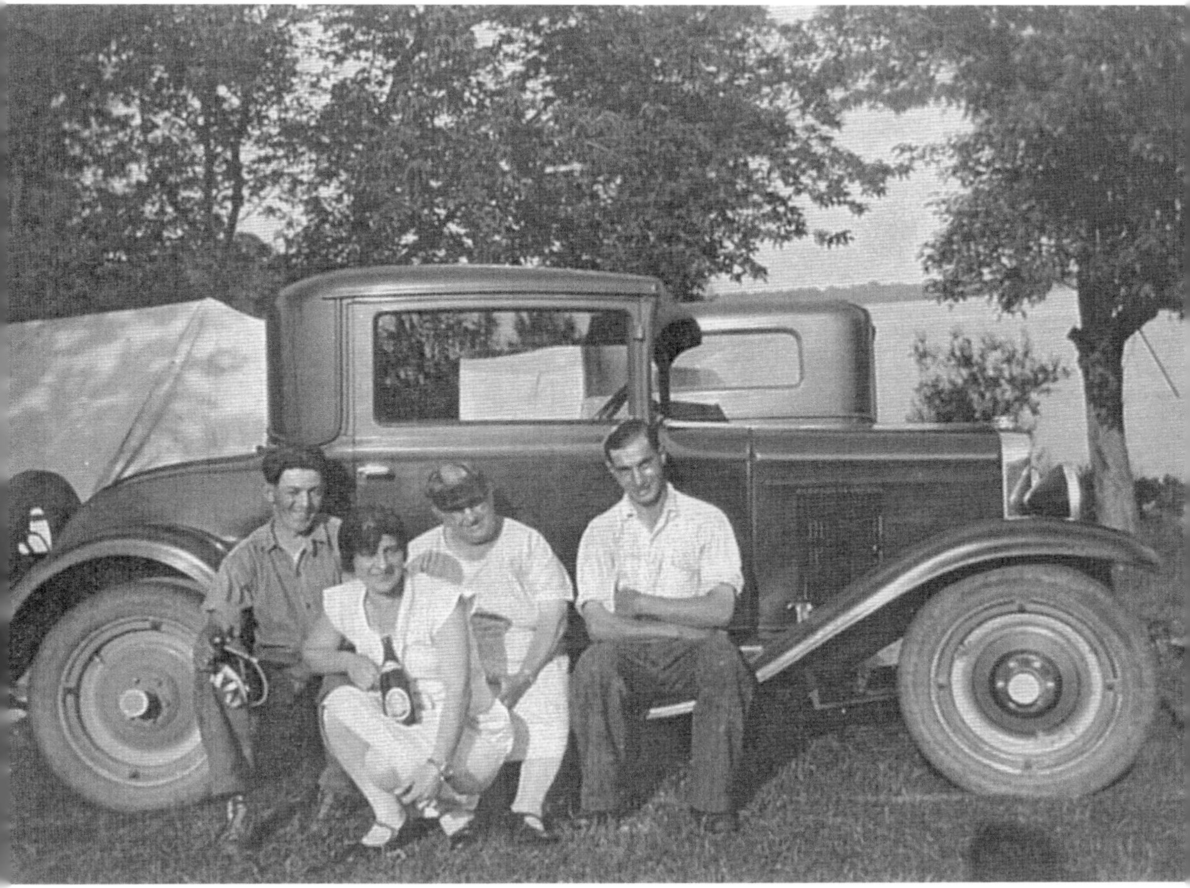

Winghart (1900–1997), seated on the left in the above photo, had the springs built up to accommodate 10 cases of liquor in the rear of his Chevrolets. He knew New York state troopers used to watch for vehicles with heavy loads. Winghart knew the tricks of the trade, making him and his brother Joe very successful bootleggers operating out of the Point Breeze area. Bernie believed bringing Canadian whiskey into New York saved people's lives because drinking homemade brews or "bathtub gin" blinded and killed many people. Joe bought land on the shore of Lake Ontario and a Chris Craft boat equipped with two water-cooled airplane engines—he discovered that liberty engines, in surplus after the war, were perfectly adaptable for rum running. His boathouse had a unique feature, an underground tunnel and storage area lined with cement that could hold over 200 cases of liquor. Metal tracks and a winch were used to haul the boat from the water into the boathouse. Thus, they could manage a perfect supply for the Winghart Grille next door and other area demand. Sadly, a fire claimed Joe's beloved rum-running boat. Arson was suspected but never proved. The family ran two successful resort area businesses, the Winghart Grille and, later, the Lakeland Hotel at Point Breeze. Bootlegging was carried out all over Orleans County in many creative ways. Area bootleggers often stored booze and cars in barns during the cold winters so the car radiators could be kept warm by cows. Local barns were places where grain could be put to many uses; more than one farmer tried to explain to federal agents why chicken feed came in gallon jugs! Booze boats were also used on the Erie Canal. Winemaking by area Italians was lucrative and forgotten bottles buried in backyards were heard exploding for years to come. (Courtesy of Joan Sullivan.)

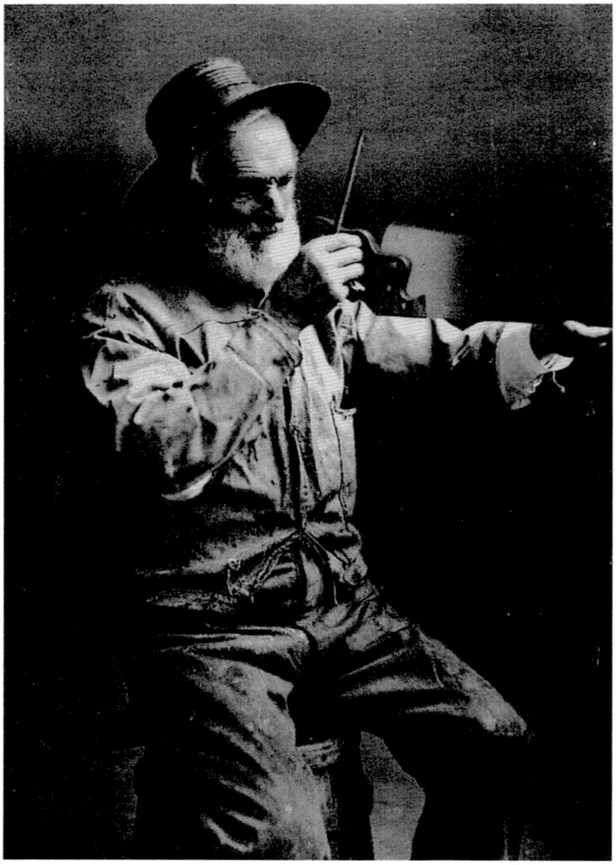

Realizing the growing county needed a larger courthouse, Orleans County Supervisors chose William V.N. Barlow, a young local architect, for the project. The courthouse would become his signature building, and the first of many contributions he would make as designer or builder. The courthouse, completed in 1858, was an ornate Greek Revival structure with a tall, 36-foot-wide gilded dome. The front columns were 50 feet tall, and the dome top twice that height. The cupola was once open to visitors, allowing for views of Lake Ontario to the north. Barlow (1810–1909) introduced other architectural styles to Orleans County over the years. Decades later, a critic wrote, in part, that "his genius as a practitioner of the true fine art of building begins to sing." (Courtesy of Orleans County Department of History.)

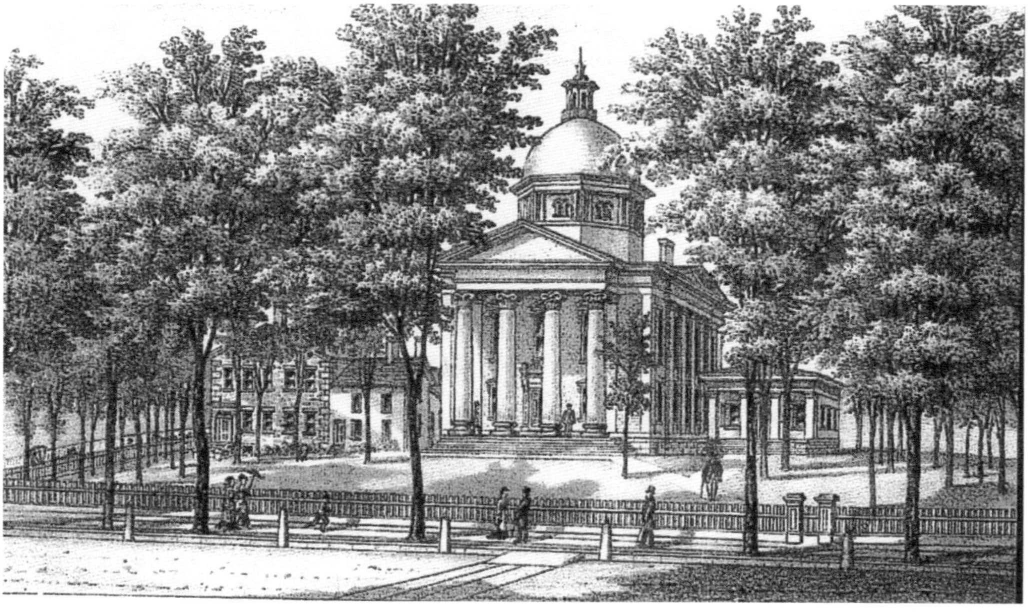

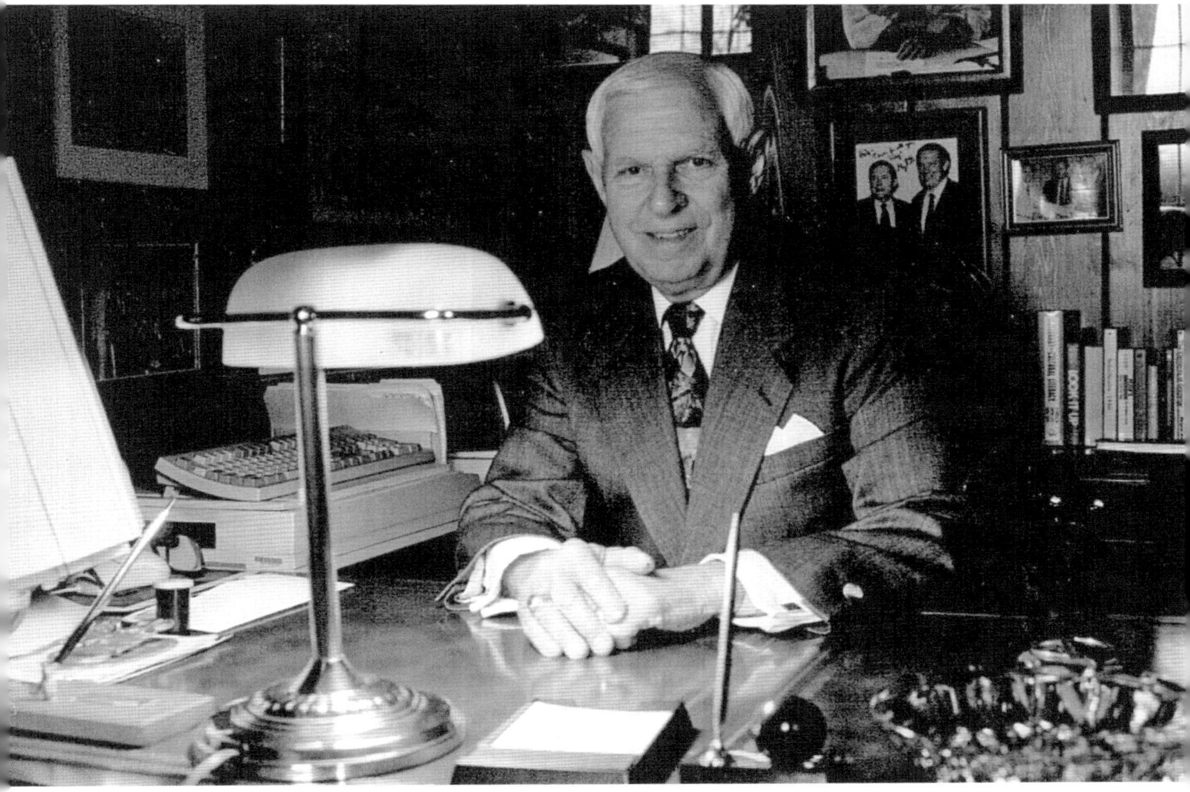

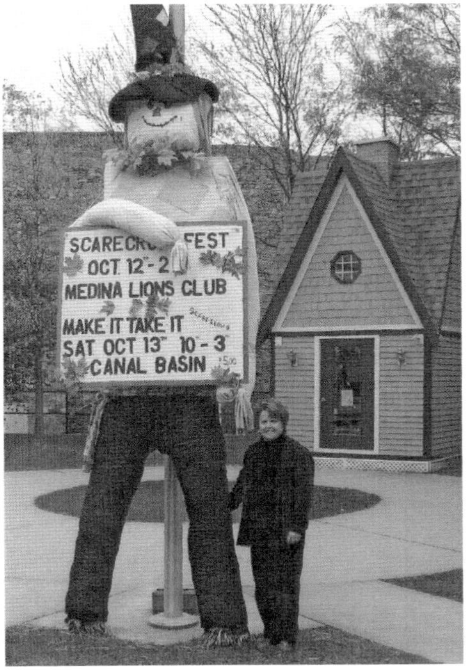

Bob Waters was an editor and publisher for the *Medina Journal-Register* and the *Albion Weekly Advertiser*. He served on the Genesee State Park Commission for 13 years and presided over the opening of the Lake Ontario Parkway's Orleans section. Waters was Shelridge Country Club's first president and is active in many community groups. He was also an aide to two senators. (Courtesy of Bob Waters.)

Wheatley takes planning seriously. She was a 4-H leader for eight years, has worked with the vision-screening program at all Head Start schools in Orleans County, and has belonged to the Lions Club for 12 years. She began the tremendously successful Medina Community Garage Sale, which attracts thousands of bargain hunters each year. (Courtesy of Virginia Kropf.)

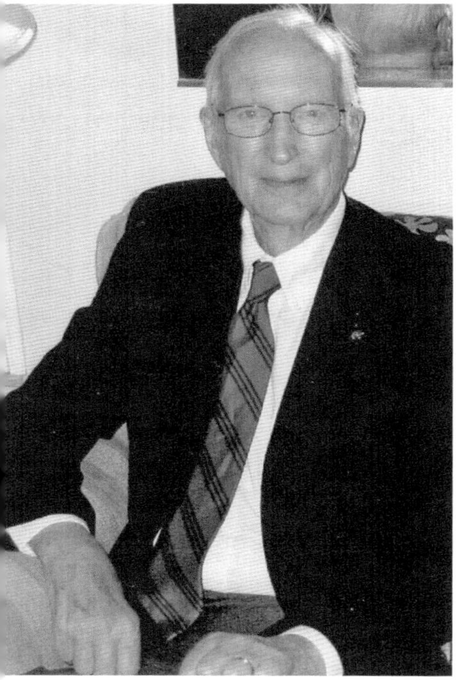

(LEFT) Eddy (1921–2011) graduated from Cornell University with a mechanical engineering degree, served in the US Army during World War II, and was president of Eddy Printing. He received the highest award in Rotary (a Paul Harris Fellow) and had perfect attendance for 60 years. He was the first campaign chair of the United Fund for Eastern Orleans County, and was former chairman of the Orleans County Legislature. (Courtesy of Kim Eddy Remley.)

Born in Michigan, Johnson moved to New York to get his PhD in anthropology at Cornell, and has lived in New York ever since. He became the Albion Village historian in 1982 and continues in that capacity today. He writes a weekly newspaper column, serves on various boards, and is active in area choirs and 4-H. We include his favorite quote, by Augustine, below:

Men go abroad to wonder at the height of mountains,
the huge waves of the sea, the long course of rivers,
the vast compass of the ocean, the circular motion of the stars,
but they pass by themselves and they don't even notice.
(Courtesy of Andrew Canham.)

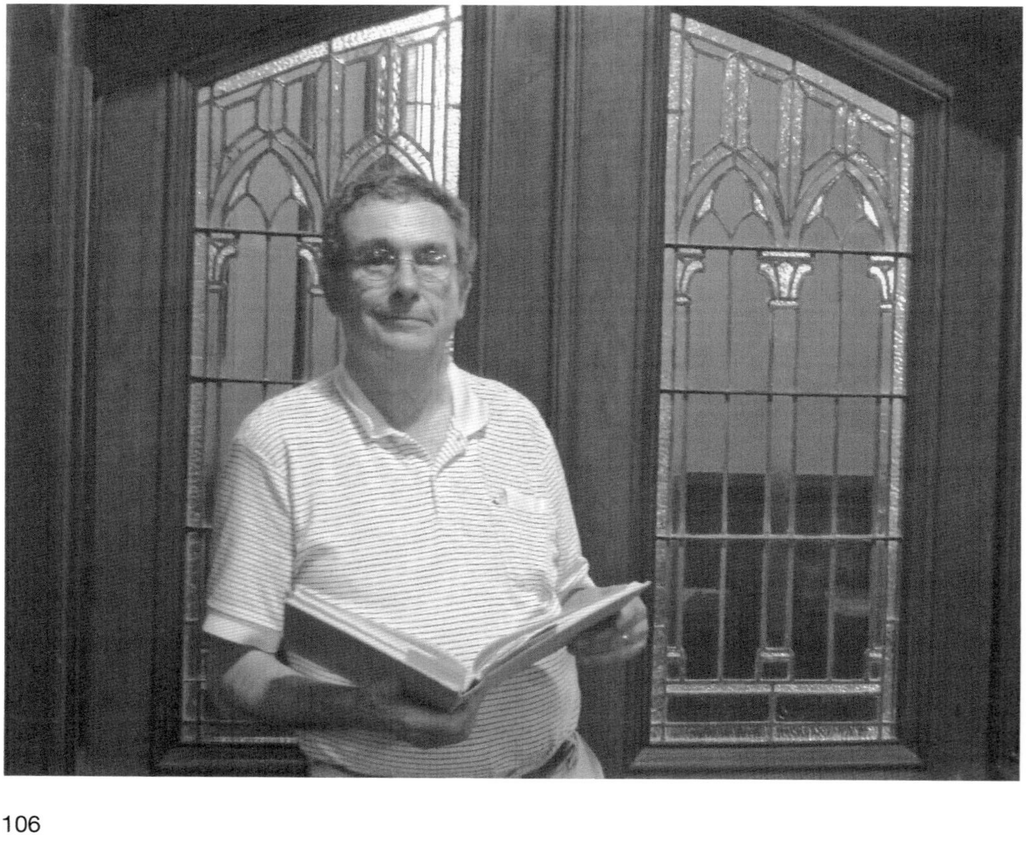

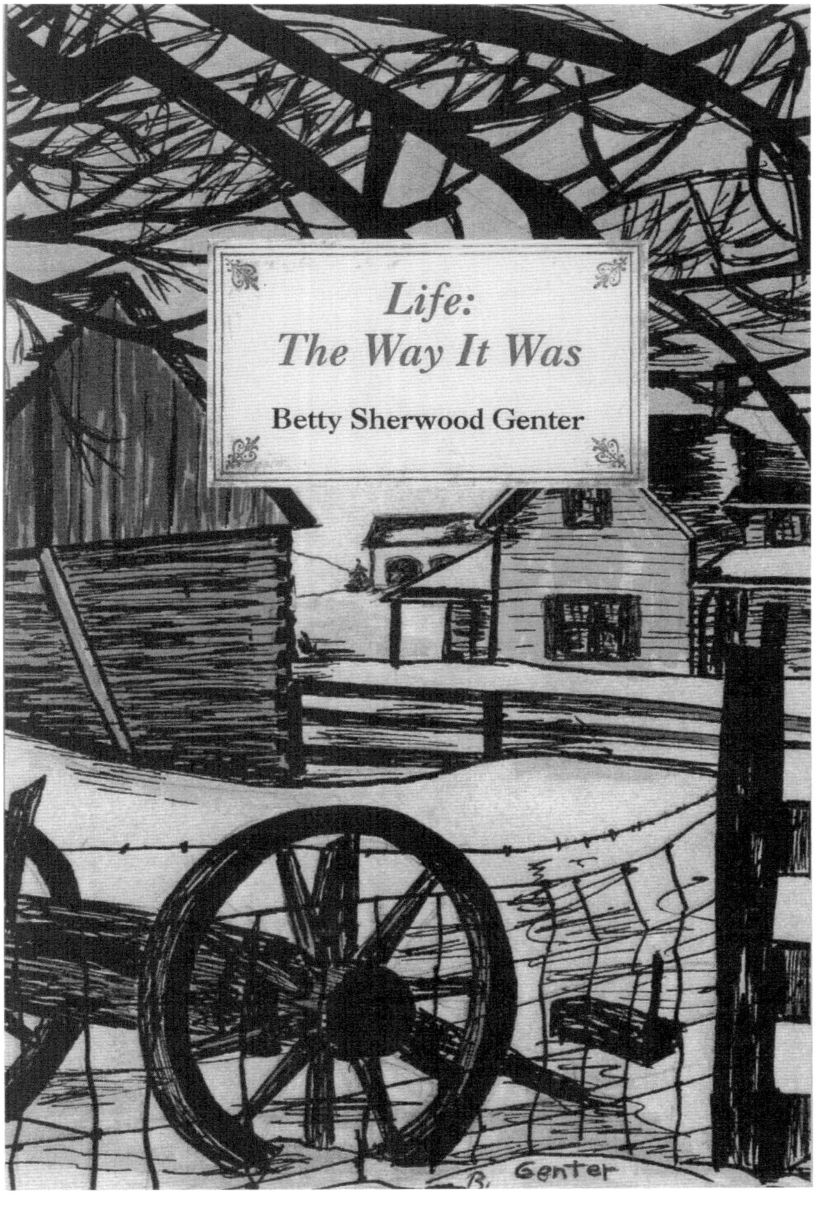

Genter wrote about growing up on her parent's muckland farm in Clarendon, New York, during the 1940s and 1950s. (Orleans County offers 11,960 acres of highly productive rich black soil, called "muckland.") Topics covered in her book include the trials and tribulations of farm life, such as the uniqueness of muck farming, the country way, and days at the Manning School (now the Clarendon Historical Society Museum). Genter helped her parents in all aspects of self-sustained farming, including mixing deadly spray materials. Her job was stirring liquid or powdered poisons into drums of water. Her mother kept a book of formulas, including medicinal recipes. Her grandmother's recipe for black salve would heal just about anything. (Courtesy of Betty Genter.)

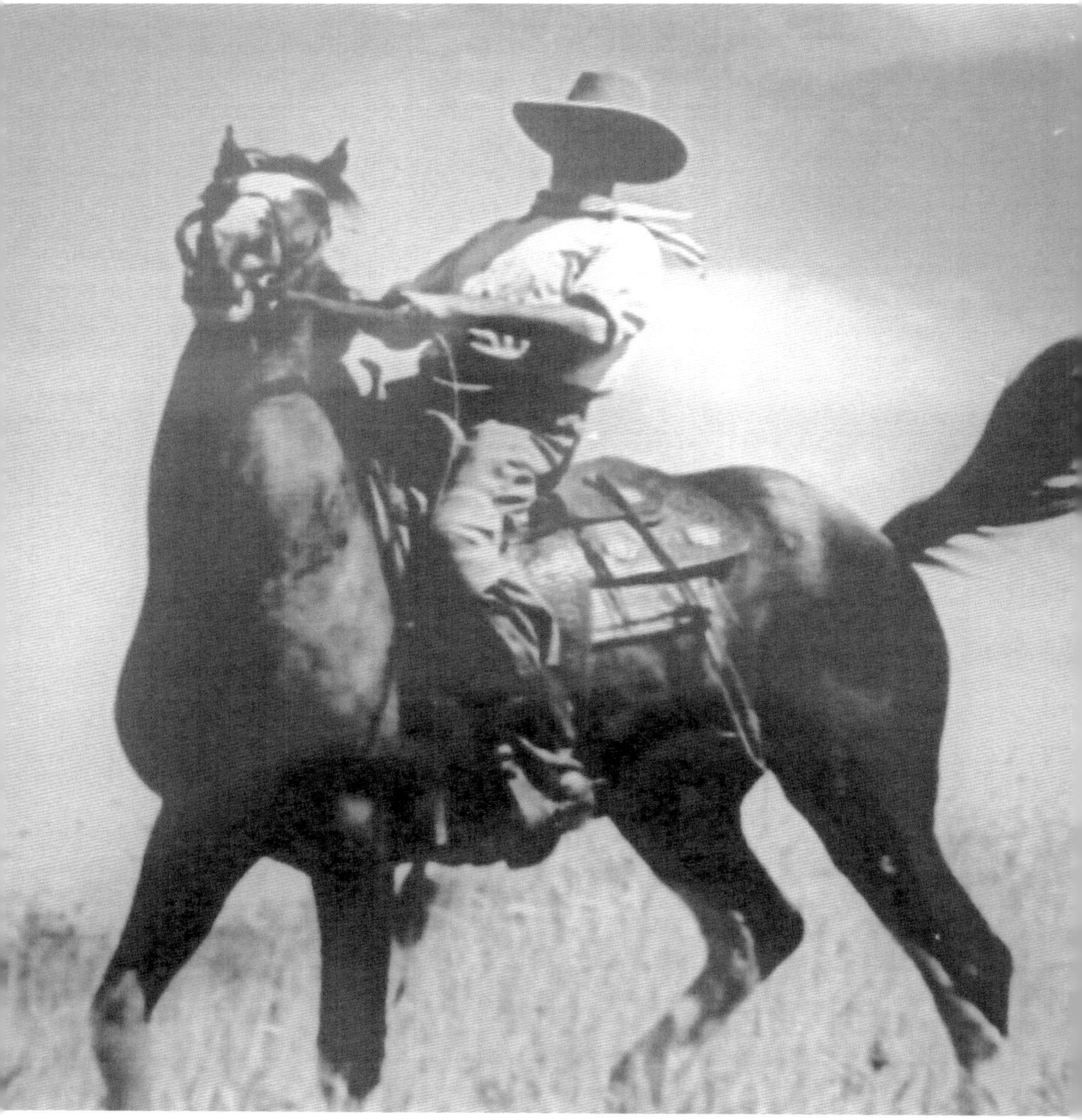

"Doc" Howes (1858–1946) was the local veterinarian for 55 years. He was an expert horseman, and trained his beloved Sandy (pictured above) to do many tricks; they were featured in every parade for many years. On August 18, 1937, Doc and Sandy appeared in a parade dedicating the new bridge over Oak Orchard Creek. During the parade, Sandy reared up and had a stroke in front of shocked onlookers. The horse had to be put down by a policeman. People still recall the tragedy with sadness and affection for the bond shared between them, and with so many. (Courtesy of Orleans County Department of History.)

Only in Orleans County

Some things found in Orleans County are unique. Some entries for this chapter are of a serious nature, and some, as the popular phrase nowadays goes, "not so much." Regarding architecture, included for your consideration is the world's oldest cobblestone church, the Medina Sandstone Soldiers and Sailors Monument, and two structures that found their way into *Ripley's Believe It or Not!* Some of the clubs we spotlight are essentially for fun, but have their ways of making important contributions to Orleans County life. Genealogy has a reputation with some as being downright dull, but the 200 members of the Orleans County Genealogical Society can attest that this "just isn't so." The society hosts a Black Sheep Picnic to prove it. The county does like to do things in big ways at times. When it comes to shoe trees, others may express it best: "Apparently there is nothing that cannot happen today" (Mark Twain), and "A child of five would understand this. Send someone to fetch a child of five" (Groucho Marx). The Orleans County Genealogical Society thanks you for your generous support and hopes you will visit us soon.

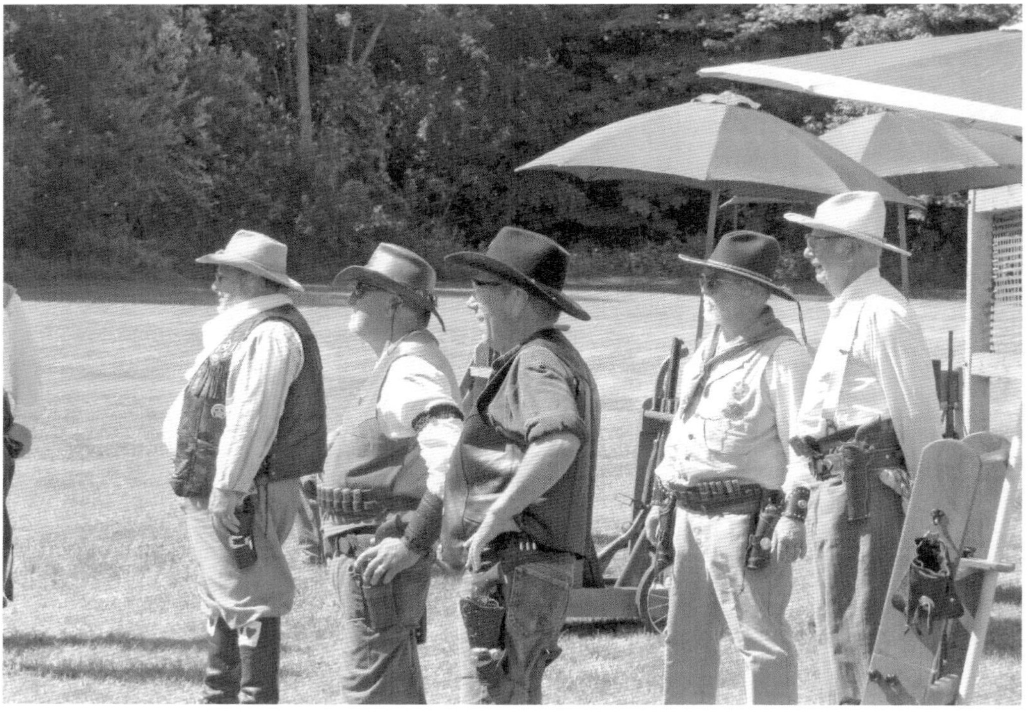

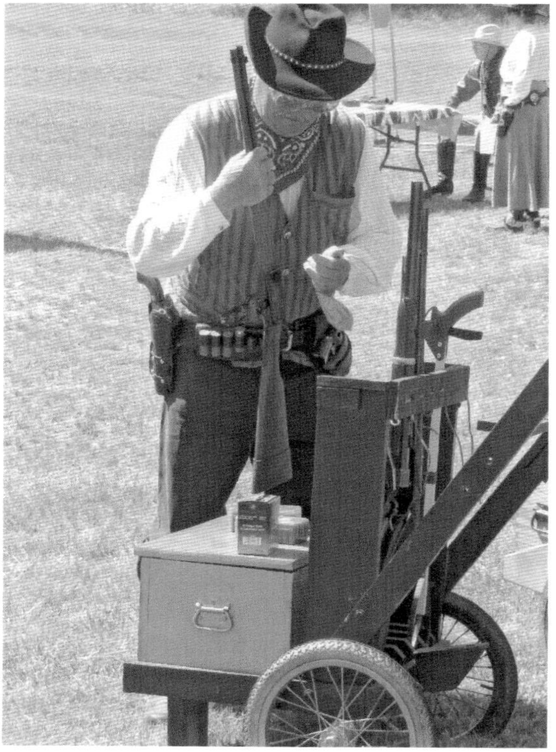

The Salt Port Vigilance Committee (named for a historic local salt spring and distillery) is the county's only club affiliated with the Single Action Shooting Society (SASS), which exists to "preserve and promote the history of the Old West and competitive shooting." The "Spirit of the Game" is essential to these family-oriented clubs' success, and requires members to adopt a unique persona somehow related to 19th-century life, such as that of a real or fictional character or profession (perhaps a banker, lawman, outlaw, or preacher) or western movie star. Participants dress in period-appropriate clothing and use weapons from around the late 1800s, such as "six-shooters," "yellow-boy" lever-action rifles, and coach guns. Real names are rarely used during events; folks use aliases, such as "Twelve Bore" (club president Jim Gommenginger, pictured above at far right), "Uncle Rog" (left), "Tombstone,", "Sassy Sue Lawless," and "Heavy Bear." (Courtesy of Elaine Canham.)

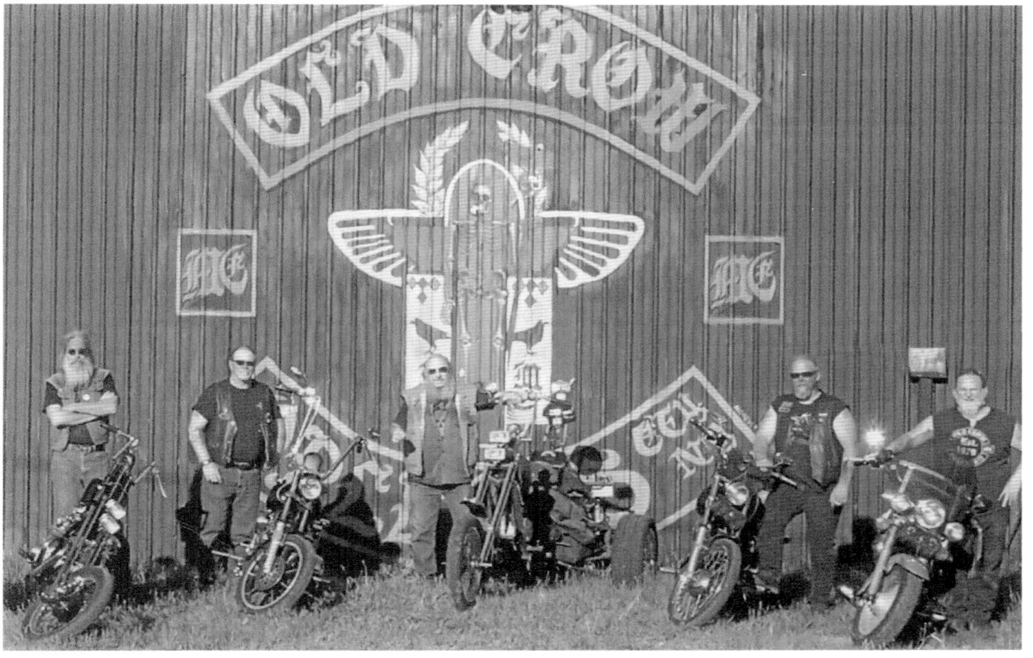

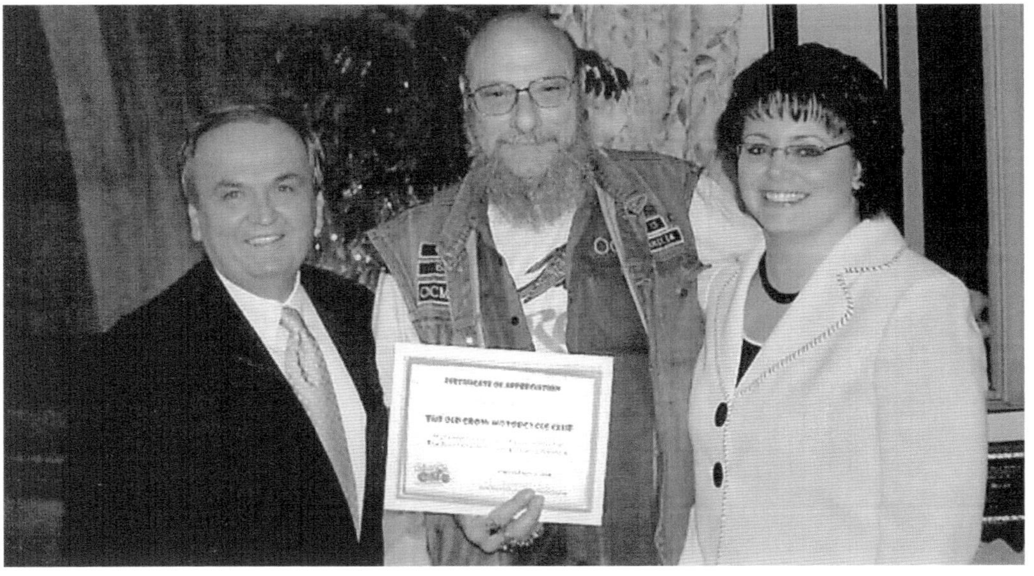

Founded in 1997, the "Old Crows" is considered a three patch club. Members must be able to take care of their family, maintain cleanliness, and be of service to the group and others. In fact, the club has received many awards over the years for their fundraising efforts. One example is shown above, where Carl Catraccia, charter member and club president for several years, accepts an award from Senator Maziarz and Kellie Spychalski of ARC. They have made numerous runs for Toys for Tots, and have helped ensure that hospitalized children have plenty of toys. They are dedicated community servants. (Courtesy of Homer Rietz.)

The applesauce stand was built (around 1929) to raise public awareness about the availability of canned applesauce—and specifically to sell the VB (Very Best) brand. The VB brand originally stood for Visscher Brothers and was later changed. Travelers could "stop and taste VB applesauce!" The roadside stand was torn down around 1950 when Ridge Road was widened, but the stand's round foundation remains visible. (Applesauce stand courtesy of Frank Berger; image of VB label courtesy of Scott Goetze; image of apple barrels courtesy of Andrew Canham.)

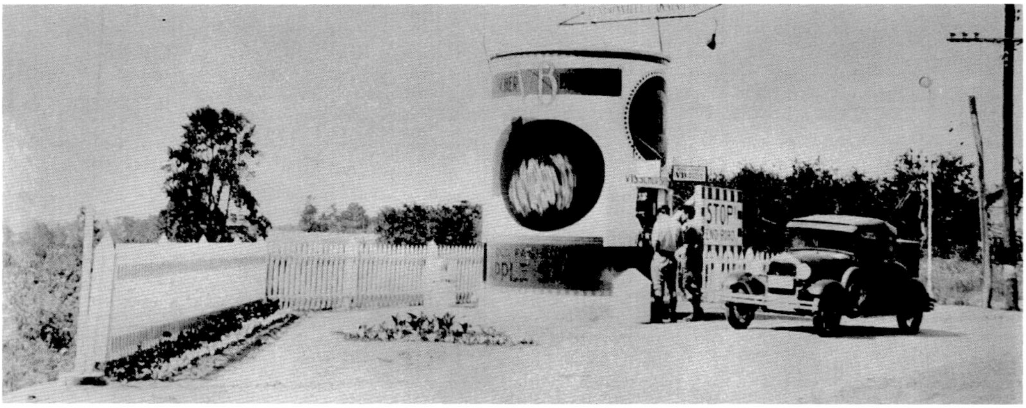

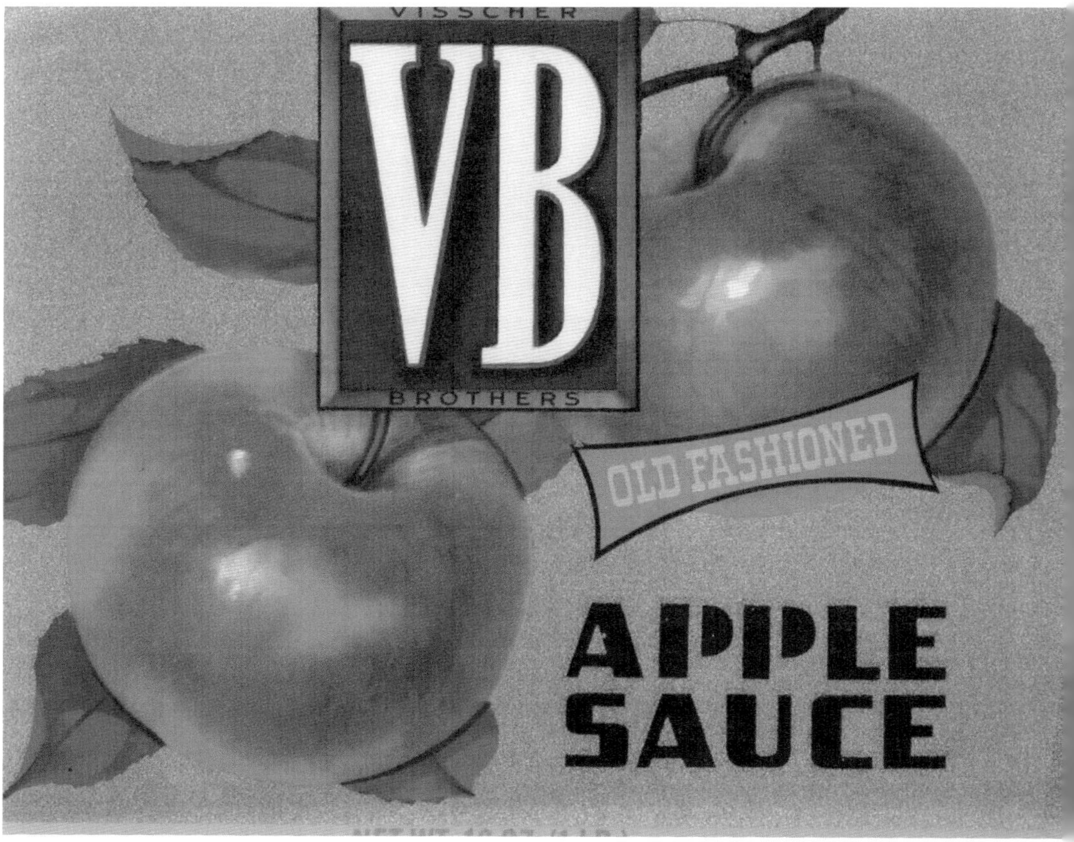

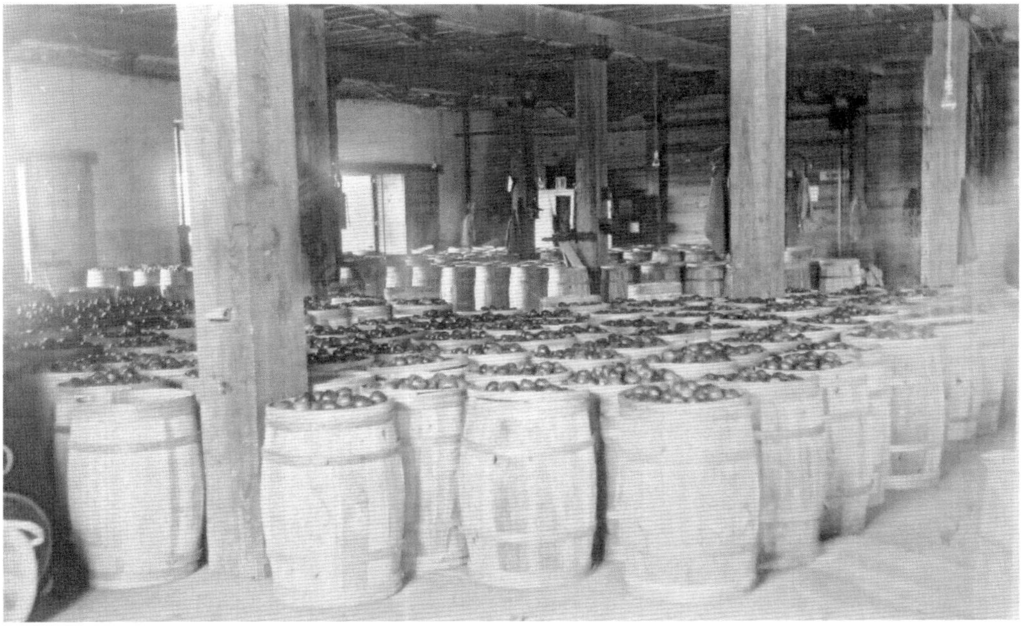

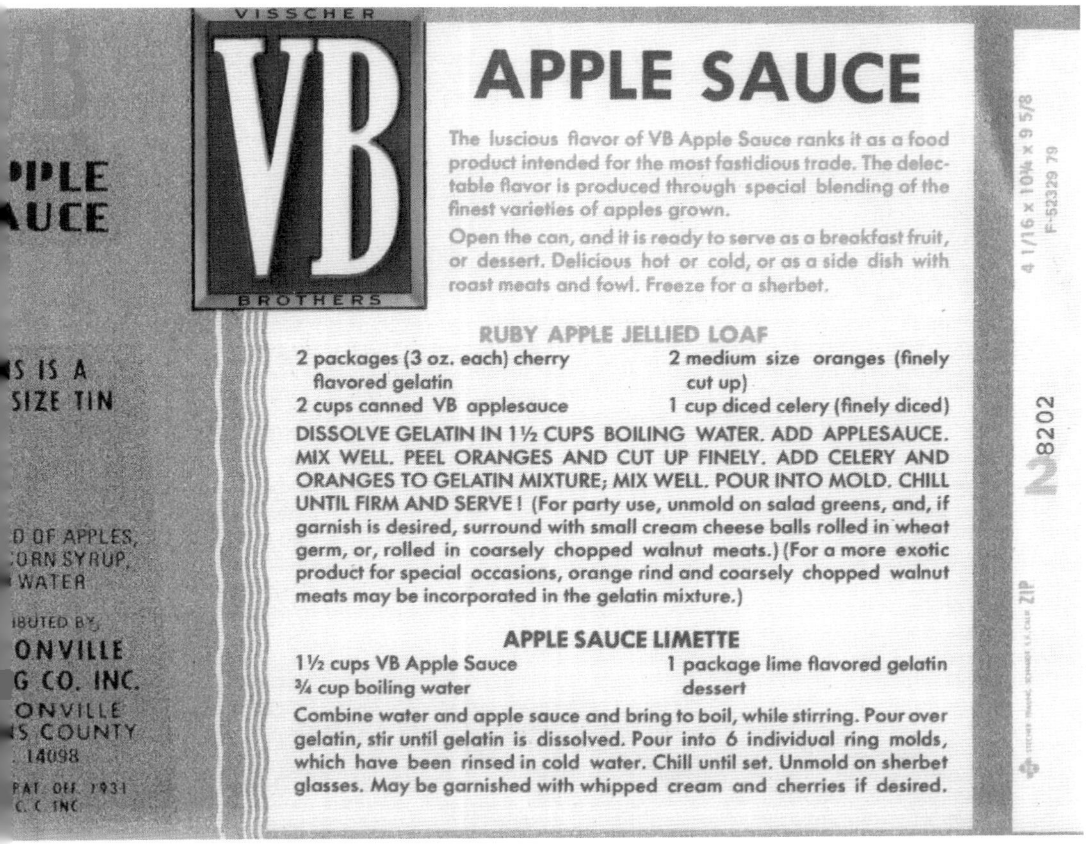
VISSCHER
VB
BROTHERS
APPLE SAUCE
The luscious flavor of VB Apple Sauce ranks it as a food product intended for the most fastidious trade. The delectable flavor is produced through special blending of the finest varieties of apples grown.
Open the can, and it is ready to serve as a breakfast fruit, or dessert. Delicious hot or cold, or as a side dish with roast meats and fowl. Freeze for a sherbet.
RUBY APPLE JELLIED LOAF
2 packages (3 oz. each) cherry flavored gelatin
2 cups canned VB applesauce
2 medium size oranges (finely cut up)
1 cup diced celery (finely diced)
DISSOLVE GELATIN IN 1½ CUPS BOILING WATER. ADD APPLESAUCE. MIX WELL. PEEL ORANGES AND CUT UP FINELY. ADD CELERY AND ORANGES TO GELATIN MIXTURE; MIX WELL. POUR INTO MOLD. CHILL UNTIL FIRM AND SERVE! (For party use, unmold on salad greens, and, if garnish is desired, surround with small cream cheese balls rolled in wheat germ, or, rolled in coarsely chopped walnut meats.) (For a more exotic product for special occasions, orange rind and coarsely chopped walnut meats may be incorporated in the gelatin mixture.)
APPLE SAUCE LIMETTE
1½ cups VB Apple Sauce
¾ cup boiling water
1 package lime flavored gelatin dessert
Combine water and apple sauce and bring to boil, while stirring. Pour over gelatin, stir until gelatin is dissolved. Pour into 6 individual ring molds, which have been rinsed in cold water. Chill until set. Unmold on sherbet glasses. May be garnished with whipped cream and cherries if desired.
4 1/16 x 10¼ x 9 5/8
F-52329 79
8202
ZIP

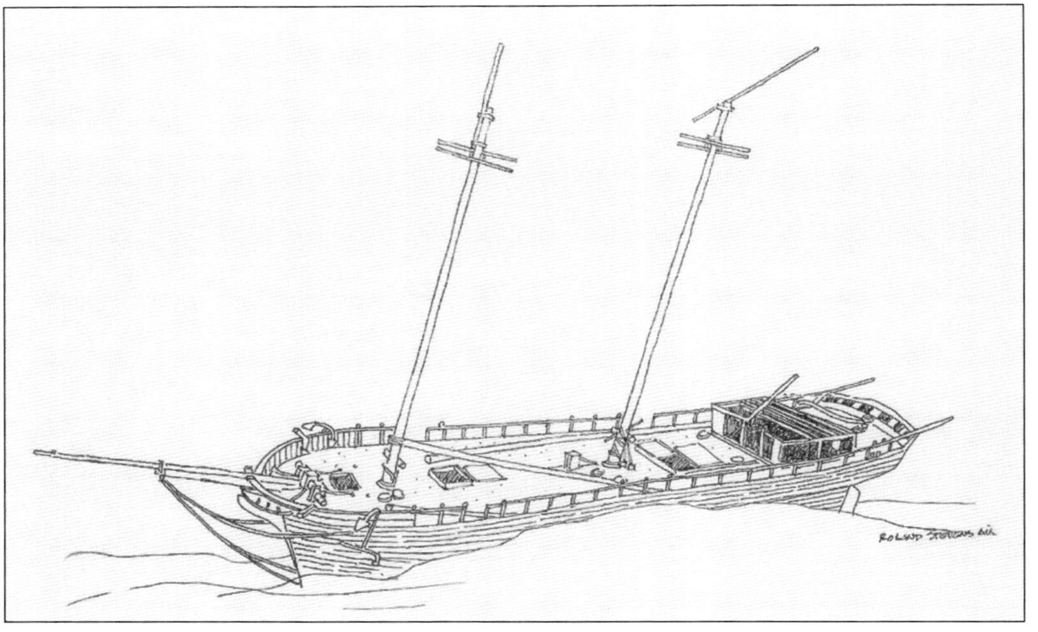

On an October morning in 1849, the schooner *Milan* sailed from Oswego with a crew of nine men, bound for Cleveland with a cargo of 1,000 barrels of salt. Very early the next morning, the men, asleep in the forecastle, were awakened by water splashing around them—18 inches of water covered the floor! Two men immediately took to the pumps while the others commenced to remove the salt cargo from the forward hold. Meanwhile, the water continued to rise. The *Milan* was turned directly south in an effort to run the schooner ashore. However, the winds were southerly and little headway could be made. Finally, in desperation, the crew abandoned ship and took to the yawl boat, just before the ship disappeared below the waves of Lake Ontario. Fortunately, a passing schooner observed the incident, took the crew on board, and brought them to the port of Rochester. At the time of the disaster, the captain of the *Milan* had on board a fine Newfoundland dog, which was trapped below deck as the ship took on water and sank. Shortly afterwards, the dog rose to the surface, swam to the yawl, and was finally saved. The *Milan* was built in 1845 by shipbuilder Asa Wilcox at Three-Mile Bay near Pt. Peninsula on Lake Ontario. She was a two-masted schooner with a beam of 19 feet, 8 inches, was 93 feet in length, and had a square stern. The shipwrecked schooner was discovered in 2005 in deep water well beyond the limits of recreational SCUBA divers (135 feet) by Jim Kennard and Dan Scoville, who located it utilizing sophisticated side-scanning sonar equipment. Scoville led a project to create a Remote Operated Vehicle for underwater exploration of the *Milan*. Many believe this early 1800s schooner is the oldest commercial vessel to have been found off the southern shore of Lake Ontario that has not been salvaged or wrecked near shore. (Courtesy of Roland "Chip" Stevens.)

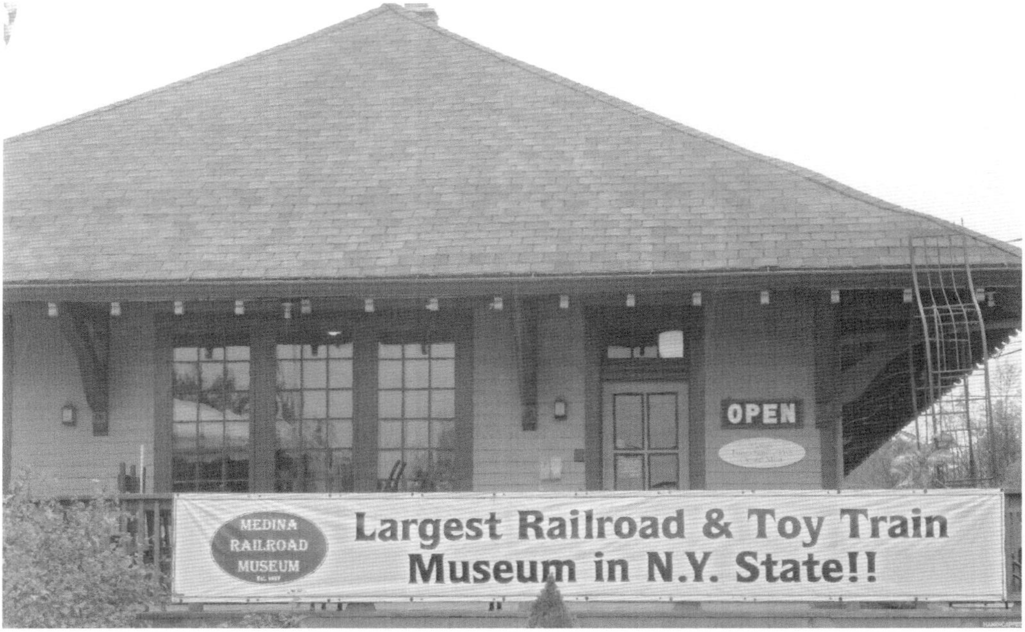

The nation's largest freight depot museum is located in Medina at the old New York Central Freight Building. Built in 1905, it is one of the largest (301 feet by 34 feet) surviving freight houses. The site showcases revolving displays of artifacts and memorabilia, and one of the nation's largest prototypical HO scale layouts. Train excursions are offered. (Courtesy of Orleans County Genealogical Society.)

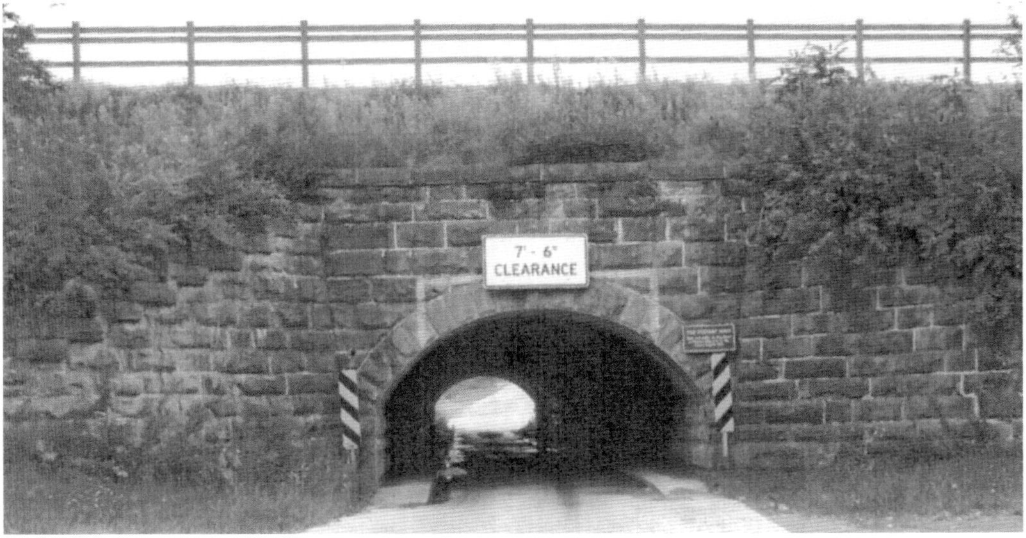

Built in 1823, a culvert was built in lieu of a bridge on this spot—the Erie Canal's only culvert. Contractors considered using a culvert because it was less expensive, and the natural berm made it possible. The site is recognized by *Ripley's Believe It or Not!* (Courtesy of Holly Canham.)

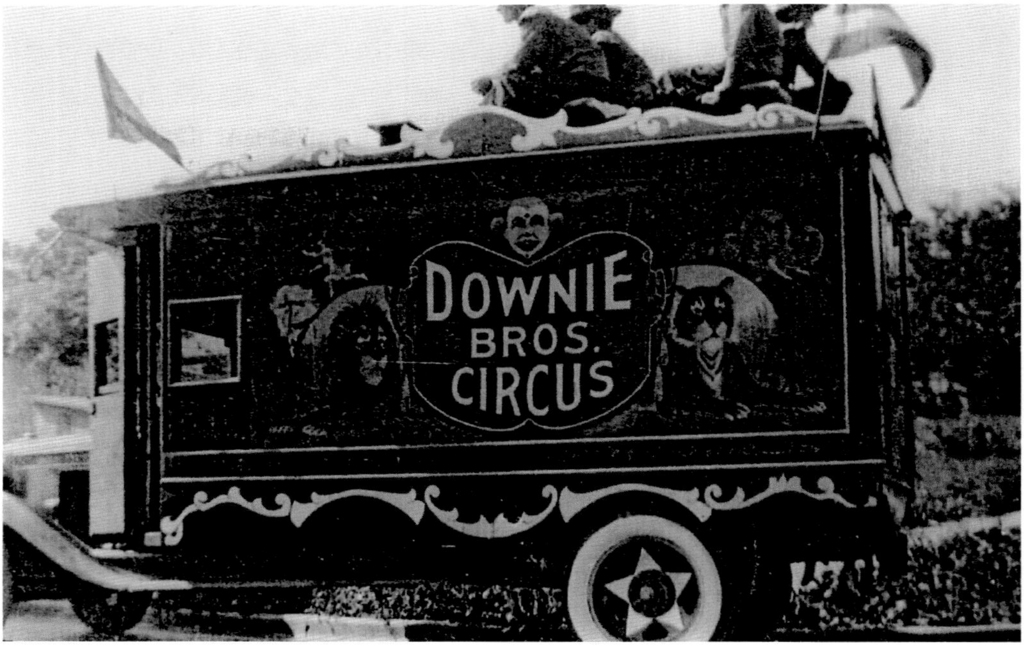

Andrew Downie McPhee arrived in Medina in 1894. Having performed juggling and tight wire acts for years, he and a partner organized the Rich and Downie Circus. He met and married Christina Hewer, sister of the late Florence Forrestel of Medina. Florence, also an aerialist, performed under the name of Millie La Tena. Within the circus world, Andrew dropped the McPhee surname and was known simply as Andrew Downie to famous circus celebrities, including the Ringling Brothers. He ran a "dog and pony show" along the Erie Canal towns. Downie retired in Medina, building a home on West Oak Orchard and Gwinn Streets. A circus elephant is buried in that backyard. His retirement was short lived. With the advent of motorized vehicles to move a circus, he founded the Downie Brothers Motor Circus, pioneering the traveling circus. (Courtesy of Virginia Kropf.)

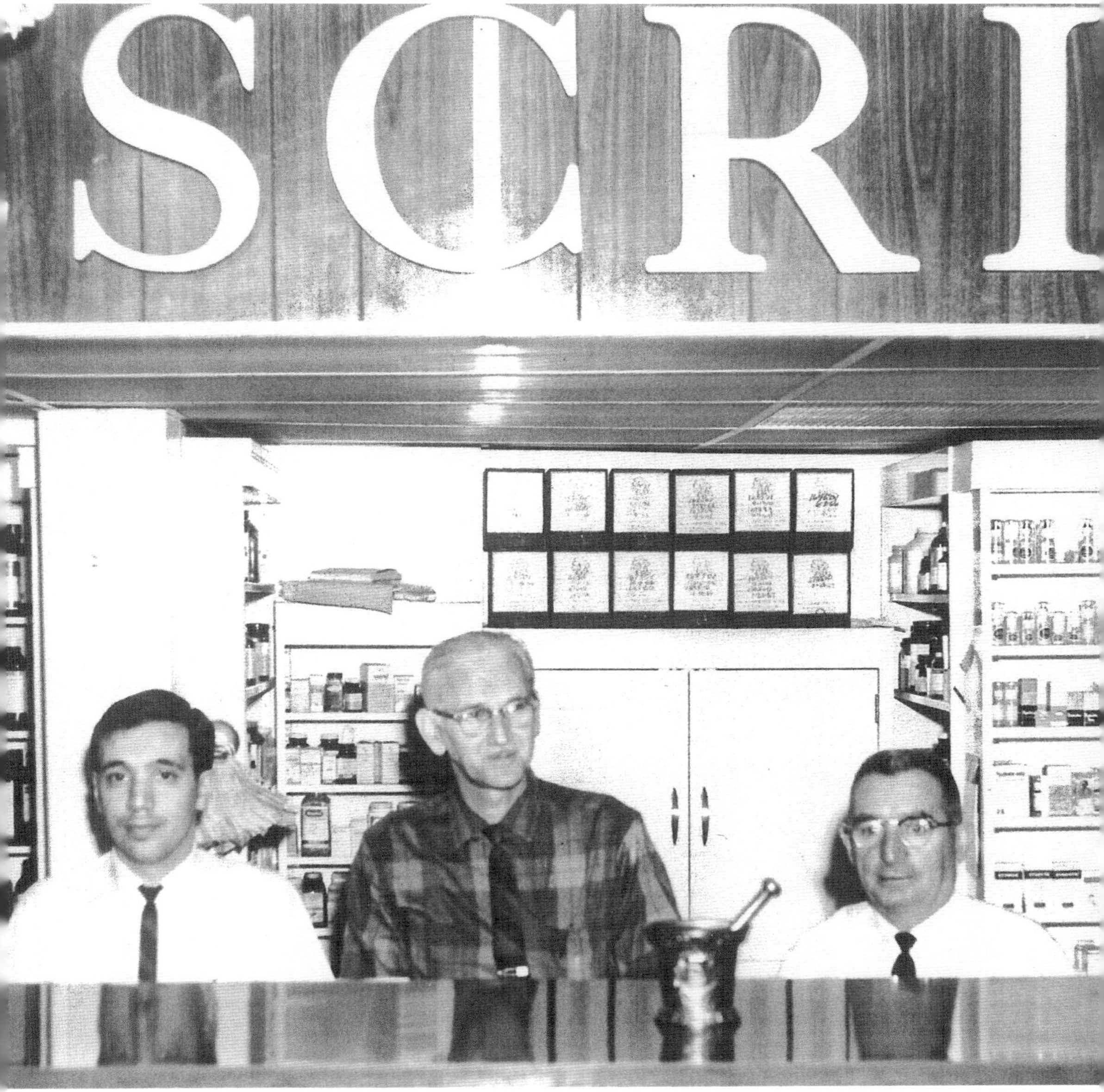

The Corner Pharmacy, located on the corner of Main and Bank Streets in Albion, was operated by genial partners (pictured center and at right respectively) Dan Wheale (business manager) and Al Kubica (pharmacist). Also shown above (left) is pharmacist "Buzz" Marone of Batavia, New York. Wheale and Kubica formed their business partnership in 1952, and by 1966 had doubled their volume—so they doubled the store's size. Locals enjoyed the site of the tiny Isetta car used for prescription deliveries. Dedicated to their community, both men were members of the Renovation Lodge of Masons and Albion Elks Lodge. Supporting staff members were pharmacists Casmir Pruski and James Jennings. Employees Fay Kubica, Pat Peruzzini, William Oliver, Dorothy Gallagher, Viola Smith, Ann London, Doris Smith, and Nedra Balcerzak served area residents for over 25 years. (Courtesy of Frank Zicari.)

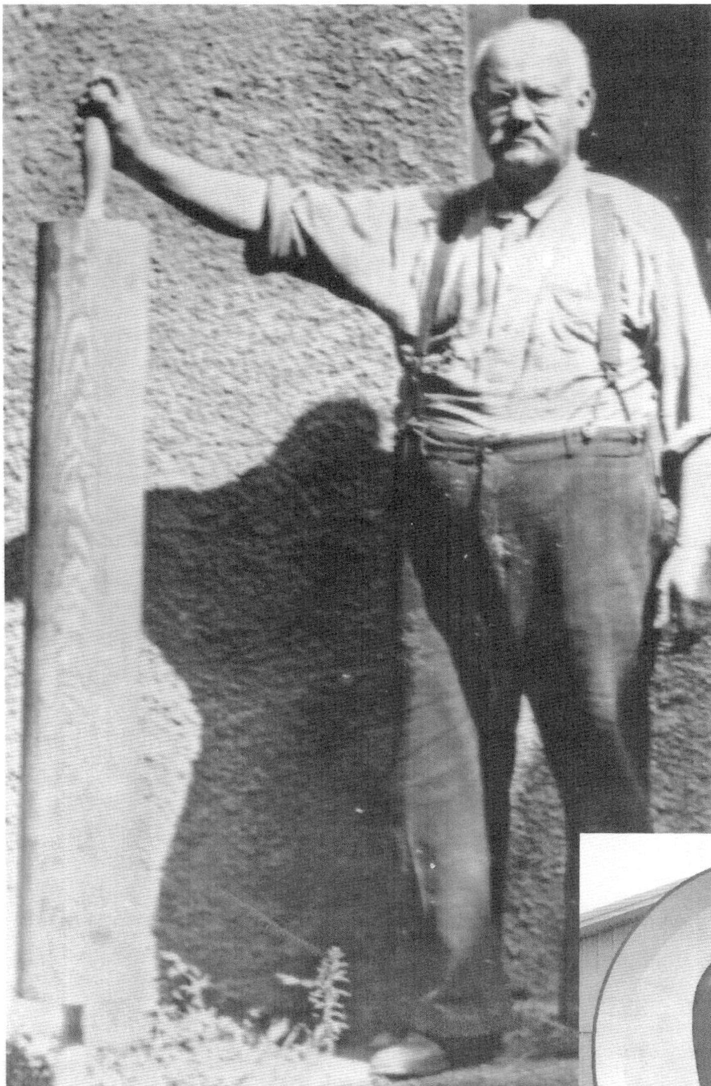

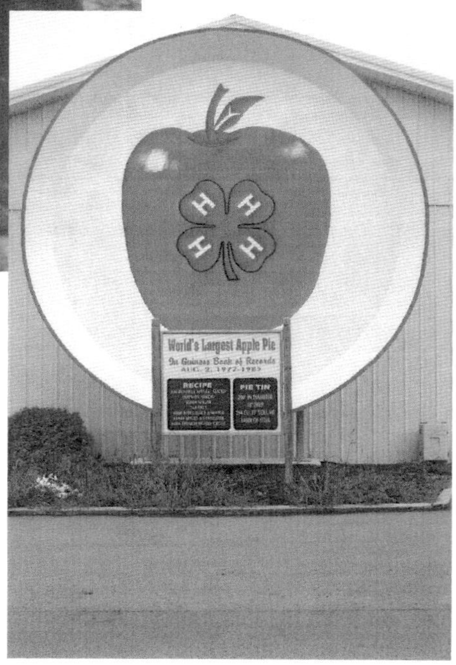

The first giant pie was baked in 1927 and weighed over three tons. Ingredients included 125 bushels of Orleans County apples, 600 pounds of sugar, 245 quarts of water, the juice of 106 lemons, two gallons of milk, 10 dozen eggs, 300 pounds of shortening, and 50 pounds of salt. The special pin to roll the crust was created by Joseph Dibley Sr. These pies were included in the *Guinness Book of World Records* until 1985. The creative idea to make the pie is attributed to Charles Howard. (Courtesy of Holly Canham.)

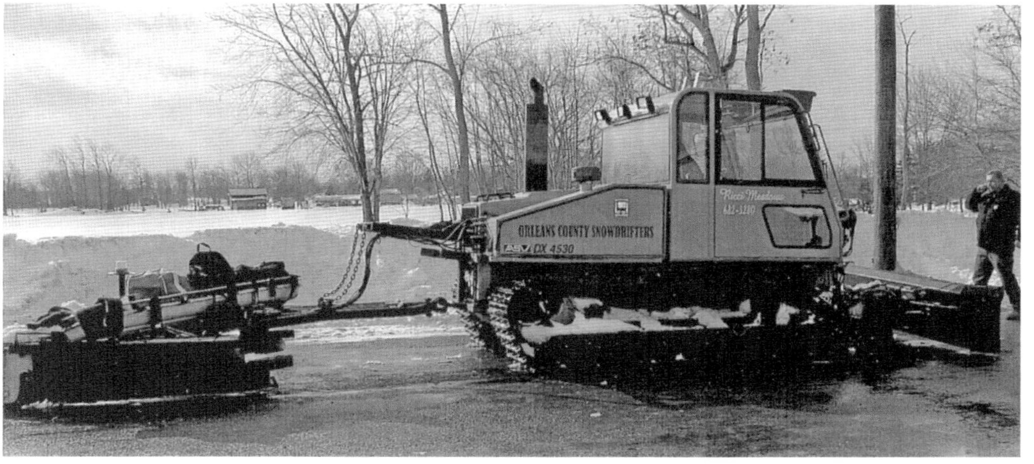

There are 3,600 Orleans County Snowdrifters, who have 76 miles of trail to enjoy. Ted Narburgh, club president, can remember the days when they first marked trails with plastic milk jugs spray-painted orange. The "groomer" (trac-truck) above is one of four vehicles used to prepare and maintain county trails; they also have a rescue sled should a community emergency occur. (Courtesy of Leanne Serrato.)

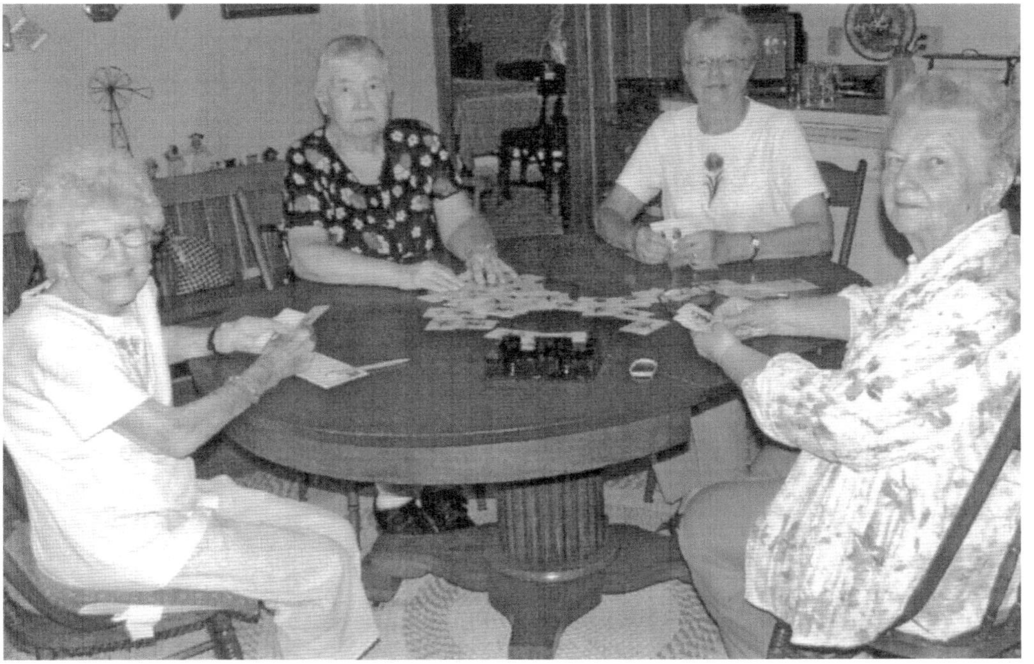

With long winters to pass, Orleans County people love all kinds of card games, especially the Great Lakes–area favorite called Euchre. In this photograph are, from left to right, Canasta Club members Veda Lemcke, Shirley Ecker, Janice Mann Beech, and Adeline Klafehn. Lemcke and Klafehn are charter members. They meet nearly every month to play cards. (Courtesy of Virginia Kropf.)

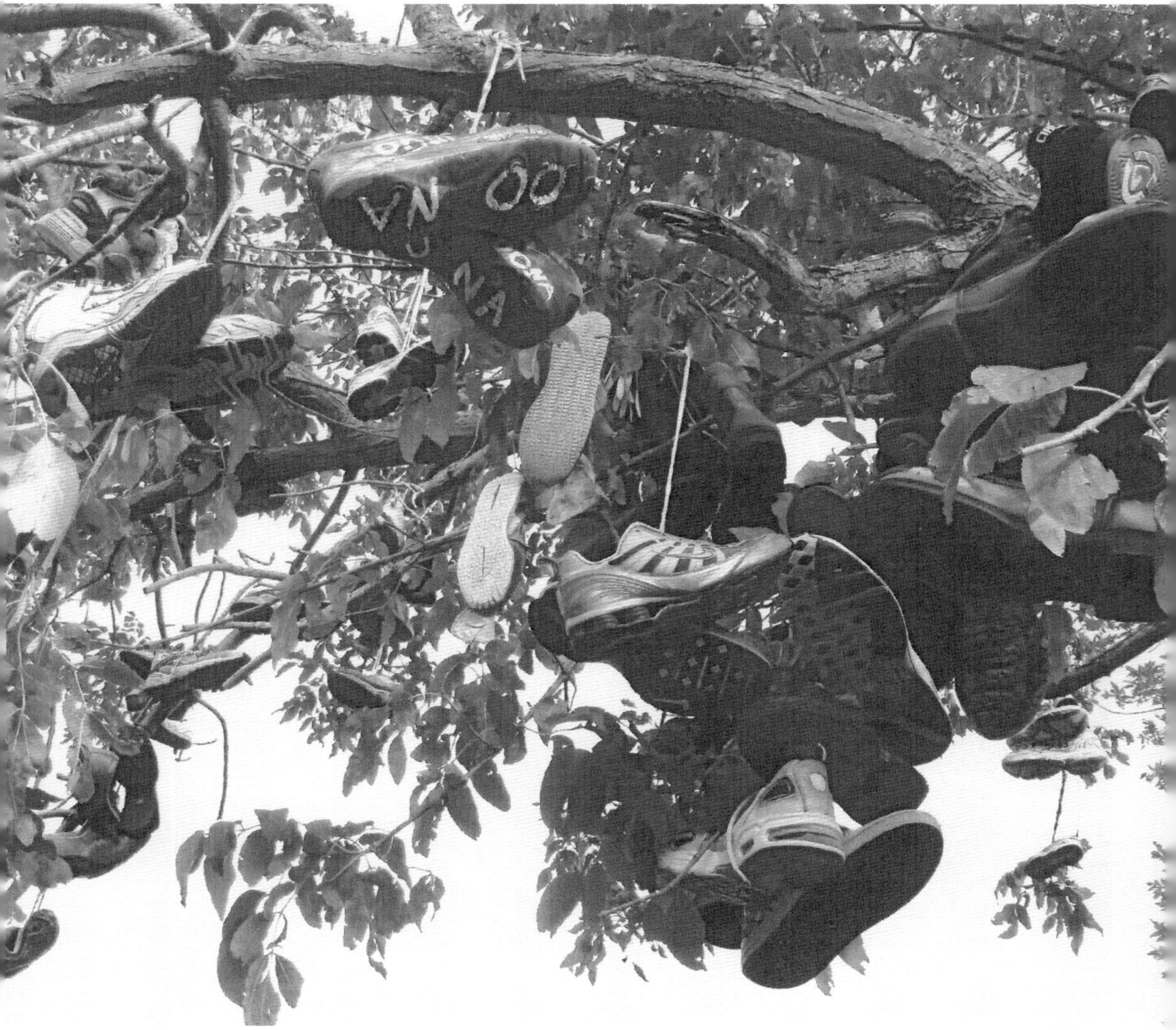

Lyndonville has four maple trees—each containing dozens of shoes. The area's dreamers believe that "if you make a wish and toss your sneakers into one of the trees, your wish will come true as long as the sneakers catch." Local legend holds that Lyndonville is home to the only "grove of shoe trees." (Courtesy of Mikken Canham.)

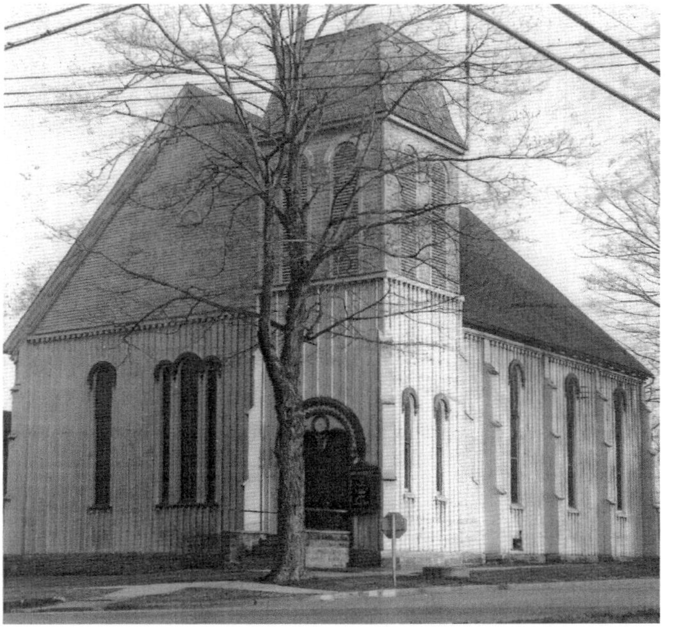

Organized in 1859, the Albion Free Methodist church was formed when Reverend Stiles was expelled over doctrinal "differences" at his previous church. One hundred eighty-five parishioners followed him. This event marked the birth of a now nationally recognized denomination. (Courtesy Orleans County Department of History.)

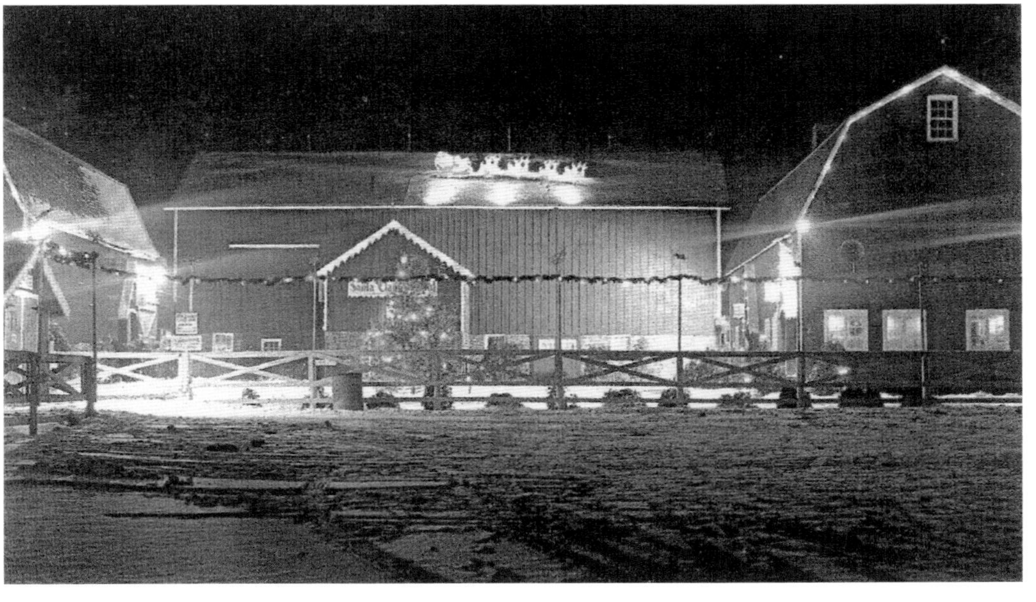

In 1940, Charles Howard converted barns on his Albion farm to use as "Christmas Park," realizing his dream of opening a Santa Claus School. Enhancements included a working campus of classrooms, dressing rooms, Santa's Workshop, gift shop, and Mrs. Santa's Kitchen. Outside, visitors could enjoy attractions such as the Christmas Park Express, a Christmas tree ride, a roller coaster, boat rides on Lake Snowflake, the opportunity to feed animals (including reindeer!) and ride covered wagons pulled by donkeys. Guests could visit Santa at Santa's Castle. Christmas Park, at its peak, attracted 80,000 visitors. (Courtesy of Frank Zicari.)

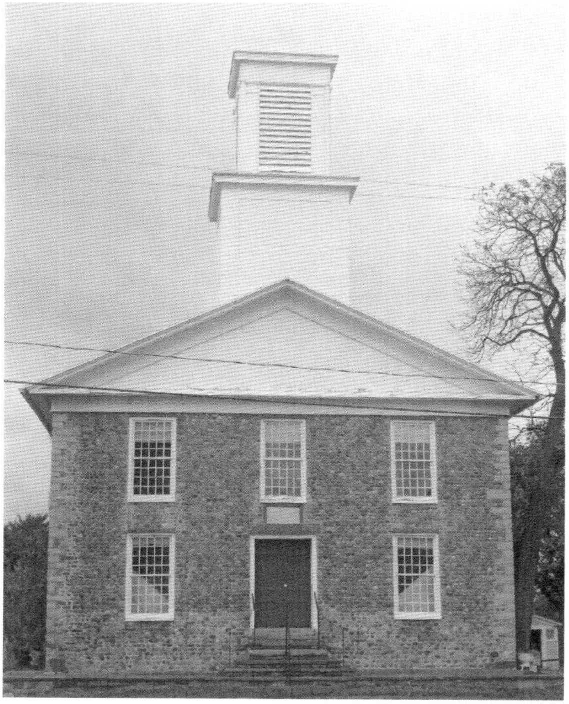

The Cobblestone Church (built in 1834) on the historic Ridge Road at Childs is the oldest cobblestone church in North America. Next door to the church is a cobblestone house once owned by Horace Greeley, the famous newspaper publisher, and a cobblestone schoolhouse is located east of the church. Together these structures were designed as National Historic Landmarks under the title "Cobblestone Historic District." (Courtesy of Bud Canham.)

This Episcopal church is the only house of worship in the world that rests in the middle of the street. It is flanked on three sides by Church Street. In addition, it faces East Center Street, causing it to be totally surrounded by roadways. (Courtesy of Holly Canham.)

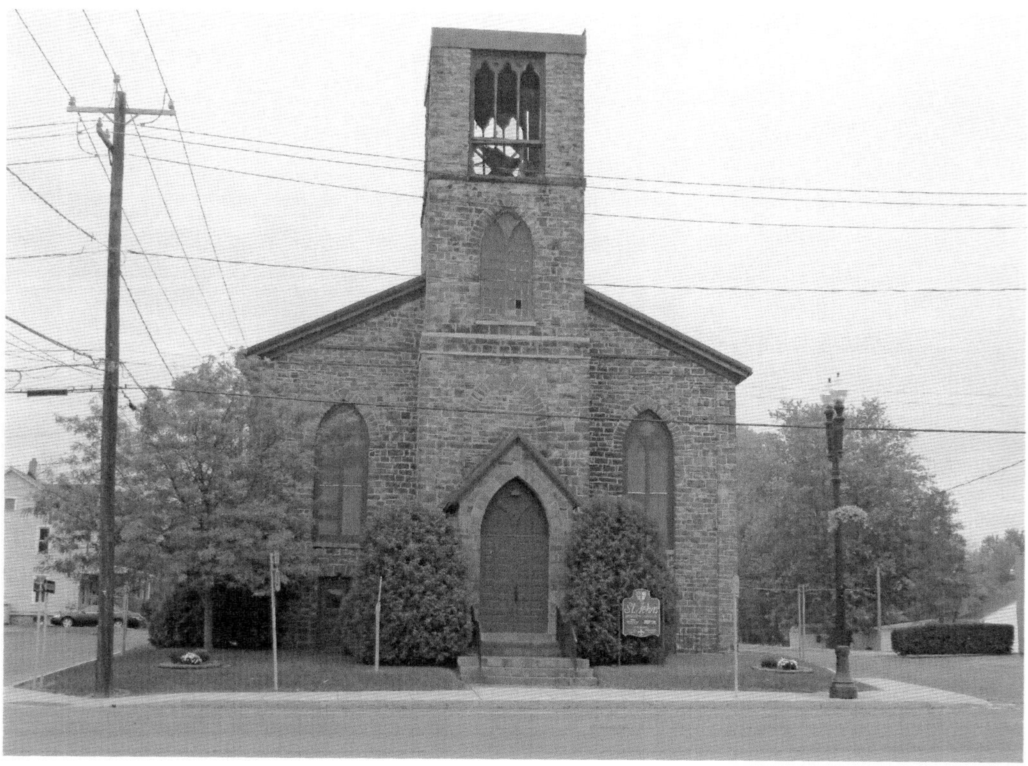

The dark pink to red/brown high-quality stone is named "Medina Sandstone" because the stone was quarried near Medina. John Ryan opened the county's first quarry in 1837. Quarry work was as essential to the economy as farming, luring Irish and Italian stonecutters and masons here for work. Concentrated near Albion, the quarry industry saved the town. Shipped via the Erie Canal to East Coast locations and beyond, the stone was used for the construction of breakwalls (photograph at right, Peter Dan Ricci, II) and fine buildings, including the "Million Dollar Staircase" at the State Capitol in Albany, and New York City's legendary brownstones. The arrival of Portland cement reduced demand for sandstone. (Right, courtesy of Mikken Canham; bottom courtesy of Christine Zinni.)

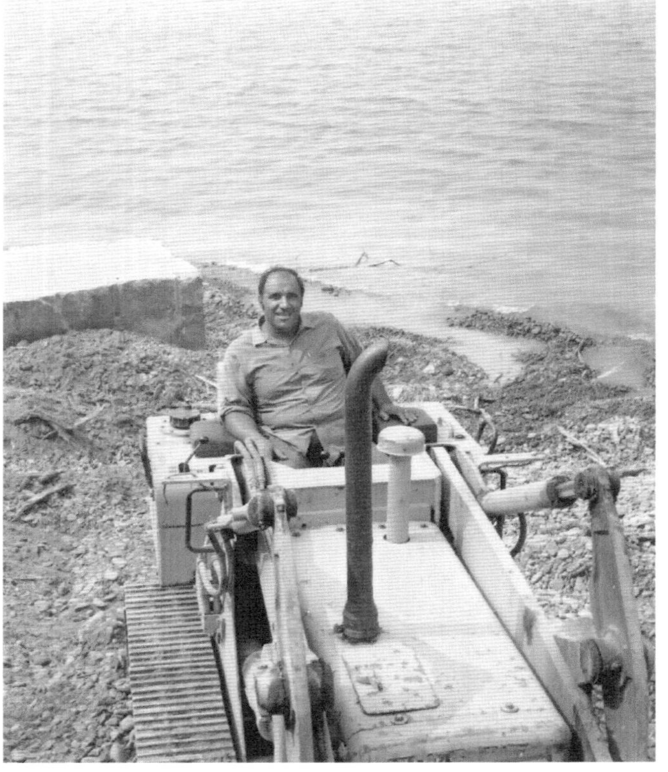

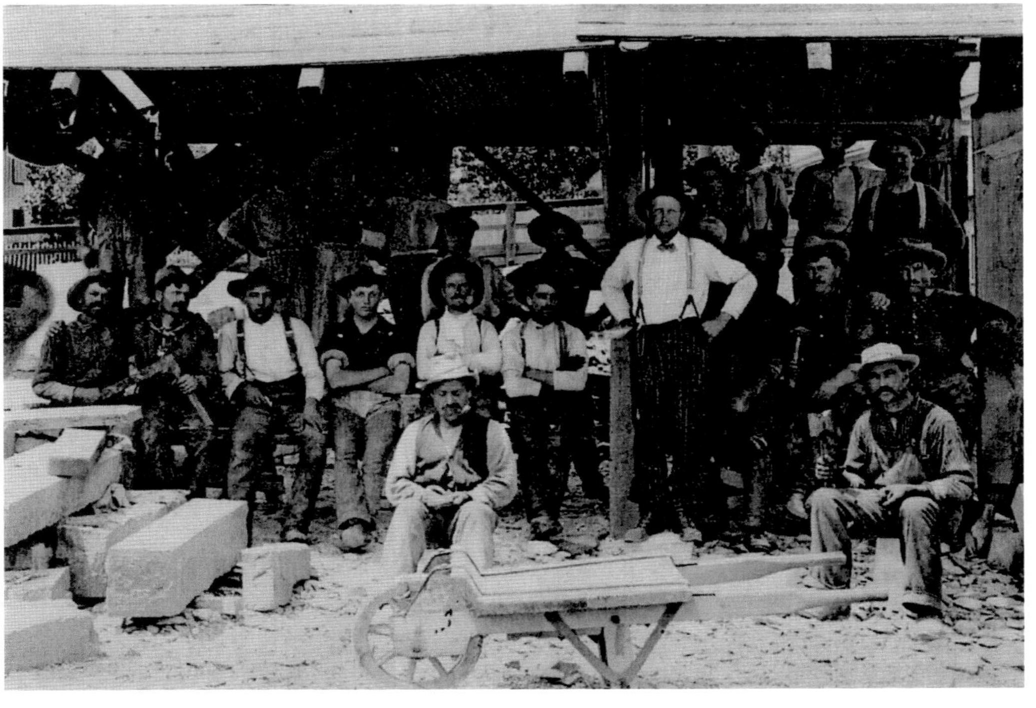

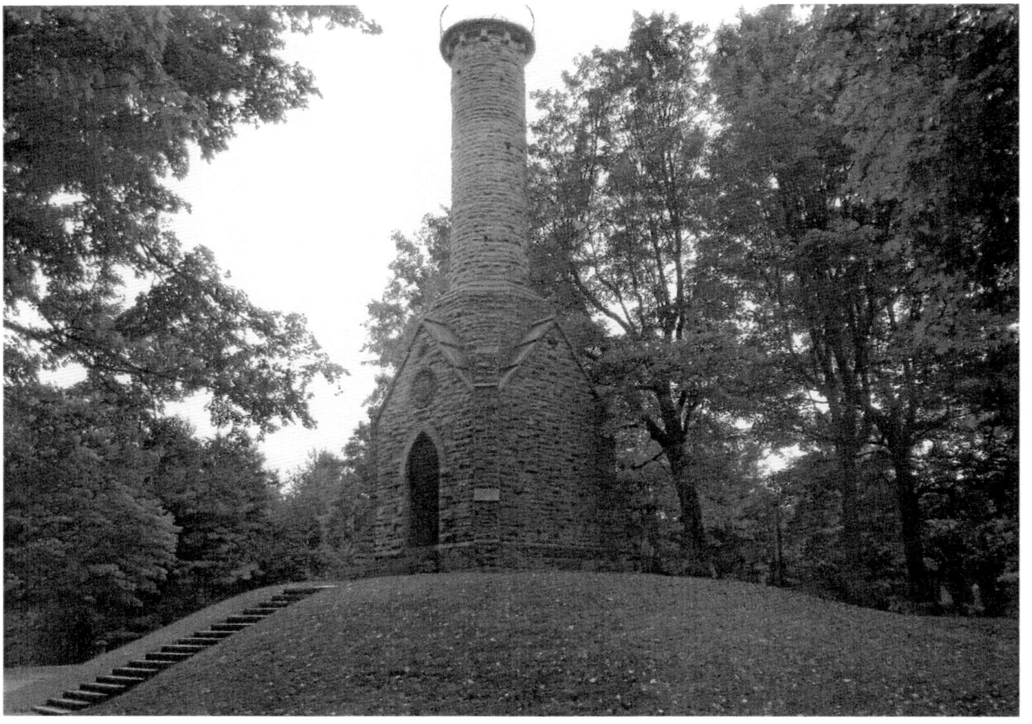

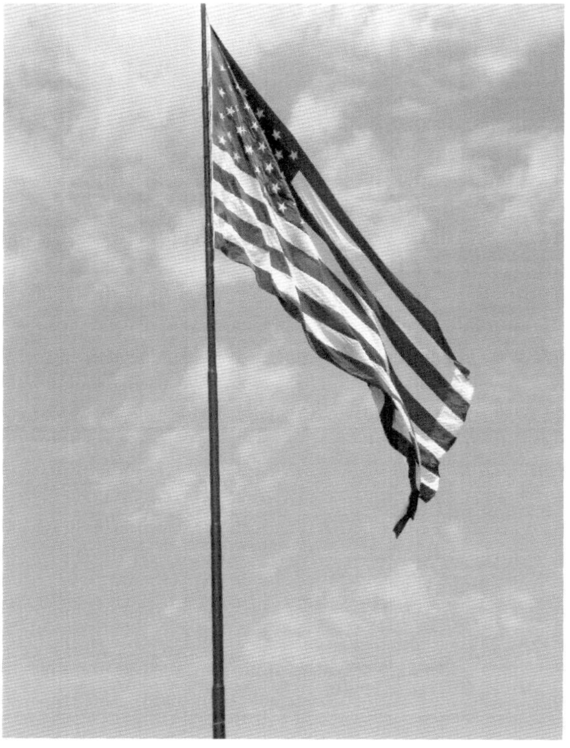

A tribute to our Civil War veterans rests in the southeast section of Mt. Albion Cemetery. Their names are inscribed on marble tablets inside the tower. The cylindrical monument is 58 feet high and constructed of hand-carved Medina sandstone. A spiral staircase leads to the overlook, which offers a 360-degree view of the countryside. On clear days, one can see Lake Ontario 10 miles north. (Courtesy of Bud Canham.)

Ridge Road Station is gone now, but the flag remains. Located on Ridge Road in Holley, the 1,800-square-foot, 100-pound flag is hoisted on a 130-foot-high, 12,500-pound metal pole. The pole extends another 13 feet underground and is secured by 60,000 pounds of concrete. (Courtesy of Holly Canham.)

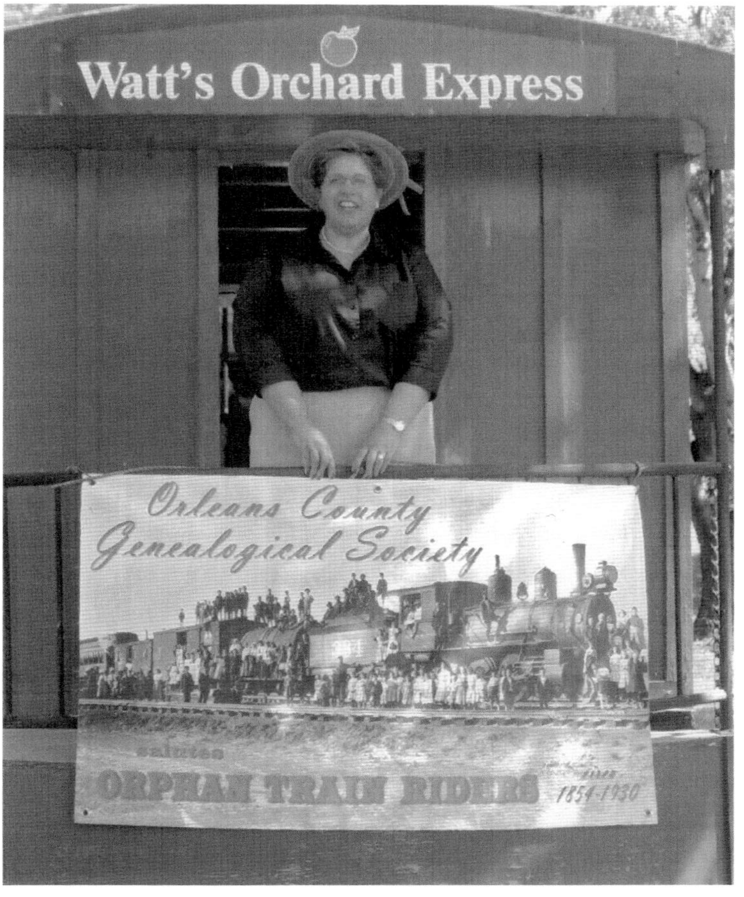

The Orleans County Genealogical Society (OCGS) dates back to 2000, when current president Hollis "Holly" Ricci-Canham (this book's coauthor) met researchers Sandra Freeman and Mark Rustay. The rest, as they say, is history. Almost immediately, the OCGS was incorporated under New York State education law and began enjoying not for profit status. The society has about 200 members, meets monthly in Albion, and enjoys an active programming schedule. The group has sponsored hundreds of exciting guest speakers and is proud to have contributed to one of the first DNA sample drives in America (2002). Living up to its charter, the group collects, maintains, and shares manuscripts about the lives of Orleans County citizens for use by generations yet unborn. The society's success is directly linked to its leadership and hardworking volunteer members—each person's effort is sincerely appreciated. Among the many successful events and programs hosted by OCGS is the "Orphan Train" project—an educational reenactment of the "Greatest American Migration." This event was planned and promoted by Holly and held April 17, 2004 at the Medina Railroad Museum. Among the 500 people attending the event were two Orphan Train riders who got off the train in Orleans County. For a 75-year period, c. 1854–1929, as many as 250,000 children were relocated across the country. The event was so successful that the Orphan Train Heritage Society of America (Springdale, Arkansas) designated the OCGS as New York's official repository for orphan train information and memorabilia. In addition to this Legendary Locals book, Holly coauthored Images of America: *Carlton and Point Breeze* (with Avis A. Townsend). She has also served on the Orleans County Historical Association's Board of Directors. (Courtesy of Mikken Canham.)

Consistent with our mission to preserve history on a local level, this book was printed in South Carolina on American-made paper and manufactured entirely in the United States. Products carrying the accredited Forest Stewardship Council (FSC) label are printed on 100 percent FSC-certified paper.